JUMP

Jump

*Black Anarchism and
Antiblack Carcerality*

Sam C. Tenorio

NEW YORK UNIVERSITY PRESS
New York

NEW YORK UNIVERSITY PRESS
New York
www.nyupress.org

© 2024 by New York University
All rights reserved

Library of Congress Cataloging-in-Publication Data
Names: Tenorio, Sam C., author.
Title: Jump : Black anarchism and Antiblack carcerality / Sam C. Tenorio.
Description: New York : New York University Press, [2024] |
Includes bibliographical references and index.
Identifiers: LCCN 2023038595 (print) | LCCN 2023038596 (ebook) |
ISBN 9781479828289 (hardback) | ISBN 9781479828296 (paperback) |
ISBN 9781479828319 (ebook) | ISBN 9781479828302 (ebook other)
Subjects: LCSH: African Americans—Politics and government. | Black people—
Politics and government. | Anarchism. | Slavery. | African diaspora.
Classification: LCC E185.615 .T445 2024 (print) | LCC E185.615 (ebook) |
DDC 323.1196/073—dc23/eng/20231024
LC record available at https://lccn.loc.gov/2023038595
LC ebook record available at https://lccn.loc.gov/2023038596

This book is printed on acid-free paper, and its binding materials are chosen for strength and durability. We strive to use environmentally responsible suppliers and materials to the greatest extent possible in publishing our books.

Manufactured in the United States of America

10 9 8 7 6 5 4 3 2 1

Also available as an ebook

*For Frances, Connie, Susan, and Ellie—
and all others who have led me here.*

And for Pip—with whom it all started.

CONTENTS

Introduction: Jumping Ship   1

1. Refusal   19

2. Collectivity   51

3. Ruination   79

4. Maneuvers   109

   Conclusion: Parsing Paradox, Escaping the Inescapable   149

   Acknowledgments   155

   Notes   159

   Bibliography   175

   Index   189

   About the Author   200

Introduction

Jumping Ship

Just bury me in the ocean with my ancestors that jumped from the ships because they knew death was better than bondage
—N'Jadaka / Erik "Killmonger" Stevens, *Black Panther*

Stick to the boat, Pip, or by the Lord, I won't pick you up if you jump; mind that. We can't afford to lose whales by the likes of you; a whale would sell for thirty times what you would, Pip, in Alabama. Bear that in mind, and don't jump any more.
—Herman Melville, *Moby-Dick or, The Whale*

What would happen after we jumped? The question never came up. You had to be free to see the horizon.
—Fabienne Kanor, *Humus*

The jumps are everywhere. This practice of the enslaved jumping from their enslaver's ships can be found across the archive of the transatlantic slave trade, from Olaudah Equiano's famous narrative to the ship log of French captain Louis Mosnier, the basis of Fabienne Kanor's *Humus*. They span contenders for the Great American Novel, blockbuster film, and most recently Lupe Fiasco's 2018 album *Drogas Wave*. Sometimes the subject of controversy, a measure of terror, or a diagnostic of bravery or succumbence, they are rarely, if ever, the matter of sustained (political) study. *Jump: Black Anarchism and Antiblack Carcerality* centers its focus on these practices, arguing that they persist as abnegations of the terms of racial order that are often obfuscated by the overwhelming political narration of that order, a narration of disorder that is meant to keep order in place. Leaping out at me in unexpected moments and places, the jumps oblige an investigation of Black dissent and refusal that challenges any facile binarism of freedom and captivity or a typology of Black resistance. They are, as Christina Sharpe reminds us, "with us still, in the time of the wake."[1] What do they tell us?

Erik "Killmonger" Stevens's provocative dismissal of King T'Challa's proposition to heal him instead of watch him die at the conclusion of Marvel's 2018 *Black Panther* is quietly piercing. As he painfully kneels on a cliffside looking out across the Wakandan landscape following his loss to T'Challa/Black Panther in the film's epic final fight scene, Killmonger sagaciously questions the former's suggestion, knowing full well that it would only amount to imprisonment, and chooses death instead. Rather than simply and emphatically marking Killmonger's last words and line of reasoning, the jumps of the enslaved come to us in the cleavage of Black politics irretrievably split between the bluntly rendered, and ultimately vilified, militancy of Black American Killmonger's hailing from Oakland, California, the formative location of the actual Black Panther Party, and the Wakandan royal T'Challa, the (super)heroic benefactor to the West, steeped in African tradition. Though brief, Killmonger's ancestral invocation necessarily complicates what is all too often an undemanding story of Black politics filtered by moral arithmetic, easy conflations, and state-centered adjudications on the utility of violence that are meant to narrate and protect our political order as it currently exists.

Jump's first jump surfaced while reading Herman Melville's *Moby-Dick*, at once the major opus of a writer thought to "[strike] a note of tragic dissonance in the established harmonies of the American political tradition" and a seemingly unlikely place for a meditation on Black political questions.[2] Political theory is a field largely uninterested in how blackness and chattel slavery shaped the deracinated democratic theory that dominates the discourse around *Moby-Dick*. Little is said about Pip, the young Black boy, amid the maelstrom and mundanity of the *Pequod*'s quest, Ahab's monomania, and Ishmael's narration. To be sure, scholars have investigated Pip's impact on Melville's major characters Ahab and Ishmael as cure and catalyst, but absent any substantive engagement with Pip's jump or Stubb's scolding inlay of the slave sale.[3]

Stubb's castigation of Pip is sandwiched by the latter's two jumps from the whaling boat when he is forced to take the place of Stubb's usual after-oarsman. On the first jump, Pip ends up choked by the line, blue in the face, and suspended between the boat and the chased whale, when he is finally halfheartedly cut from his entanglement, much to the anger of Stubb and the rest of the crew. On the second, he is left behind, drowning in the miles of shoreless ocean, "the intense concentration of self in the middle of such a heartless immensity" as the boat continues after the whale.[4] When he is finally rescued by the trailing ship, his body "jeeringly kept [up]" by the sea, Pip is no longer himself.[5] His remaining days are marked by the ostensibly incoherent uttering of "ancient tongues," which include the third-person recitation of his own imagined runaway slave advertisement, that lead the crew to designate him mad.[6] What interests me is the absence of analysis and general lack of regard for Stubb's excoriation of Pip as the context in which he jumps and generates his non/being, "the terrible spectacle [that] dramatizes the origin of the [enslaved] subject."[7] Unhitched from this racial antagonism, dominant political interpretations of Pip's fall into madness have pursued it as a transcendental experience and a foreshadowing of the crew's tragic demise.[8]

This was a scene of subjection, the "original generative act."[9] In it, Pip, nominally free aboard the whaling ship but generated by a "violence so totalizing it prevents the closure of [his] bodily schema," is meant to carry the burden of the calculable value he cannot bring as property—indebted and at the same time structured by enslaveability no matter his distance from the plantation or that he hails from Tolland County, Connecticut.[10] The reference to the auction block signals the specter of chattel slavery that haunts the ship and reframes the relation of second mate and after-oarsman as master and slave. Yet Pip, caught between the legal statuses of free and slave, is lost as such in the innumerable studies of Melville's novel. The scholarly elision impresses the deracination of Pip within the text as he and his jumps come to us via Ishmael's narration, where understanding of Black suffering is suspended by Ishmael's advocacy of Stubb's unintentionality and his own self-reflection. Ishmael names the "ruthless detestation" felt toward Pip's fear of whales yet ultimately concludes that Stubb "did not mean to" abandon him.[11] As Ishmael proffers the benevolence of Stubb, he concurrently ignores the invocation of the chattel slave, an ignorance that scholars have extended in their examinations of Ishmael's "unforgettable melancholic witness" and sympathetic identification to Pip's traumatic drowning.[12] The scholarly extolling of Ishmael, "the novel's embodiment of fair-minded common sense and liberal tolerance," on the one hand clouds the Melvillean examination of US society's capacity to witness the experience at the enslaved position and on the other divulges the violence of bringing the suffering of the enslaved close, to render it legible within the liberal frame.[13]

This is clearest at the conclusion of the chapter in Ishmael's remarks: "The thing is common in that fishery; and in the sequel of the narrative, it will then be seen what like abandonment befell myself."[14] As Pip is displaced for Ishmael's own relationship to the world, he becomes a vehicle of speculation and speaks to the "difficulty and slipperiness of empathy" where "good intentions," Saidiya Hartman maintains, can channel the "fungibility of the captive body."[15] In the same pages that Pip seeks himself through his own fugitive-slave notice, Ishmael's question obtains: "Who ain't a slave? Tell me that."[16] The displacement is meant as an appeal to a common humanity incommensurable with the reality of antiblackness, which in part explains how appeals to theses of Ishmael as a "prophetic voice of America's dispossessed and disinherited,"[17] Ishmael's "true" witnessing, or Pip as harbinger of the crew's demise may illustrate the deleterious absorption of blackness to a kind of universal liberalism, reproduce the violence of Ishmael's power to negate Black suffering, and unsee Black dissent that fails to align with the assumption of shared cause with the crew. While scholars want to recognize the centrality of Pip's character, they may do so in a way that does not fully appreciate the insistence of chattel slavery and his slave position to their own political cogitations.

Of the most capacious studies of the Melvillean tragedy is that of C. L. R. James, who famously claimed it as a representation of modern civilization where the "harpooners and the crew are the ordinary people of the world," a "world-federation of modern industrial workers."[18] His notation of Pip's lowliest status in 1851 America sits within what he deems to be Melville's major theme for critique—totalitarianism in the service of capitalism.[19] Unlike Melville authorities Donald Pease and Jason Frank, James does not share an affinity with Ishmael, whose intellectualism is as blameworthy as Ahab's tyranny for the fall of modern society. His disdain for Ishmael's intellectualism to some extent explains his interpretation of Pip's drowning as "the attainment of the ultimate wisdom" because he has made "contact with the reality around them" juxtaposed against the "profundities of philosophy and religion" that characterize true madness.[20] James also reads Pip as ignorant, of "simple faith and good-fellowship," and uninterested in "the political reorganization of society," noting that "Pip plays no great part in this book, as the Pips play no great part in the world."[21] James argues that Melville rightfully gives Pip the moral high ground, but his reading, equally disengaged from the ship's structural antagonism, de-emphasizes Pip's action. The political elision of Pip's jump is in part a function of James's famous, but candidly Marxist, study that centers the capitalist economic system that produces and reproduces wage labor and separates the crew from Ahab's quest. As James argues for Melville's illustration of the promised failure of a world built on modern capitalism and its social relations, he offers a universality of labor (the common man) as the binding force of those oppressed by this society and of capital as the source of the oppression itself. He implies the resolution of this flawed social relation as the possibility of correcting society's downfall. In locating the pairing of labor and capital as the ship's mode of organization, the racial antagonism is not understood as the fulcrum of order, but rather insists that racial "lowliness" will be incidentally eradicated through the correction of capitalism.

For James, the story of Steelkit, who leads an uprising against a tyrannical figure on another vessel but for which success results only in "everything [going] back to just where it was before," demonstrates Melville's dismissal of revolt's viability.[22] But what could James have seen in Pip's jump had he diagnosed the structure of society differently? Anarchism's contestation of Marxist political philosophy has often been aimed at the latter's recuperation of state authority, that is, its embrace of the state as an instrument to be used for the benefits of working-class power.[23] As it attempts to retain authority while critiquing capital, this embrace has resulted in a political horizon similarly encumbered by Western democratic liberalism.

Alternatively, Pip refuses a governing structure of antiblackness, revealing the processes of violence that both establish and maintain ontological difference between master and slave—the very relation that structures his and Stubb's coherence. Among the crew and the officers of various creeds and positions, it is the lowly Pip's jump that invites a disruption of the political horizon set by narrator and protagonist Ishmael's vision amid Captain Ahab's monomaniacal quest for the white whale that had bitten off his leg during a previous encounter. Pip's refusal is a refusal of the master's authority, of authority in toto. His supposed idiocy, then, is simply an idiom that the rest of the crew fails to understand. Said another way, Pip's jumps propose a political renunciation that confronts a crisis of incomprehensibility, one established and sustained by the foreclosure of the challenge's referent, the order that is disordered. Signaling what Tina Campt has called "practicing refusal" that specifies the "urgency of rethinking the time, space, and fundamental vocabulary of what constitutes politics, activism, and theory, as well as what it means to refuse the terms given to us to name these struggles," turning to Pip forces these interrogations.[24] His jumps anchor our attention to the elsewheres denied by others, the conditions of his oceanic vault, both Stubb's malediction and

Ishmael's narrative displacement, as illustrative of the confines of authority that Pip necessarily presses against.

Jump begins in the unlikely place of *Moby-Dick* because the political story of Pip's jump, hidden in plain sight—disavowed by Ishmael but also by the dint of those who study it—cues what Barnor Hesse and Debra Thompson call the "anti-political logic of antiblackness," itself defined by Moon-Kie Jung and João H. Costa Vargas as an antisocial logic, a generalized abjection of blackness.[25] The anti-political logic of antiblackness demonizes and violently polices political forms of Black life if they are unabsorbable to "the desires and ideals of white hegemony" or are otherwise unauthorized by white authority to exist where and how they do.[26] The manner in which Pip's jump undergoes a narrative foreclosure elaborates this anti-political logic and mirrors the elision of its historical referent, the enslaved who jumped from slave ships, from the historical record. As I will argue later, such jumps have been conventionally dismissed in favor of studying more direct forms of resistance like ship takeovers. They have also been mis/understood as practices of either cowardice or misery, whose value is limited to demonstrating the horror of slavery. The jump upends and interrupts, but it also confronts narrative obfuscations that preserve the horizons of Western liberal democratic traditions.

The disruption of crystallized ideology bares the risk of illegibility (the loss of legibility promised by ideology) but also the possibility of practice, the anti-pre-figuration unburdened by our imagined horizons. Rather than offer us an altogether dissimilar or organized political ideology, the enslaved who jump the slave ship orient us differently to questions thought settled in the roots and routes of Black freedom struggles. As Pip pushes off the boat's structuration, he rejects its socio-spatial arrangement and leaps into a deeply expansive, but altogether uncertain, ocean with no knowledge of what is to come. The collective leap from this space of captivity, Kanor tells us in her critical reimagination of the 1774 jump of fourteen enslaved women from the French slave ship *La Soleil*, is not bound by any assumption of outcome, because liberation cannot be objectively known from within the confines of antiblackness and its structural order; you had to be free to see the horizon.[27]

Studying the jump through the loupe of Black anarchism brings new understanding to political refusal, interrogating the foundations of authority, questioning consensus and resolution, spurning the crystallization of political ideology, and upending the givenness of conditions. To study the jump as a preliminary outline of Black anarchist practice arouses the rethinking of practices often thrust beyond the hem of politics proper, while also providing a new aperture for understanding the ontologically antagonizing relation of the world.

Black Anarchy

A Black anarchist reading breaks through the parameters of *Moby-Dick*'s conventional liberal or Marxist readings even if the imaginaries that Pip proposes are disavowed. Peeling at the resonance of Pip's jumps, this loupe allows us to cultivate a political understanding of his act as an oppugning and disruptive practice. His oceanic landing signifies the action's threat, its excess beyond the temporal and spatial boundaries that set the terms of political participation and to which the polis seeks to confine him. It exerts a racial chaos, where chaos seems to be the only appropriate term for the attempt to fracture order itself, the "coherence of humanity writ large."[28] The coupling of Black and anarchism, then, is not superfluous. Black anarchism begins at a radically different position from that of white Anarchism and emerges from an entirely different understanding of the foundations of the world. Unlike the white horizons posed by the critique of capital's antagonism, a Black anarchist reading centers the antagonism that births Black abjection and non/being as the outside to the human as the foundational antagonism that structures Stubb's authority, authority in Western modernity.[29]

Classical Anarchist theory has largely suffered from an absence of engagement with the deep histories of the racial paradigm emergent in Western modernity. The Black Rose Anarchist Foundation has pointed out that Black anarchist politics have been deceptively absent in the existing literature, and that capital-A Anarchist thought has historically denied its relationship to Black politics.[30] The silencing of antiblackness, chattel slavery, and colonialism as foundations of empire and the state are often sourced in class-based understandings of society's functions.[31] For white, Western, and European Anarchism, not unlike Marxism, class is both the reason and the stage on which the war with the state is waged because class is the primary hierarchy imagined structuring and determining white life. White life has long focused classical Anarchism's adherence to Western universalism. It is of little consequence to the larger political ideology that Black populations have sustained extra-state political resistance inflected by Anarchist modalities in centuries of struggle against the structural violence of antiblackness and that Anarchist movements, for their part, include a lengthy history of Black militants and adhere to a philosophy of antiauthoritarianism that has strong links to Black movements. The Anarchist movement is almost always thought of as originating, practiced, and applied in nineteenth-century Europe and then "imitated in other parts of the world."[32] This origin story not only places Europeans as central to the project of Anarchism but defines it as a set of ideas that then flourishes into a practice to be emulated elsewhere, implying that all anarchist practices have an ideological root and that it is found in white and European Anarchist tenets.

In 1910, when Emma Goldman wrote to correct the narrative of what Anarchism "Really Stands For," she declared that "Anarchism urges man to think, to investigate, to analyze every proposition."[33] Yet its very essence to question remained undisturbed by the question of racial antagonism. Classical Anarchist thought has not simply alienated Black political thought but has declared itself impervious to its many invocations and provocations borne of the experience of chattel slavery and its afterlives. My exegesis of Black political practices refracted through Black anarchism reflects Goldman's call to think against the grain as much as it offers a rejoinder to the epistemic violence endemic to classical Anarchist thought. This is to say, it follows the anarchist impulse, not only in recapitulating its anticipatory and antiauthority stance within existing Black political practices but in questioning classical Anarchism for its failure to account for antiblackness as the structure of *the* authority itself, which, I argue, sows its continued proposition of "analytically consistent [alternatives]."[34] By this I mean that in its misplaced oppositions, it ultimately can only offer the retention of the racial antagonism of the world.

This retention animates *Jump*'s turn away from prefiguration as a necessary foundation of the Black anarchist lens it assembles across its chapters. Anarchism's relationship to prefiguration is often paraphrased in the claim that revolutionary means must mirror desired ends. To be sure, while Anarchism's desired coherence of means and ends may stem from a concern with egalitarian organizing practices and arguably does not presume to know how actions will exceed intentions, the certainty with which it has assumed to know the trajectory of means and ends has shaped and displaced its engagement with Black political practices on many occasions.[35] The prioritization of white Anarchist vision over the Black anarchist practice has functioned as an assent to Anarchist imperialisms and white imaginations, making those pernicious violences that shape Black everyday life even more extant yet invisible by placing the ongoing relations of slavery under further cover.

To consider Black anarchism through the practices explored in the following chapters is to examine the productive intersections of anarchist modalities and Black radical politics that often contravene the foundations of white Anarchist thought. Black anarchism stands counter to the requirement of a vision that fits within Anarchism's constraints. As an accretion and substitution, the Black in *Black anarchism* signifies an exertion against and beyond containment, an introduction of racial disorder that undermines the material and epistemological governance of antiblackness. As such, the Black anarchist practices discussed herein are also reorientations, appeals to new geographies of Black life that refuse to labor through a mere reconfiguration of the current order. Rather, the deviant and often neglected practices, what Richard Iton has called "minor-key sensibilities," are read against our archives of resistance and politics because they demonstrate a "willingness to engage time, space, and other modalities outside of the given parameters."[36] The turn away from prefiguration is thus rooted in the agnosticism required of this willingness, to proceed without the alternative in view in a refusal of speciously predetermined outcomes and a horizon, to borrow the words of Iton again, "characterized by the dismissal of any possibilities beyond the already existing."[37] The understanding of Black anarchism offered here does not only stand in opposition to a centralized authority in a unitary state but rejects the prefigurative and fully fledged political ideologies in which this centralized authority finds its essential support that cannot help but remain extant in the horizon of the human. I am thus also offering Black anarchism as a method or practice of reading that at once rejects and reveals the social order's boundaries as not only exploitative, but imprisoning to the world as we know it .[38] As such, taking a Black anarchist orientation means thinking of jumps differently, how they may exceed and oppose the confines of the ship's polity and the structures that establish it. So rather than focus on the myriad intentions of Pip's jumps, which are nonetheless important, the reading of Black anarchism is meant to invoke his jumping overboard as an anticipatory opposition to the structural order that is otherwise meant to orient him.

Pip brought to me a question that is central to the rest of this book: How can we better understand a politics of refusal of racial authority? In truth, while building off other work in Black anarchist studies, the purpose of this book is not to apply Black anarchist theory to specific practices in the hopes of defining them as Black anarchism. Like the black fantastic, Black anarchism is also what Zora Neale Hurston could term a double descriptive insomuch as Black politics and anarchism seem to emerge and exist as disruptions of authority's validity.[39] Instead, this project seeks a new understanding of Black anarchism through the entanglement of Black political thought and anarchism *emerging from* Black practices of refusal, those nonrepresentational and nonreproductive jumps from the slave ship in other places and times. It is as much a critique of white Anarchism as it is a critique of the Western liberal tradition. It also works to intervene in discussions of Black politics that privilege the state and civil rights, by taking seriously the "right to struggle for freedom by any means necessary" and reconsidering the Black in Black politics as not simply an indication of the race of its participants, but an "oppositional thinking" and "oppositional risks."[40] In the practices discussed throughout this book, disorder and disruption are refusals and abstentions of the structural antagonism that reiterates Black abjection. They are the wading in the wake, where I offer wading to think about these restive movements, proceeding with difficulty, as a form of attack, as "living within the un-existable" without the attempt for resolution.[41] Rather than attempt repair or coherence on which we can all agree—for as Brittnay Proctor has reminded us, agreeance is a trap, an "anti-black logic that hinges on the idea of legitimacy"—examination through the loupe of Black anarchism that dislodges us from political accounts of means and ends situated within the world of the human moves us beyond the horizons set forth by existing Western political traditions in anticipation of something else elsewhere.[42] In so doing, they rupture the very "dictates of legibility" for radical political thought.[43]

Tracing Carcerality

Practices of *dis*order are part of what William C. Anderson identifies as the "process of destruction" necessary to produce "a *complete* ruination," what Marquis Bey calls "critical in the destructive sense" and "disruption toward freedom," or what Hartman summarizes as "tumult and upheaval" and "wayward experiments."[44] Taking on these preliminary descriptions of what we might call Black anarchism, *Jump* works to ground them in non-teleological spatial subversions, those that are often left to politically void interpretations but actually undermine the assumed legitimacy of architectures often thought of as purely aesthetic and separate from racial power, locating them as spatialities that hide the order of antiblackness in plain sight. The link between anarchism and architectural agitation is not new. Conceptually, *anarchitecture*, a portmanteau of the two, first emerged as the name of a 1970s New York artists collective unofficially headed by Gordon Matta-Clark. Defined by Matta-Clark, it described work that subverted architectural convention, questioned its "privileged and removed position," and unearthed its reality as an "apparatus of social control."[45] Black history is littered with this spatial reality; the Black sociopolitical position has been stringently produced through a series of oppressive environs whose reach stretches across the slave castles and ship holds to redlined ghettos and maximum security prisons. Methods of containment and surveillance, like those Rashad Shabazz, Simone Browne, and Dennis Childs have shown us, have generated the conditions of Black social death, where carcerality is etched deeply into the everyday landscape. Both Browne and Childs have located the provenance of contemporary security technologies and mass incarceration in the slave ship.[46]

When the Clotilda, known as "the last slave ship," was discovered on the coast of Alabama in mid-2019, it was unearthed as a tomb. A schooner scuttled in an effort to protect from prosecution those involved in the then illegal trade, it was a well-preserved reminder of enslavement's brutality and of our close proximity to it no matter the attempt at concealment. The slave ship has equally functioned as womb, indeed in the ontological linking of disparate people passing through the vestibule of enslavement, and also in the birthing of new but similarly formative captive places.[47] "The semiotics of the slave ship continue;" partus sequitur ventrem.[48] *Jump* undertakes this thesis of carceral evolution by examining the multiple forms and measures by which Black unfreedom is constructed and extended alongside the multiple ways that Black(ened) persons contested, refused, and always imagined and acted otherwise. Peering through these practices provides us with a different view of how antiblackness lives as a spatial order and how its regulatory power endures in part through its depoliticization of abstentious, destructive, and non-assimilative subversions. In tracing the wading, *Jump* equally traces the wake in which they are extant. It offers an extended rumination on the carceral sites and the carceral conditioning in the afterlives of enslavement and the slave ship that tie the forms of spatial captivity and the narrative foreclosure of this captivity and Black dissent, which together constitute antiblack carcerality, or maybe better still, that index antiblackness as carcerality.

Antiblack carcerality and antiblackness as carcerality summarize the connection of, and transition from, the slave ship to the modern prison industrial complex marked by violent regimes of policing, surveillance, and confinement that reify the structural antagonism of blackness and the human, where blackness and Black people "have served as the counterpoints to safety, rationality, belonging, and life" since the birth of modernity.[49] My use of reification is borrowed from what Brett Story has argued is a carceral disappearing act: the mystification of social relations into "things that appear to us as pregiven and self-contained but whose historical formations and social contingencies are thoroughly obscured."[50] To link carcerality and antiblackness may admittedly be a conceptual redundancy, but one that is meant to flood light on the antiblack historical formation and continued antiblack propagation of the carceral "things" we take for granted. As I have argued elsewhere, carceral here is not limited to "that which resembles or functions like a prison (e.g., detention centers) or uses its technologies (e.g., surveillance via ankle monitors)" but is "defined by the existence of the punitive relation that manufactures the criminal and the innocent."[51] It is more diffuse than the prison but just as violently generative of Black social and physical death. By thinking the antiblackness of carcerality and the carcerality of antiblackness, *Jump* gathers the many vestibules—the geographies that animate Black suffering and engender the structural positionality of blackness as nonbeing—that have themselves emerged from the vestibule of chattel slavery.

The Chapters

Jump contributes to the theorization of Black anarchism and antiblack carcerality through its turn to spatial subversions of our antiblack world catalyzed by the jumps of the enslaved from the slave ship. It does not intend an exhaustive explication of the jumps and the slave ship nor a definitive explanation of what Black anarchism is or should be. Rather, refracted through these lenses, we see refusal and disruption differently, in practices of dissent too often disregarded as ineffective to gain access to the world of the human as if inclusion and humanity are what must be sought. Chapter 1, "Refusal," seeks the jump through Black anarchism and Black anarchism through the jump. Guided by Hortense Spillers's notion of "vestibular cultural formation," the chapter introduces the concept of vestibular subjection as a way of reading the slave ship's spatial technologies as shaping its metamorphic capacity, the practices that arrange and divest meaning on the flesh of the enslaved. This provides the frame through which the political force of spatially disruptive practice is gleaned, itself a contestation of readings of the jumps of the enslaved as irrelevant to foundational questions of politics. Further, in examining its nonreproductive thrust against racial authority as an indication of Black anarchist politics, this chapter explains how and why the jumps from the slave ship are sometimes eschewed as rebellion's less worthy cousin, interrogating the pressure the jump places on our political imaginaries. In part, this includes a consideration of how race and gender simultaneously structure Black anarchist possibilities and the limits of their common consumption. Working through the political anatomy and carceral geography of the jump from the slave ship lays the groundwork from which to understand the sites of the remaining chapters as new iterations of the slave ship, each carrying their own vestibular force and the spatial disruptions of each as offering their own recapitulation of Black anarchism: collectivity, ruination, and maneuver.

Chapter 2, "Collectivity," considers the voyages of the Black Star Line, the shipping line of Marcus Garvey and the Universal Negro Improvement Association, to reconceptualize the Black diaspora as an anti-state modality, one that highlights the "participatory connection between the individual and the collective" in defiance of the unfreedom initiated by white imperial authority and that upholds the sanctity of the nation-state.[52] It argues that the line's voyages and global symbolic force mobilize a Black collectivity in direct opposition to the national consolidations of white dominion, those which secured white belonging through the noosing of a Black populace into an ever precarious and exploitable space of nonbelonging. As such, it works to unsettle the overwhelming narration of the Black Star Line as an economic failure and tethered to Garvey's imperial machinations. Further, in reconceptualizing Black diaspora as an expression of Black anarchism, it offers an alternative way of reading a global cohesion of antiblackness across national boundaries. It ends with a consideration of Black nationalism that stands counter to the popular Anarchist dismissal of Black social movements that interface with the state, determining that the state contested by typical Anarchist thought and the state contested by Black anarchism may indeed be different.

Chapter 3, "Ruination," reconsiders the Watts Rebellion of 1965 and its destructive disruptions, like arson, theft, and vandalism, as a cataclysm that clears material and discursive ground and proffers its own questions of property. Running counter to characterizations of senseless and cathartic or criminal and useless, these subversive practices interrupt the state's propertied analysis and solutions and refuse fealty to law and order. It argues that the cataclysmic vantage of the Watts rebellion overflows on a narrative meant to misapprehend both the political subjectivity of Black people and their conditions of possibility that locates transformative possibility in the state and the law. As such, it asks us to think differently and productively about destruction as offering its own intellect of refusal, a disruptive leap from white society's Black ghettoization, antagonistic to both state and civil society. The state's response is explored through both policing and public housing, the latter of which ascribes to notions of privatization and self-empowerment to muster property as the solution to crime, disorder, and urban malaise. Focusing specifically on Oscar Newman's concept of defensible space, the chapter suggests that the invocation of property endorses a US national fable that effectively shifts antagonism from view but also dematerializes the history of property that has created this structural inequality in the first place.

Chapter 4, "Maneuvers," examines the prison, expanding antiblack carcerality, and the criminalization of Black politics through the example of Assata Shakur, including her physical escape from prison and its textual reflection in her autobiography. It returns to the slave ship as a third origin story of the prison that interrupts dominant genealogies within carceral studies typified by the works of Michel Foucault (*Discipline and Punish*) and Michelle Alexander (*The New Jim Crow*) by centering the Black imprisoned subject and the history of chattel slavery, and which enunciate the entanglement of movement and punishment. Exploring this entanglement, the chapter argues that vagrancy emerges to paraphrase a prohibition of Black political practice and movement. With Shakur's abscondence from prison and the autobiography's arguable "absenting" of it, the chapter examines how Black surreptitious movement, as dis-incarceration, transmutes vagrancy to contest carceral practices and spaces. I argue that the absenting of her flight in the autobiography demonstrates an abolitionist interruption of cycles of reproduction and representation, those "declarative cul-de-sacs" that often mire Western politics and Black politics alike.[53] Initiated by the enslaved who jumped from the slave ship, this book deliberately finds its end with a return to abscondence to think about how secrecy and ultimately abandonment may maneuver an alternative aperture for Black liberation from this world.

Oceanic Elsewheres

With its impetus being Pip's leaps in *Moby-Dick* and the jumps of those enslaved held captive in Middle Passage slave ships, it is of little surprise that this project begins on the ocean. The ocean, the Atlantic Ocean in particular, has long been central to any understanding of Black history and contemporary Black life and positionality. In many ways, the history that has been foreclosed is in the ocean, littered among its depths in debris, wood and metal, flesh and bone. Yet to simply look to the ocean for artifacts is only to skim its surface. The sea also lends us a method, one that forces us to consider the simultaneity of past and present—the debris spanning centuries across the same oceanic floor, coming up for air across the same epipelagic zone. To look to the ocean invites us to consider across, between, and through chronological time, asking us, maybe even telling us, that we must move beyond discrete temporal periods. It becomes imperative to think through a collection of jumps from racial ships that have long been separated from simultaneous consideration. We are moved to consider not only the *longue durée* of Black confinement and capture but their oceanic connections rooted in a history of slavery and its contemporary afterlives. When moving past a land bias, it becomes apparent that the ocean, rather than separating, is actually connecting. While many believed, like those captains of the *Leusden* and the *Zong* who sent their cargo to their deaths, that the ocean would cleanse a violent history, this is merely an illusion.[54] An oceanic method instead elucidates a story of human life at the expense of Black death, one that must be examined with new optics that are not beholden to the West's colonizing discipline and violent temporalities.

In the same way that the slaves' jumps from the slave ship seem to come up for air in the unlikely place of a novel about a whaling ship, Black anarchist practices bubble just below the surface of our studies and observations on Black politics. They introduce a new modality of Black politics, an exertion of racial chaos that bridges the individual act with the collective, an anticipatory ruination, and nonrepresentational maneuvers. They are a radicalization that often does not, or cannot, make sense within traditional Western political spheres. In this way, the slaves' jumps from the slave ship do not only embody a rejection of the existing world as a set of material relations but also exemplify a frustration of this world's political logics, delineating their racial shape. Despite Ishmael's disavowals and displacements, Pip's jumps emerge from and animate Melville's story until the very end, demanding that we reckon with this refusal qua dissolution—the deed that exceeds the demand—even though this world often fails to. I turn now to these refusals, these deeds—these "lines of flight out of Empire"—as their own intellectual analyses of the world.[55]

1

Refusal

It requires much caution at first, in allowing them to go on deck, as it is a common practice for them to jump overboard to get quit of their misery.
—John Woolman, 1883

In the daily log for the British slaver *Lawrance*, on October 4, 1730, alongside a note about the breeze, there lies a clipped line that goes almost unnoticed in the countless yards of microfilm: "last night two of our woman slaves Jumpt overboard but being brisk loosed the boats and got them again."[1] References such as this by Abraham Dumaresq are not easily found, often lost among the litany of abuses experienced by the enslaved and perpetrated by a white master class. Scholars have done quick work of naming these moments when they can be found, but across a slave ship literature already marked by a "fundamental silence" and wider source material on the experience after Middle Passage journeys, they have been superseded by armed uprisings and plantation runaways in analyses related to resistance.[2] While these enslaved people, oftentimes women, launched themselves into the oceanic expanse of the Middle Passage and oppugned the relationships constitutive of the slave trade, the sheer strength of the practice has nonetheless garnered little attention to its political anatomy in comparison to allegedly more direct forms of resistance.

What provokes this hesitation about the enslaved who jumps? The answer to this question is of course manifold. It is no coincidence that the rebellious acts primarily carried out by enslaved Black women have been repeatedly neglected. As historian Jennifer L. Morgan has demonstrated, the claim of passivity "constructed African women as a panacea" and lifted their market value.³ Rather than revolutionaries themselves, enslaved women are culled as both antipode and salve in slave masters' ideologies of rebellion. As both byproduct and producer of these persuasions, the very spatial structures of slave ships gather our conceptual frameworks for understanding how, where, and to what end Black liberatory practice takes place. While Black women were of course involved in ship takeovers and armed insurrections and often used constructed docility against the crewmen who held them, their participation in this arena has been entangled with assumptions that such tactics were in greater part the result of enslaved men. Whether or not this is factual has little bearing on the ways this gendered premise has continued to shape our mis/understanding of revolutionary dissent. The belief that armed resistance was more often than not a male enterprise and more effective because of it meant that armed resistance was given a more sustained analysis. Concurrently, the forms and sites of protest that were by majority the pursuit of enslaved women have often been overlooked and understudied. That the jump from the slave ship has been held at arm's length from substantive political study is steeped in its equation with suicide, suicide's comparisons to surrender, and the feminization of this entire composition.⁴

Suicide among the enslaved was a major point of emphasis in antislavery campaigns across the eighteenth and nineteenth centuries. White abolitionists, especially those of the evangelical sort, often depicted these suicidal acts as "peculiarly feminine capitulations" where the enslaved have succumbed to "utter humiliation," while Black abolitionists like Henry Highland Garnett and Joshua Bowen Smith would later venerate them as acts of enslaved men and their principled resistance to tyranny.⁵ Where white abolitionists used Black bodies to punctuate the aberration of slavery, Black abolitionists powerfully recognized the slave's desire for freedom, but both camps remained wedded to gendered questions of morality and the heroism of enslaved men. In modern scholarly accounts of slave resistance, the anxiety has been quelled through a series of political typologies that effectively squirrel away acts of self-inflicted death. Indeed, in some scholarship, the distinction has been made between "subtle resistance," to which jumping overboard has been assigned, and "band resistance."[6] Eric Robert Taylor, famously studying shipboard revolts, even defines *revolt* as an action that must involve at least two individuals "with the intent of reclaiming their freedom." Practices he understands to be suicidal or an effort to escape are relegated to the term *resistance* because they are "singularly concerned with personally rejecting it."[7] These systems of classification occasion the argument that shipboard mutinies receive the attention that the enslaveds' jumps do not because the former invokes the mass while the latter is restricted to the individual. Yet they also hold presuppositions of political efficacy and a tenuous delineation of insurrection from its allegedly lesser counterparts. Peeled back, Taylor's overdeterminations of efficacy reveal the sinew of Western liberal traditions of politics' function and methods and recirculate the "numbers, ciphers, and fragments" of the master's archive.[8] Different but inseparable from the cynical dismissal in the ship log that opened this chapter, maritime insurance law and litigation, I will argue, urge the system of outcomes and measures of success that base Taylor's claims.

But beyond a retort against typologies and white Western genealogies, this chapter initiates a larger argument for Black anarchism and the socio-spatial textures it invites. Recent scholarship in and of Black anarchism, greatly attuned to the matter of Black liberation, are aware of its "existential threat to white supremacy" and the impossibility of reform for this purpose.[9] Charged by the necessity to "change course" away from the democratic promises of the West and liberalism and expressly concerned with the collective, Black anarchism mobilizes a crucial question: "Which fear is greater, the fear of the pain we know or the pain we do not?"[10] *Jump* emphasizes the agnosticism that undergirds this query, which is central to the Black anarchist thought and practice discussed herein. This insistence is genetically different from those accounts of resistance during the Middle Passage animated by diagnostic descriptions of intentions. As such, *Jump* chooses not to use the word *suicide* to describe jumps of the enslaved to resist the urge of assigning justifications to their practices. Too often, the term *suicide* implies and applies intentions to deny a relevance to politics strictly understood. It is not that *suicide* lacks a political quality but rather that its politicization is a primary reason that the term cannot account for the form of dissent that this book attempts to examine. Refusing the conventional lexicon is not to ignore the importance of death as an interruption of enslavement, but it is to recast it in the political without recourse to measurements of the *desire* to die, or, for that matter, to live. The politicality of jumps from the slave ship rests in the practice, rather than the desire, *of* death, mobility, and destruction that confronts, opposes, and interrupts the system of enslavement. The principal point is not to disavow the desire for resistance but to consider how and what the jump refuses to offer as an alternative approach to defining its political form. This methodological approach is dictated by the archive of slavery itself, where access to the interiority of the enslaved, which is arguably a prerequisite to define something like suicide, is largely unavailable. The Black anarchist lens employed here also distrusts the sense of agency inherent to the stamp of "self-destruction" that runs counter to the nonhuman conditions of compulsion and coercion that structure the world of enslavement for the enslaved.

These structures of enslavement are imperative to any study of Black political practice and have been central to discussions of carcerality within Black anarchist scholarship. However, a substantive engagement with the socio-spatial environment from which Black anarchism leaps has not yest been endeavored. The jump from the slave ship parses Black anarchism from a new socio-spatial vantage point that allows us at once to rethink often maligned practices of refusal and to retheorize our carceral state. Doing so requires breaking from an explication of the slave ship as simply a place where slavery occurred and instead resetting the central role played by the ship as a spatial apparatus that constituted the chattel slave. This explication follows in the lead of those like Simone Browne and Dennis Childs who trace modern surveillance and incarceration from the slave ship.[11] Holding the jump of the enslaved and the slave ship together in this way marks the refusal of not only a single space but the social order that was both constituted and maintained by its built environment.

Enslaved Black women's jumps from the seafaring architecture of enslavement illuminate an ever-expansive authority of the master (that is, of the human) at the necessary dehumanizing cost of the slave position that is as materially extant as it is politically enduring. Expressing an "abolition of all constraints," these leaps bear a refusal of both, the physical "production and containment of [raced and] gendered difference," as well as the interpretive valuations reducing the jumps of the enslaved to unfortunate circumstance.[12] They provide a new anarchistic map for Black politics that lays bare a topography of racial boundaries that constitute classical Anarchism and Western liberalism alike, problematizing raced-gendered definitions of rebellion and refusing the thrust of reproduction. This is not offered as a corrective to the historical record that has heretofore failed to substantively undertake the scene of the enslaved jumping the slave ship as Black politics. Instead, it is what the jumps can teach us that bears out this opening chapter, illustrating the multiple and converging ways in which assumptive logics of form, site, and progenitors of protest circumscribe our interpretations of what it means to practice radical politics as well as encouraging an appreciation of unrecognizability guided by the agnosticism of practice rather than the security of ideology.

To approach the jump in this way aims to comprehend its critical purchase as it enunciates the limit of our political understanding and offers one glimpse of the antagonism of Black anarchistic protest to the West and Western political thought. This means reckoning with the conceptual difficulty of destruction as Black politics, with cataclysm in excess of demands, with the anticipatory promise of abolition but also the risk of death. While the countless ripples of her splash signal the extent to which the jumps from the slave ship generate a force against enslavement, the perils of the oceanic space also illustrate their precarity. Ruptures along the boundaries of a socio-spatial order of containment that depended on white rule and Black abjection, they were also an almost certain death. We are reminded, "When death is a synonym for sanctuary, political engagement is, to say the least, a paradoxical undertaking."[13] This suggests the ethical emptiness of engagement that animates the exigency of refusal and limns the unease of death as such refusal. In this way, the jumps indicate a tension in our understanding of disorder and the im/possibility of new worlds. They mobilize our thinking beyond prefigurative politics, the deed that exceeds the demand, and force a serious undertaking of the unknowable and unimagined as fertile ground for Black politics. They refuse our imagination's dependency on those forms of politics that may reorganize, but still reproduce, the world that we already know. The jump posits, as Fanon argues, that to "change the order of the world" requires "total disorder."[14]

The Vestibule

As the log of the *Lawrance* can attest, the documentation of the jumps of the enslaved are dispassionate accounts, marking the deaths of the enslaved alongside the brief, but always more detailed, descriptions of the weather. The archive of slavery tells us very little of enslaved life except to tell us it was disregarded. A single sentence across two lines is the only reference to the two women's jumps from the slave ship in the entirety of the log, the archive as fleeting and momentary as the act of jumping itself. Yet while there is little formal documentation as to the number of enslaved people who jumped from slave ships during the transatlantic slave trade, jumps were happening as long as slavers were sailing. In his narrative, Olaudah Equiano recounts a moment when numerous slaves aboard the ship to which he was sequestered "preferred death to such a life of misery."[15] The account of British surgeon Alexander Falconbridge mentions instances of enslaved women leaping from the slave ship admitting "circumstances of this kind are very frequent."[16] In 1714, while aboard the *Florida*, four enslaved women, one of whom was pregnant, jumped overboard while the ship was departing. In 1732, six enslaved women jumped from the slave ship of Captain James Hogg in the middle of the night.[17] There are also the fourteen enslaved women who jumped from La Soleil in 1774.[18] This was not only a problem for the British and the French, as evidence shows that Spanish ships were also quite accustomed to these breaches.[19]

Jumping from the slave ship was widely practiced by the enslaved and widely feared by the crew, and in both their formal and informal instructions, merchants warned captains. While instructing the crew to keep a vigilant watch, captains, for their part, requisitioned numerous accoutrements and alterations, all in the effort to keep the enslaved under control. Still, there are cases when large groups of thirty to one hundred enslaved people were known to have jumped. Oftentimes, though not exclusively, these jumps from the slaver were practiced by enslaved women who went about the deck relatively unfettered in comparison to enslaved men who were typically chained to ringbolts when outside of the hold. The jumps of enslaved women often occurred when they "gave [the crew] ye slip," spontaneously plunging into the sea if they were able to dodge the netting and the rescue parties desperate to return them.[20] Faced with unknown and indescribable danger, the enslaved jumped anyway, exhibiting the radicalization of an urgency to escape the constrictions, violence, and overwhelming governance that enact the structural antagonism of enslavement.

One of the difficulties in proposing the jump from the slave ship as a practice of sociogeographic force is the postulation of the ship as simply the setting of the struggle over power. This postulate claims the innocence of architecture, which is itself birthed in what Henri Lefebvre has called the "illusion of transparency" that asserts the full comprehension of space on simple sight alone. Transparency dictates that space is free of secrecy and the realm of action given free rein.[21] Space is thus assumed to be devoid of meaning and power until ideology brings its meaning into being. Within this schema of innocence, the slave ships are retold as a bastardization of an otherwise respectable history of maritime architecture. Further, with space understood to be absolute, sutured closed, and impenetrable to change, the ship schematics are offered as if they tell us the entirety of a spatial story. The counter, provided by Michel de Certeau's famous vignette "Walking in the City," is that the bird's-eye view is not an absolute truth, because the movement through space is also its enunciation. It is the interaction with space that actualizes a selection of the possibilities that are organized by the spatial order, that "makes [these possibilities] exist as well emerge," and it is through these improvisations that space is remodeled.[22]

As an alternative to the blunted geographic story offered by ship schematics, the jumps of enslaved women provide a blueprint for what Katherine McKittrick and Clyde Woods call a "black geography," a Black vantage point from which to understand the production of segregated space as they "disclose how the racialized production of space is made possible."[23] They are Black tactics that map even as they reconfigure the boundaries meant to maintain enslaved Black life. To use Lefebvre's phrasing, the enslaved who jump the slave ship reveal it as a social space that is a social product.[24] According to his spatial triad, while the slave ship is conceived in its design and commercial production, its meaning and its reality as a space are formed and transformed by how it is perceived and lived by social actors. The slave ship comes into being as a ship for and by the system of enslavement where its use is its very constitution; its physical space lacks reality "without the energy that is deployed within it."[25] This is not meant to imply that each spatial mechanism has a fully developed intentionality behind it but rather that the social forces that produce the ship are the very mechanisms and operations that orient, situate, and make the space function.[26] These mechanisms, actuated only by movement within and around them, are what constitute and codify relationships in the social order. Put simply, it is in this ordering of space—the violent practices of division, distribution, extraction, exploitation, appropriation, and obliteration—that the social order is created.[27] Mercurial and accumulative, the ship in its multitudinous mechanisms of brutality is best understood as a "living, micro-cultural, micro-political system in motion" through the enslaved's experience of it, the linchpin whose antagonistic relations shaped the modern world.[28]

FIGURE 1.1: "Slave Ship Fredensborg II, 1788." *Slavery Images: A Visual Record of the African Slave Trade and Slave Life in the Early African Diaspora*, http://slaveryimages.org/s/slaveryimages/item/2058

The intimacy of the slave ship brought with it an anxiety of maintaining divisions. While the captain and officers resided in the higher quarters, the crew and the enslaved were "neighbors in [the] space belowdecks."[29] To keep the distance clear, the carpenter, boatswain, and gunner were in charge of spatial practices by which the enslaved were kept aboard. Before the late eighteenth century, when slave ships were not yet being produced for the slave trade and instead employed retrofitted vessels, alterations were made to the existing structures, the most crucial of which was to increase the size of the hold and modify the hatches to be "fit" for human cargo.[30] In all slave ships, this fitting included providing a means for air to reach the enslaved in the hold that maintained the upmost security, which came in the form of iron grates at the hatches or the attachment of collapsible canvas funnels. As the ship was loaded on the African coast and awaited departure for the Middle Passage, the crew fashioned a makeshift holding area of wood lattice walls on the main deck to "prevent the purchased negroes from leaping overboard" and to flaccidly shelter them from the elements.[31]

Upon leaving the port, this temporary pen was replaced with netting hung along the ship's sides, again to ward off any vaulting pursuits.[32] Employed alongside chains and bolts, this aggregate of accoutrements evidence what late historian Stephanie Camp has argued in her work on plantation slavery, that "enslavement was containment."[33] But aboard the floating barracoon, while all these mechanisms might singularly define this axiom, it was the barricado that could signal the slave ship from a distance. Described as "a strong wooden barrier ten feet high that bisected the width of the ship near the mainmast and extended about two feet over each side of the vessel," it was spiked and fitted with swivel guns at the top, as well as peep holes through which the crew fired pistols and muskets.[34] The provisory wall was primarily used to separate the enslaved men and women, but it also acted as a defensive barrier behind which the crew would retreat to the women's side to quell insurrections on the deck.[35] Together, the draconian composite of barricades and latticework in wood, rope, and iron mark the perennial impress of violence on the body yoking precaution, domination, and subjection. In their attempt to secure the enslaved to the ship, they exist as landmarks of the constitutive foreclosure of the self and the transmutation to chattel.

By colonial extraction and bodily extirpation, the slave ship is the site of what Hortense Spillers has termed "vestibular cultural formation" that makes and unmakes the Black subject/object nautical mile after nautical mile.[36] To think with Spillers's formulation posits the slave ship as a/the primary vestibule of racial formation at the forging of the New World and clarifies the spatial technologies that shape its metamorphic capacity. More than additions to a regular vessel, the aforementioned spatial mechanisms of domination and coercion are fundamental to the "ship's optimal function," constituting its operative architecture.[37] In this light, the slave ship as vestibule is a passageway, a container, an interregnum, a "birth canal" that ushers blackness as abjection and non/being.[38] From the barracoon on the shore to the barricado on the ship, the spatial practices that lacerate and wrench as they divide and discipline are both

FIGURE 1.2: "Revolt aboard Slave Ship, 1787." *Slavery Images: A Visual Record of the African Slave Trade and Slave Life in the Early African Diaspora*, http://slaveryimages.org/s/slaveryimages/item/2060

producers and byproducts of the social relation of enslavement. In their brutality and regularity, they repeat blackness as the constitutive outside and abject to the human, shaping the order of the modern world as expeditiously as the slave ship sails. With each spatial interaction comes execution of the relation of difference between Black and white as enslaved and person. Every hatch, ringbolt, and barricade reiterated this relation as a condition of abjection for all the enslaved rather than as a singular instantiation of difference between individuals; each use of each device differentiated users from targets, masters from captive bodies. This vestibular subjection glosses the architectural expression of order, the production of racial blackness as a structurally antagonistic difference via practices of discipline, captivity, and coercion.

Indexing a mode of domination that is metamorphic, that transmutes blackness as nonhuman, vestibular subjection suggests that the racial order is birthed in the very production of space. Its series of spatial elaborations, even or especially those violently sedentarizing techniques, both discursive and material, that are employed when Black people are "out of place" endure untethered from consciousness. This is not a preamble for absolving participants of the trade but rather an argument that brutal intent was not necessary for the brutality of relation that (use of) the mechanism enacts. In the latticed corral and the drawing of the hatches, the practices of containment and policing produce space as distribution, confinement, and order(ing) of all those who inhabit it. Race here is a constitution rather than a given, an enactment of order inscribed on the body, a political relationality instituted by "extremity of force" rather than an identity.[39] The drawing of lines and the creation of containers mechanized from the hold to the barricado classified and divided an entire master race over and against enslaveable blackness and in this separation produced these very positions. In this way, the slave ship instantiates the very conditions of possibility for the carceral geographies that ride slavery's wake.

The mobile, seafaring nature of the slave ship is itself crucial to understanding that the spatial creation of the social order is wrapped up in its reiterative maintenance. As antechamber "literally suspended in the oceanic," the slave ship renders the enslaved "nowhere at all," and meaning is both lost (kinship, person) and gained (property, cargo) on and through the body.[40] The ocean, far from the coherence, support, and security of land, signals the uncertainty of being that must be quelled by the repetitious, if not unsteady, variety of fixive spatial practices regulating the life of the enslaved. In short, the recurrent recapitulations of the relation of black to white as slave to master were repetitions crucial to order. In order's incomplete state, categorically short of absolution (what Oliver Marchart via Ernesto Laclau calls the unreachability of pure systematicity of the system), the slave ship demonstrates race governance as a process of continuous territorialization necessary to the constitutive relation of domination.⁴¹ The fluid quality of the slave ship was made even more salient through the flexibility and of its temporary structures and adjustable components that bespeak the maintenance of order as less fixed barriers and more adaptive conditioning of subjection that can shift as needed. If this ephemerality and systemic instability appears to decrease the gratuitousness of violence imagined to condition the life of the enslaved, it only does so by making it more difficult to hold it up to the light of greater scrutiny.

Engendering Race

Once past the Door of No Return, the hold and the barricado produced the positions of the enslaved woman and man through intimate violations of the body. Arguably two of the slave ship's most defining spatial characteristics, together they demonstrate how fluidity and flexibility are integral to the simultaneity of race and gender formation through the vestibule. Beneath the hatches and along the decks, the engendering of blackness was a matter of socio-spatial positioning that again did not simply describe categories of difference but were intrinsic to the production of categorical meanings inscribed on the bodies of the enslaved and concretized in the minds of slavers.⁴² The articulation of spatial mechanism and the body concerned the maintenance of order tied to the production of knowledge, where meaning fulfilled on and through the Black body meant knowing it as outside the position of the human. This outsideness, constituted through enslavement's condition of Black flesh as absolutely exploitable, unequivocally complicates any assumption of gender's separation from blackness.

Spillers has argued that while the enslaved woman and enslaved man were subject to different conditions, they were also "ungendered" as quantifiable property, whose only difference was how much space they took up in the hold. That "every man slave is to be allowed six feet by one foot four inches for room, every woman five feet ten by one foot

FIGURE 1.3: "Transport des négres dans les colonies." *Slavery Images: A Visual Record of the African Slave Trade and Slave Life in the Early African Diaspora*, http://slaveryimages.org/s/slaveryimages/item/3000

four, every boy five feet by one foot two, and every girl four feet by one foot."[43] Slave ships were consciously overpopulated, deliberately stacking the enslaved to lie in the crescented curves of each other's bodies along every rounded corner of the hold, careful to maximize space and, as slave trader Theodore Canot has implied, to ensure that they did not sit aboard as passengers.[44] Occupied spaces were "[shrunk] to their minimum," directly contributing to their physical death and sharply marking their social death.[45] The hold, in this way, signifies how gender provided no coherence to challenge the enslaved's structural position as nonhuman. At the same time, practices of enslavement aboard the slave ship did divergently produce the categories of enslaved woman and enslaved man in overwhelmingly violent ways.

The barricado's use as a dividing line was meant to mitigate the damage of rebellion by keeping, and violently striking down, the insurgent men from the protected side of the allegedly less dangerous enslaved women and children. It exemplifies how the hierarchy of engendered race developed through its practice, here through its exacerbation of sexual violence. Often because of the barricado, enslaved women, while at times shackled like enslaved men, were more often left unchained on their dictated side. Coupled with the precautionary netting hung along the sides of the ship, the barricado provided crewmen even greater sexual access to enslaved women's bodies out of sight. Their relative liberty meant that the disciplinary production of the classification "enslaved woman" often occurred through their illimitable sexual exploitation by white slavers that positioned them "irrevocably outside the category of the feminine."[46] Numerous journals write of common sailors and officers sexually abusing enslaved women, noting that many had unlimited license.[47] The fact that they occurred in the open air only intensifies the well-accepted and illimitable vulnerability that defined the enslaved woman, what Christina Sharpe calls the "monstrous intimacies," which are "breathed in like air" but go unacknowledged as horrors.[48] The barricado and the hold compound as much as they exemplify the "exposure of female captives to sexual predation" that is foundational to creating hierarchies of engendered race.[49]

This is not to argue that enslaved men were not also brazenly violated. On the contrary, the frequency and the secrecy surrounding the rape of enslaved men similarly shaped the heteropatriarchal violence at the heart of chattel slavery. As historian Thomas Foster has demonstrated, the sexual violation of enslaved men's bodies was rampant under slavery, even if its extent is not yet well understood.[50] The gratuitous disregard and general disavowal of sexual violence as an "offense not affecting the existence of the slave" was built into enslavement for all of the enslaved.[51] Legally, the rape of the enslaved was not recognized in the same way that murder *could* be, with the rape of the enslaved impossible within the context of the law. The impossibility of rape was in part made possible by the assertion of the "rapacity of the Negro," effectively linking blackness with sexual excess.[52] For the enslaved aboard the slave ship, the physical boundaries produced social divisions; devices that devise as they divide, they conjured qualities such as violence and sexual lasciviousness and named them inherent, marking differences between the enslaved but also between them and their captors.

The issue, then, it seems, is not whether the enslaved can be said to have gender and whether this is given by the hold or barricado but that articulation with these spatial practices enunciates what it means, as Saidiya Hartman terms, to be "possessed by gender."[53] The very meaning of enslaved Black woman is engendered simultaneously by the practice of illimitable sexual violence and the disavowal of the practice as anything other than the everyday conditioning of the enslaved. Thus, the barricado unveils the engendering of the enslaved woman not as a lack of the protections assumed to be generated by gender and embodied by whites, but as a totalizing access to the body that renders her distinction from the human. The fluidity of ascriptions enacted on and attached to the enslaved woman in the barricado alone—"how gender, and its variations of terms, are made to mean"—disclose the possession, which, as Patrice D. Douglass argues, "obscur[es] rather than clarif[ies] where violence enters the condition."[54] The constitution of gender as such in the structural antagonism of blackness as nonhuman illustrates their inseparability and their incapacity to stand as coherent identity categories from which to claim any viable protection in the world birthed by the slave ship.

Narrative Silencing

As these partitions and reticulum geographically consolidated vulnerability to sexual violation that became essential to the captive body's fabrication as sentient property—and this cannot be overstated—the meaning-making power of these spatial structures extended to the very knowing of rebellion and its endemic formulation of feminine passivity over and against masculine aggression. Unlike the plantations that would be a primary geography for the enslaved upon landing, especially in the English Americas, where enslaved men had a more elastic relationship to confinement, aboard the slave ship it was enslaved women who had a greater opportunity for movement.⁵⁵ In this way, the slave ship produced its own "cleavages of the social order" and different possibilities for political refusal that also imbued the enslaved with gendered meanings.⁵⁶ As a mechanism of discipline, the barricado named men more willful than women, not to offer any gendered semblance of protection but in the service of concretizing racial ideologies, that is, in the conditioning of discourse. The barricado's separation of enslaved women and men conjured the former's docility in terms of the will to rebel and feigned the ease with which it was assumed that enslaved Black women could be controlled. From chain to net, the architectures of the vessel shaped and were shaped by the trope of the hypermasculine African man as rebellion's source and by the docile African woman as its beneficiary, which together continue to determine our grasp of what dissent looks like and who practices it. Where the barricado unsees the willfulness of enslaved Black women, the nettings holding the jump at bay named enslaved Black women as hyper-affected and irrational.

Taylor's own rebellion typology, mentioned at the outset of this chapter, inherits these notions of passivity as he celebrates armed rebellion as the effect of those enslaved who "managed to transcend their differences and come together for one common cause," distinct from those who "would sit by passively as their shipmates fought and died."⁵⁷ As Taylor argues that ship takeovers are "*true testaments* to the ability of severely oppressed people *to find the will* to capably stage highly effective rebellions" and characterize the pursuit of "true freedom," he sits comfortably in the conventions of rebellion's study that attempt to render the interiority of the enslaved and the will to be free.⁵⁸ In truth, the only convention that Taylor contests is in the "definition of slave resistance" where he attests, "it is the effort we celebrate rather than the result," in which, of course, lies the rub.⁵⁹ While it is not my intent to diminish the bravery of the enslaved who participated in armed takeovers, Taylor's multiple invocations of heroism and of results as the testimony of will, like the barricado's formulation of insurrection, beg the question of what we make of other forms of dissent. The implication of dismissal of those other practices fashion the notions of freedom we continue to inherit and, despite Taylor's claims to the contrary, demonstrate that the convention has always been results.

Whether armed or nonviolent, our conventional definitions of rebellion, of what makes resistance, have come to depend on questions of outcomes, retroactively ascribing meaning to those practices that are deemed successful within our frame of what politics is supposed to do.[60] The survey of "success" attempts delineations that disavow forms of critique and promote measurements of progress that ultimately keep our political order intact. But trafficking in such appraisals and developing classifications quite indifferent to the jump from the slave ship finds its roots much deeper than Taylor's choice to celebrate the takeover at the expense of other forms of dissent. Insurance litigation, a primary archive of slave ship resistance, demonstrates how its modeling predetermines the jumps' excisions from our political landscape. While slave ship litigation during the late seventeenth and eighteenth centuries has been widely discussed by scholars interested in the dehumanization of the enslaved and the inherent contradictions of the enslaved as human cargo, I argue that it may also be the primogenitor of the immutable outcome structure governing the nexus of politics and intentions and dangerously tabulating the desire to be free.

The insurance litigation archive largely begins in 1698. Prior to this, the Royal African Company of England monopolized the trade in enslaved Africans, which allowed the company to spread risk; this makes it difficult to assess whether voyages undertaken prior to 1698 had to be insured. After 1698, however, merchants in the Atlantic slave trade became more numerous, and independent insurance underwriting became much more frequent. Insurance litigation from this period indicates a history of slave valuation and evinces how the language and procedures of insuring slave ships has, in fact, played a formative role in the intellectual lineage of slave rebellion. Our definitions are shaped by the same concerns that structure the work of insuring slave ships against loss in their attempt to *know* resistance.

Perhaps the most widely known and regularly cited case is the 1781 *Zong* massacre and its subsequent insurance litigation, a series of horrors in which 133 of the enslaved were jettisoned from a British slave ship under the auspices of saving the remainder from dehydration. This was perpetrated under the agreement that the ship's owners would then bring a coverage case against its insurers, which they did, claiming "general average" and assuring that it was of absolute necessity to cast off a portion of the enslaved for the purposes of keeping the rest alive.[61] Along with the *Zong* case, there is considerable literature describing ship owners' claims and the insurance coverage of human cargo, including claims based on losses by "perils of the sea" and by rebellion. Although there was no officially recognized rebellion aboard the *Zong*, scholars often refer to losses by rebellion as a counterpoint from which to understand insurance litigation concerning the enslaved being thrown overboard. Often amiss in these readings and recitations is the fact of the enslaveds' *jumping* overboard—as a practice of dissent. This lacuna is constructed in part by the insurance law that constitutes rebellion and positions the jump awkwardly against other forms, the excess of risk that cannot be financially accommodated.

When the *Zong* set out across the Atlantic from São Tomé on September 6, 1781, it was overpopulated. A relatively smaller ship, the *Zong* should have carried only about 193 enslaved persons, but instead it set out with 459 when leaving Accra, greatly exceeding a "full complement."[62] Around 133 were thrown from the English-owned *Zong* when, allegedly running short on water, Captain Luke Collingwood ordered that they be killed in three batches to ensure that "marketable" slaves would make it to their destination in Jamaica.[63] Between the evening of November 29 and December 1, enslaved women, men, and children were dispatched through cabin windows or cast from the ship's quarterdeck.[64] The massacre would have gone relatively unnoticed had it not been for the legal case that the owners of the *Zong* raised against the ship's insurers to secure payment. To turn its "lost cargo" into profit, the ship owners attempted to make a claim against the ship's insurance.

In a trial held in March 1783 at the Guildhall in London, a jury found in favor of the owners, thus deciding that the insurers were obligated to dispense compensation under the terms of the insurance policy. This decision was appealed, but when Lord Chief Justice Mansfield along with Justices Buller and Willes made their decision for retrial in May 1783, they were not making a judgment on the act of killing but on whether the killing could be legally compensated.[65] To this end, during the proceedings, it was to be decided whether the mass killing was "a matter of necessity" as the owners claimed.[66] John Lee, the solicitor general representing the owners, argued that this was not a moral issue, for the enslaved were thrown overboard as property "for the preservation of the Residue. . . . That if a hundred did not die in this way 200 must in another."[67] The insurers denied this, believing that the only legally acceptable basis for compensation of the dead enslaved would have been death due to a shipboard revolt.[68] In response, Lee claimed that had the killing not taken place, "there must have been such an insurrection," but more so that as things, the killing of the enslaved "constituted a sensible jettisoning of objects."[69]

Insurance is based in the question of risk—the risk of loss by dehydration and the risk of loss by rebellion. In terms of slave ships, rebellion is the most prominent example of an excess of risk in insurance underwriting, as it was understood as almost guaranteed. To be excessive in terms of insurance is to be "too predictable, too likely, too probable for any underwriter to promise compensation."[70] The obvious juxtaposition to those that are thrown in response to risk, are those who are in excess of risk because they jump. The question is then what differentiates them from "rebellion" as it was alluded to in law and in insurance underwriting. The archive will say it is the difference of "inherent vice." While the insurance coverage of rebellion shifted throughout the eighteenth century—where at times death in general was not covered at all or rebellion was covered only if a certain mortality threshold was met—it was always marked in contradistinction to other forms of death on the ship.

Slave "suicide," under which the jump from the slave ship was often organized, also has a shifting history in the lineage of maritime and life insurance litigation. While for a time it was listed separately, British insurance policy in 1781 included suicide under the appellation "natural death." This shifted again with *Jones v. Schmoll* (1785), wherein the death by suicide was narrated as an "inherent vice," which then determined its exclusion from the ship owners' recovery.[71] In other words, it is a foreseeable circumstance of the slave trade that the enslaved would try to kill themselves and as such would not be covered by insurance. *Jones v. Schmoll* decided that those who committed suicide after a rebellion were not covered due to inherent vice, but those who attempted to escape were part of the general average. This line was drawn with the belief that the nomination of inherent vice did not include "the desire to be free."[72] It reveals the uneasy attempt to set standards on the confluence of the terms of rebellion, escape, and suicide. While the archive is unsettled in its delineations, what does become increasingly clear is how the archive of insurance litigation and underwriting depends on outcomes that retroactively determine intentionality.

The status of the enslaved as sentient beings—property that is both physically living and socially dead—emerges in the various rationales offered to arbitrators and annotates the antagonism of Black life and white preservation. As property, they are absolutely subject to the will of the master, but as sentient property, they are also and in all cases considered a threat, a risk, "regarded as enemies . . . enemies who might revolt."[73] The *Jones v. Schmoll* decision marks insurance and the discourse of risk dependent on intention, and presupposes a desire for freedom that continues to skew our understanding of rebellion. Maritime insurance litigation already constitutes a definition of rebellion that requires the loss of control over the ship to the enslaved, inferring a direct and physical interaction between master and the enslaved, by differentiating itself from escape—this is Taylor's inherited typology. In the move to differentiate between suicide and escape in the terms of desire, insurance litigation increasingly impacts the larger narrative of rebellion. How does one measure the desire to be free?

It is not a coincidence that the language used to describe the jump from the slave ship is couched in giving up, preference of death over life, and getting "quit of one's misery." Often absented from the modeling of rebellion, the fact of the jump was and is reduced to a suicidal surrender to the conditions of slavery, where suicide is often coded as feminine. This is in part due to the descriptions of slave suicides that littered newspapers and autobiographies in the nineteenth century, circulating images of enslaved women taking their own lives that would become icons in anti-slavery writing.[74] While there are examples of suicide that are read as male, such as "self-sacrifice in war or a republican challenge to tyranny," those instances of suicide that "appear to constitute surrender rather than a choice" are mapped as the practices of women.[75] Such a gendering of suicide presumes a legible intentionality, but more importantly, it is also circumscribed by a narrative structure that names men more willful than women.

The outcome model's pursuit to explain desires for liberation, its use of race-gender logics and measurements of rebellion, resistance, and threat, push the jump outside the frame. How has this affected our knowledge of the extent to which jumps were occurring? How so has it continued to affect our inherited understandings of what dissent aboard ships looked like? How, too, has this affected what dissent continues to be? The terms of suicide, escape, and rebellion that we have been given are steeped in a moral calculus of both failure and honor, an arithmetic that is ultimately dismissive of the jump as a practice of refusal. Among these specifications, the practice of jumping ship retains its political affect only with the survival of the enslaved. It reduces us to a particular trajectory for the successes of "resistance" and analytically forecloses the jump from its attack on the master, his property, his rule, and his sovereignty. The outcome/intentionality model is a dismissal that eases us out of the conundrum of what Iton calls "difficult data," those acts that put pressure on our narrow understanding of political practice.[76]

While some scholars, including Taylor, have perceived the enslaved's jump as a self-inflicted death and a form of defiance, there are still others who further downplay its significance.[77] Like the insurance underwriters before them, those taking stock of the jump have assessed importance depending on if one dies and how one dies and dangerously tied the intentionality of the enslaved to the outcome of their act. This only extends the "archival structure of knowability" that is often silent when it comes to the most radical acts practiced by the enslaved, in particular by the enslaved woman.[78] To look to the jump is to look at a practice that is generally ignored, one that unearths a productive tension that mobilizes political thought. How have our specifications undermined the agnostic power of the enslaved's jump? When the possibility of death unflinchingly demarcates a move beyond "a life of misery," how have we dismissed different modalities of Black liberation? As the litigation and subsequent reappropriation of such archives has shown, the jumps of the enslaved are a practice that fails to find purchase in Western political discourse. It is a practice of refusal that eclipses the narrative of emancipation and its legal apparatuses. Rooted in paradox and tension gleaned through a Black anarchist lens, it also troubles any conventional construction of Black politics.

To Thieve the Self

Scholars and activists, both enduring and contemporary, of what can be admittedly generalized under the banner Black anarchism have authored a capacious and necessary philosophy that has subverted the oft-trotted-out course of liberalism and classical Anarchism as much as it has transformed our grasp of the Black radical tradition.[79] In this vein, the jump from the slave ship indicates the conjunction of blackness and anarchism, the "radicalization of radicality," that the former is always the latter or that the latter is a condition of the former.[80] Our appreciation of this relationship is rooted in the practice itself rather than in the concretization of an archetype. To attune oneself to this is to at once reveal and refuse the material and epistemic bonds of society. The jump is neither loyal to any centralizing authority nor bound to any preordained alternative, and in this way it disrupts our typical ways of thinking and doing politics, inviting new perspectives of enduring contexts. Further, the jump evidences, as Morgan's locative work of enslaved women in revolt has argued, that attention to their practices promises to powerfully shift our understandings as they produced a particular critique of power.[81] Rather than reread a limitation to the corporeal or to further buttress a general disregard steeped in the assumption of individualism, the jumps of enslaved women teach us that the action of an individual, in its contestation of the order that defines and assembles collections of people, is always an invocation of the collective.

In the preceding sections, I have demonstrated how the power to dictate the place of the enslaved emergent in the very architectures of the slave ship was an expression of racial order, of vestibular subjection. At the same time, the jumps from the slave ship are practices that interrupt the centralizing authority of enslavement. In attempting to live outside the parameters of meaning-making indelibly inscribed on the flesh—that is, the production of blackness—the jumps from the slave ship emerged as a "living force," antithetical to the processes of enslavement that produced the African as enslaved in defiance of sovereignty over both life and death.[82] At its root, the jump refuses, and it reflects the material and theoretical possibilities of withdrawal from structurally antagonistic authority as the architect of transformation, even as the enslaved faces the ocean knowing full well that the gratuitous conditions of antiblackness seem insurmountable.

The jump offers us a particular vantage for the politics of refusal. Unlike an armed uprising, the jump rejected the racial governance of the slave ship by a literal leap. In the case of jumping ship, the enslaved did not take over the ship and steer it in a new direction but abandoned the ship altogether and bore questions about the possibility and meaning of destroying its object, the enslaved. The jump of the enslaved was antagonistic to the West, both in and beyond the spatial violences that contained and regulated Black life and death about the ship. It embodied the threat of opening up possibilities of being that precipitated the gratuitous violence that came as punishment and the immobilizing narratives that attempted to name it a consequence of insanity. As Margaret Higgonet has argued, "Above all, [suicide] creates a rift in meaning" because "by cutting short the 'natural' span of life, the person who takes his or her life both turns it into a metaphoric ruin and breaks the frames that society relies upon to produce meaning."[83] In the case of the enslaved, where the "natural" span of life included the "perils of the sea" and dying at the hands of master and his crew, the jump interrupted the system of meaning on which the slave ship sailed and that it served to constitute. Rather than simply an assertion of a new subject, a "new entry on the balance sheet of identities," the enslaved's jumps from the slave ship signified a "violent, practical, active desubjectivation, the rejection and betrayal of the role that has been assigned to them."[84] As such, in interrupting the very antagonistic relations that structure enslavement, the jump was an exertion of self, predicated on the refusal of self.

If we can understand the West as the "environment that is hostile to us" deployed through various spatialities of capture and control, then the jumps are both revelations and rejections.[85] Taken here as the anatomical force of Black anarchism, they reveal new cartographies. Rather than understand them as escape tactics, as we must stay attuned to the overwhelming capacity of the West, the jumps refuse the reproduction of relations of domination that are sometimes endemic to political practice. In other words, they are less representative of liberated space—for empire need not fear delimited space—and more so thought of as a mode of disorganization.[86] It is in this mode of liberating practices rather than liberated outcomes that the jump beyond the boundaries may exert new social relationships and new imaginaries. Thinking in this way is aided by the scathing critique deployed by Lucy Parsons, anarchist communist and eighteenth- and nineteenth-century labor organizer, toward representational government and political parties, wherein she argues that the possibilities of anarchism are in part due to their distrust of "crystallized ideas" that structure other schools of thought and are meant to dictate what is possible.[87] Parson's words clarify that Black anarchist practices are meaningfully incomplete, what Richard Iton calls those "in-process notions of autonomy and emancipation" that do not necessarily embody the "most advanced ideas" but what Ashanti Alston calls a politics of "trying to live," of "[working] it out as we go."[88] Unlike the outcome models dictated by the archive and reproduced by some scholars of resistance, the practices of Black anarchism move away from prefigurative political opposition. They are agnostic, proceeding without the alternative order in view, unlikely to adhere to "hidden imperialisms" that sometimes mark ideologies of progress and the universal.[89]

In other words, the jump from the slave ship appeals to new geographies of Black dissent that refuse to labor through a reconfiguration of the current order susceptible to reproducing antiblack domination. This agnosticism is often the reason that anarchism generally, and Black anarchism specifically, are disregarded as inviable and unsustainable. But the Black anarchism of the jump invokes this unviability as a disengagement with order. This is not meant as a claim to idealism or utopianism (it also is not necessarily *not* that either) but a refusal of a capitalist-inflected cycle of reproduction that so often stalls our practice and understanding of Black politics. The Western liberal tradition proposes a linear and allegedly progressive trajectory, but this linearity comes only to mystify and dematerialize a historic cycle of violent assimilation to a Western order of things. The enslaved who jump the slave ship jump in excess of that order, refusing reproduction in a multitude of ways. While refusing to replicate Black submission to white will and impeding Western liberalism's linear and continuous rebirth of itself, the enslaved Black woman was also absconding from her literal sexual reproduction. As the actual reproducers of the slave labor force, the Black enslaved women who jumped—pregnant or not—were interrupting the West's means of production. The nomination of Black anarchy is thus meant to invoke the slave's jumping overboard as a phenomenal practice in excess of order. If the captive body is the terrain of the master's power, then the escaping body, the body that dies at the hands of the self, was a direct threat to dominion.

Indexing Difficulty

Hartman warns us that because of the enslaved's particular position as both object and subject, the question of agency, which so often shapes examinations of rebellion and resistance, requires careful consideration so as not to simply "gift" it in scholarly wrapping.[90] Tendencies in the appraisal of the jump from the slave ship—demonstrated in the maritime insurance litigation, the abolitionist discourse of suicide, and scholarly study—have fluctuated between calculating loss, claiming heroism, and assessing the horrors of the Middle Passage. As Hartman's caution alludes, sometimes the general penchant of studying resistance has been to romanticize, celebrate, and privilege to the point of elision. Take, for example, Taylor's assertions of shipboard rebellions' power:

> Fearless, organized, and desperate, the actions of slave insurrectionists confronted even the most hateful of slave traders with the reality that Africans were human beings, forced to do what any other group in their position would do. By fighting, and sometimes winning, these Africans proved their humanity in a way that later abolitionists could never do. They stood toe to toe with their oppressors, challenging them at every turn, and in so doing, powerfully dismantling the argument that they were meant to be slaves.[91]

While Taylor's arguably extreme assertion is hardly the only one, it is emblematic of a larger conflation between agency, resistance, and supplication to the trappings of humanism that tend to paper over the central antagonism of chattel slavery and its terrible reach. The facile assurance of humanity's proof only confirms obeisance of the enslaved's strength at the expense of understanding the extremity of slavery's domination and Black ontological non/being. The other side of these appraising proclivities is the absolutist reduction to nothing but a condition of domination, which can also disappear the forms and sites of dissent that may sharpen an understanding of politics' paradox in the state of domination's ontological antagonism. In the case of the jump from the slave ship, a vantage shift to the practice as an index of precarity provides a whetstone on which we may hone a more trenchant examination of the political imaginaries and Western liberal traditions that attempt to circumscribe the horizons of the Black radical tradition. Moreover, focusing on the jump as practice, its transience, difficulty, and even impossibility ushers us into a reflection on the parameters of both personhood and politics while at the same time further speculating about the threat posed by the deed.

I have argued that the jump from the slave ship is the "chaotic violation of order itself."[92] Yet in the order of the human, the enslaved could not be incorporated as the subject that the jump attempted to invoke. The African, converted by the colonial-racial system of chattel slavery from person to nonperson, from human to commodified sentient being, sat at a position that Alexis de Tocqueville highlighted in his 1851 *Democracy in America*: "The Negro has lost even the ownership of his own body and cannot dispose of his person without committing a sort of larceny."[93] The very position of the enslaved absented the capacity to secure a relational status to the social order that did not require her objecthood.[94] In this, the jump became a kind of Pyrrhic victory, wherein to inflict death on one's own was prohibited, and if achieved or attempted, its consequence was gratuitous punishment. This is not an attempt to sabotage my own argument of the jump's political importance but an assent to the careful consideration of the fungibility that is fundamental to the state of domination and its conditioning of the jump. While the individual enslaved's death by jump from the slave ship may have been seen as negligible, it threatened white dominion to the point that its reassertion required an expression of the enslaved's fungibility. By beheading an enslaved person already dead or by killing a recaptured one, the master was effectively communicating the insignificance of slave life while simultaneously marking the boundaries of their movement with violence.[95] In the spectacle of violence performed by the master is the adumbration that it was not the death of the enslaved that was inimical to the master's claim but the power to kill oneself.

This fundamental antagonism is relevant to our construction of a liberal political horizon, as the practice of jumping the slave ship sits antithetically against traditional analyses of political dissent. As argued throughout this chapter, the jump has been largely overlooked, an epistemic violence that effectively doubles the brutalization of the enslaved. If not resulting in return to the ship, the oceanic leaps of the enslaved were often met with physical death by the indirect hands of the crew, who often chummed the ship's wake for sharks to terrorize the enslaved and combat the "rage for suicide."[96] These frenzies were public spectacles, another form of conscious degradation, that existed alongside the possibility of drowning that literalized the precarious position of the enslaved in what Hartman calls a "loophole of retreat," a space of both freedom and captivity, or, relatedly, what Tocqueville calls a "climax of affliction" where "slavery brutalizes [the slave] and freedom leads [her] to destruction."[97] Both Hartman's and Tocqueville's phrasings reflect the limit of the jumps' salience, insomuch as the brutalization does not simply end with physical death or gratuitous violence but continues epistemically within the discourse of the political horizon that dismisses its practice.

Throwing into crisis a central tenet of the white authority—the containment and immobilization of its enslaved Black population—the jump is subsequently immobilized, moments of rupture, however brief, obscured and suppressed as apolitical or unproductive. In reality, the jump from the slave ship communicates a question of freedom that fails to align with Western expectations. The liberal democratic frame simply cannot account for the seismic yet interstitial shift that this practice introduces. Some historians and witnesses of slavery have made the mistake of neglecting the jump as a political practice, calling it either immaturity or hysteria. Such an assertion is at best an oversight and at worst an indication of the West's specification of Black political (dis)engagement in the moment of rupture, where white jurisdiction and the ablation of Black political practice is normalized without any reference to slavery's structural positions. It is what Sharpe, in reference to suppressed hysteria, calls a "double repression: the repression of the traumatic event that becomes manifest through the symptom, and the repression of the symptom through which the trauma attempts to become visible."[98] So by way of its presuppositions, the designations of insane or immature preemptively exclude any reference to social death and the positions it engenders, easing us out of the conundrum we face when the lexicon of racial order cannot account for the Black nonhuman life that endures as its foundation. In other words, within the confines of Western meaning-making, by foreclosing the referent, the enslaved's jump from the slave ship is easily excised from our political landscape and "refused a narrative structure."[99] Any understanding of the Black anarchist practice against their vestibular subjection as political practice becomes untenable.

The jump from the slave ship becomes stuck in what Bataille refers to as a state of mutism; if the jump "spoke it would cease to be what it wanted to be, but if it failed to speak it could only lend itself to misunderstanding."[100] Like the slave ship, Western liberalism's political horizon is orientating, keeping one—again to use the words of Parsons—"caught and impaled between the planks of long platforms."[101] Just as archival omissions are evidence of the ideological productions crucial to the maintenance of slavery, our present disregard of the jump offers evidence of a political horizon where we "feel at home" and how we "find our way," which continues to calibrate our vision of what is to be.[102] The enslaved who jump from the slave ship refuse this line, casting off the repressions immanent to its preservation just as they thrust themselves off the bulwarks and into the ocean.

Interstices

With the mark of immaturity, fear, depression, and sometimes even religious belief, the jumps from the slave ship have often been the provenance of the master's truth, at times understood to reflect negatively on the courage and fortitude of the enslaved to survive terrible conditions. In some respects, the distress of a practice when faced with possible demise can inspire political solidarity, as it focuses our attention on the will of the enslaved in the face of insurmountable violence, but in others, the misery of an ostensive self-destruction can be the terminus of political purchase. While strife is often used to measure the significance of a political practice, in the case of the enslaved jumping ship, which could not promise viability, where the certainty of death was almost overwhelming, the misery of the practice becomes the threshold for its exclusion from political analysis, as it names an absence of choice and underscores a life of coercion. In other words, the enslaved who jump raise concern because of our increased reliance on the agentive, which is subsequently tied to questions of intention, and later still, to success. For too long has the practice been absent from our studies of the Black radical tradition, as it pressures understandings of what political practice is and how this intersects with the paradoxical positioning of the enslaved as sentient property. The life of the enslaved, and a politics based in her practices, is not a simple matter of agency and consent. It is instead a complicated nexus of survival, coercion, and the foreclosure of agency, where "compulsion eclipses choice, as neither right nor protection secures the line between consent and nonconsent."[103] The free-willed subject is an inadequate point of reference for the enslaved's position that assumes both choices and rights that are unavailable. For the jump, the term *self-destruction* is somewhat of a misnomer, meaningfully imperfect, as this "giving of the self" presupposes autonomy.

To destroy oneself is always already a theft of oneself, for the enslaved's relation to the self is one of wrongful possession.[104] As such, the jump remains in the interval, between a dissent from slavery and any possible future outside its ever-extending reach. At the same time, it offers a new lens, one meant to frustrate the "racially bound, unproductive labor" that has become commonplace within the standard liberal narrative and the political participation it calls for.[105] In troubling our reliance on the "self" for the purposes of defining politics through intents, desires, and autonomy within the confines of enslavement, the jumps of the enslaved may reveal more questions than answers, but they may still present necessary questions to those answers we have assumed to be concrete.

2

Collectivity

I know no national boundary where the Negro is concerned.
The whole world is my province until Africa is free.
—Marcus Garvey

When we think of the Black Star Line, we have generally been taught to think of failure. It has become the hallmark of Marcus Garvey's contested legacy as charlatan, often decried among his contributions to the Black freedom struggle and his ideological and organizational work with the Universal Negro Improvement Association (UNIA). His lifework is necessarily complicated and sometimes overly simplified by his arrangement in the Black political tripartite with W. E. B. Du Bois and Booker T. Washington. Washington's ardent belief in self-sufficiency is known to have in some ways inspired Garvey's own political ideology, and the two corresponded briefly before the former's death only several months before Garvey would come to the United States in 1916. And like Washington, Garvey and Garveyites were publicly maligned by Du Bois, labeled demagogic and lowly by the founding leader of the National Association for the Advancement of Colored People. Yet unlike Washington's strategic accommodations of white influence and Du Bois's talented tenth-driven coalition politics, Garvey's "constructivist theory of self-determination," blatantly untrusting of white patronage, pushed for separatism and nationhood, a desire primarily understood through the global establishment of Black unity and the Back to Africa movement.[1] From within the Tombs prison of New York City awaiting the verdict of his appeal for bail after his conviction for mail fraud, Garvey queried, "Where is the black man's government? Where is his king and kingdom? Where is his president, his country and his ambassador, his army, his navy, his men of big affairs?"² It was a pointed series of questions that reflected the absence of both Black autonomy and state representation and a clarion call for Black nationalism as a way out from under the thumb of white nations. His aim was the creation of a "new world of black men," a "nation of sturdy men making their impress upon civilization and causing a new light to dawn upon the human race."³ Starkly gendered and highly grandiose, Garvey's call fomented a strong following of both men and women who believed in the mission of self-reliance and establishing a new Black nation beyond the ostensible reach of the United States. It was steeped in a deep pride and celebration of African culture but also mobilized a desire to "redeem" Africa with himself as the harbinger of its restoration.

Garvey was deported to Jamaica in 1926 after his appeal was denied and amid the financial ruin of many members of the UNIA and its related investors. In the arena of fiscal irresponsibility, the Black Star Line is offered as the prime example of Garvey's and the UNIA's missteps.⁴ Yet despite dismissals as failure and fraud, these maritime endeavors are much more capacious and compelling than the record has heretofore revealed. This is not to say that the discussions of Garvey's financial failures and the critique of Garvey's imperialist aspirations do not hold weight but that these narratives abrogate a deeper appreciation of the voyages as salient refusals of carceral arrangements meant to keep Black populations in place.

Garvey has been equally characterized as imperialist, nationalist, and transnationalist, both celebrated and denigrated. One perspective claims Garvey as a Black nationalist whose sole focus was the sovereignty of an independent Black nation-state.⁵ A second argues that while Garvey was a nationalist, this narrative misstates his more noble diasporic or transnational motives, especially of the Black Star Line, with which Garvey meant to provide a global, steamship-driven network of communication and to institute communal ties.⁶ Building across these two perspectives, Desmond Jagmohan argues that Garvey's constructivist ideology was both nationalist and transnationalist, shaping his understanding of nationhood, political subjectivity, and self-determination in which transnational unity was necessary to "acquire the attributes of nationality."[7] Considering these various entanglements with nationalism, the purpose of this chapter is not to bring Garvey, the figure, or Garveyism, the ideology, into a taxonomic fold of Black anarchism. For its part, any such analysis must recognize the dangers of Garvey's imperialism. While not akin to the white Western imperial conquest, Garvey's desire to establish a sovereign Black state on the African continent has been understood as reappropriating settler colonial logics and repurposing statehood in the fight against global white supremacy.[8] Still, in the "cultivation of Black autonomy," some recognize Black nationalism as a tactic rather than a strategy, or in the words of Ashanti Alston, "beyond Nationalism, but not without it."[9]

This chapter is not about Garvey, and yet to attempt to think about the Black Star Line wholly removed from him would be a fool's errand. That said, to read the Black Star Line as practice against the deeply etched grain of his charismatic leadership and political ideology requires a reorientation to the line's voyages loose of Garvey's intent, imperial or otherwise.[10] In this way, the use of a Black anarchist analytic is not to challenge Garvey's imperialist rhetoric. It is also not meant to excuse the problematics of Garvey's ideology, nor is it an attempt to sidestep a long-standing debate. The Black Star Line cannot be ushered as a definitive answer to the question of whether Garvey was conservative, nationalist or transnationalist, wrong or right. This chapter's focus is, however, an attention to the voyages of the Black Star Line as practices that invite a Black anarchist perspective disentangled from Garvey's shadow, eschewing denouncement and recovery of Garvey's political philosophy. As Jeffrey Howison propounds, while Garvey and the UNIA have often been written about and understood as multidimensional, diasporic, political, and complex, the Black Star Line has not been given the same theoretical attention and nuance.[11]

Shaking the constraints of an economically fueled reading and narrow concentration on Garvey's ideology, this chapter encourages new understanding of the voyages in light of their political symbolism, effects and possibilities and the threats they posed to white nation-building and white sovereignty. Given the history of the Middle Passage and the fortitude impressed by the lives and practices of the enslaved aboard slave ships discussed in the previous chapter, Black people on ships will always bear significance. In the case of the Black Star Line, this became especially true within, beyond, and against the physical and ideological borders of the United States, a "nation of immigrants" that imagined and established itself as a white nation in the hegemonically white West. Emphasizing the diasporic force of the line itself reconceptualizes the voyages as salient practices elucidating and interrupting the demand of white sovereignty borne of nation-states in the West and reads diasporic collectivity as a facet of a Black anarchist optic.

Black Ships

The Black Star Line was a shipping line meant to transport goods among Black businesses in North America, the Caribbean, and Africa. The idea was first raised in 1919 by Black seamen who were in search of job opportunities since being increasingly replaced by white soldiers returning from World War I, and in the same year, the first ship was launched.[12] During its short run, the Black Star Line was used for international produce trade, and under the development of Garvey and the UNIA, it was meant to become the linchpin of a global black economy, but as a "revolutionary undertaking," it was also much more than that.[13] The Black Star Line consisted of three ships, the SS *Yarmouth*, which was to be christened the *Frederick Douglass* and handle coastal trade from the eastern United States, the Caribbean, and Costa Rica and took three trips across three years to the Caribbean;[14] the SS *Shadyside*, a river ferry that lasted only a season before it sank; and the *Kanawha*, a yacht that failed mechanically on its maiden voyage. The ships were all in poor condition at the time of purchase, and scholars have noted that the UNIA was overcharged and the organization overpaid—much

FIGURE 2.1: Black Star Line broadside. Collection of the Smithsonian National Museum of African American History and Culture, ca. 1921.

of this due to a lack of experience with the shipping market and to brokers who did not ensure proper scrutiny—reportedly spending tens of thousands more than the ships were worth.[15] As a business venture, the Black Star Line's collapse was marked by the loss of many investors' life savings and various mechanical disasters aboard the ships. The Black Star Line was publicly terminated April 1, 1922, and went bankrupt in 1923, the same year that Garvey was convicted of mail fraud for using the US Postal Service to sell stocks in a potential ship for the line, which catalyzed his deportation to Jamaica, the country of his birth.[16] Because of this, the Black Star Line endeavor is often pinpointed as the beginning of the end for Garvey's success in the United States and is linked to the commencement of his troubles with the law that painted him a swindler.

A voyage by the SS *Yarmouth* from Jamaica to New York that carried a seven-hundred-ton cargo of coconuts is commonly offered as emblematic of the Black Star Line's miscues. While on the journey, Garvey ordered that the ship stop in Philadelphia and Boston, and by the time they reached port in New York, the coconuts had rotted in the hull.[17] In the autobiography of Hugh Mulzac, the captain of the ship, this is given as further proof of Garvey's negligence and ineptitude that explains the Black Star Line's failure as a shipping line.[18] Yet taking Mulzac's criticism that Garvey was more concerned with propaganda than business invites a more sincere attentiveness to the political nature of the voyages. Given the political threat Black travel—and Black geographic autonomy more generally—posed to global white dominion, the fate of the Black Star Line behooves us to assess its story dislodged from determinations of success rooted in the accumulation of capital. Had the purpose of the Black Star Line been purely economical, then the threat it posed to the governments of the West would have been an empty one, as the UNIA's Black Star Line posed little concern, at least financially, for the economic giant that was and is US capitalism. Readings of the Black Star Line that use these determinations tend to employ conceptual frameworks that privilege class and capitalism over, and at the expense of, a racial and political analysis. This is due in large part to the public musings of Garvey, who often and loudly proclaimed the importance of economic prowess to sociopolitical equality. Garvey's project of "social and political physical separation of all peoples to the extent that they promote their own ideals and civilization, with the privilege of trading and doing business with each other," appealed to a nationalist agenda, to "race purity," and to a separation of the races that sought an economic relationship.[19] Largely unsurprising given the time, it was brazenly masculinist, citing the brotherhood of men and demonstrating a paternalistic relationship toward Black women. Within the wider logic of business and trade was his ultimate aspiration of raising a "strong and powerful Negro nation in Africa" that would consolidate the race into a national stronghold that was meant to stand alongside it Western peers.[20]

While the Black Star Line emerged from Garvey's brain trust and was imagined as a financial steppingstone within his political orientation, it also exceeded this particular Black political frame. Neither his nor any political philosophy can be given sole responsibility to translate political meaning. To be sure, it was a capitalistic enterprise, but this can be taken in turn with its conflict with the world, as a mobilization antagonistic to the comportment required by (white) nation-states. The antagonistic relationship between the Black Star Line and Western governments maps the West as a project of containment long after emancipation. Taking shape in the wake of the slave ship, the West and its white nations endure as a system of carceral processes that depended on the socio-spatial "fixing" of blackness. The threat, then, of the Black Star Line can be best understood by taking seriously the international dispersion that government officials so seemed to fear. Housed in an "attempt to restore to black people a sense of worth and nationness," the line's voyages contested white authority as a propulsion of autonomous and collective Black mobility.[21] This nationness was not, however, white nationness, even if such aspirations of equal national footing may indeed have been Garvey's endgame. Charles Carnegie argues that Garvey's nation may be better understood as a "transnation," where national unity was constructed via race rather than territory, measured qualitatively in symbolic power rather than quantitatively in the number of international branches, followers, or institutions bearing his name.[22] With the rhetorical deployment of maritime iconography and the circulation of their *Negro World* publication, the Garvey movement reached beyond and across national boundaries to foster a new political identity and empower those in localized struggles, but it was the Black Star Line that archetypically elaborated the movement's global reach and constructed collective.[23]

The iconic image of coconuts rotting in the hull may, in fact, say less about the failure of the Black Star Line and more about the sacrifice required for the discomposure of the confines of white Western control, celebrated by large parades of onlookers like the one in Philadelphia that precipitated those spoiled fruit. In the context of increasing segregation and subsequent antiblack violence in the United States, the stops of these ships, crewed and owned by Black men, were attemptive of a self-governing Black mobility, the first of its kind to be seen by Black populations from New York to Cuba.[24] This autonomy directly contested white jurisdiction both within and beyond the deepening threat posed by Garveyism. Yet, locomotive autonomy is not offered as an argument with or for new measures of success even as the line's economic dimension becomes less useful as a measurement of political impact. The twinned turn to geography and political symbolism denies the requirements made by conventional paradigms of success that are often, if not always, steeped in Western political traditions that befog a besmirched appreciation for the Black Star Line. It is in a tenor of dissent that the Black Star Line's geographic, symbolic, and yes, even economic function might then be best understood.

The arenas of industry and commerce were assumed to be the sole provenance of white men believed to be the only ones capable of entrepreneurial feats. Under this white schema, commerce was capitalistic and individualistic. Yet the Black Star Line posed an alternative way of doing business, one that was necessarily diffuse, where people in various countries bought into the venture and no one was allowed to purchase more than two hundred shares. This meant that shareholders were coming from a variety of income brackets and often humble economic backgrounds. As such, while it was an instantiation of Black power that employed the capitalist tools and symbols of modernism, the Black Star Line did not wholly imitate, and rather critiqued, Western individualism and state-centeredness by redeploying these tools as a means of assembling a collective.[25] The Black Star Line resonated particularly with Black struggles in Africa and the Caribbean as a symbol of self-determination and Black liberation. Threatening the exploitative relations of Atlantic capitalism, the Black Star Line appealed to the growing revolutionary sense across national and continental boundaries. At a time when there was a systematic effort by colonial powers in the Caribbean to ban the *Negro World* inundated with adverts for the shipping company, there was also a strong effort by colonized peoples in the Caribbean to take up the call of economic self-determination. This manifested as strikes and seditious rhetoric in local Black newspapers that referred to Garvey and the Black Star Line as models for a new basis of organization that was highly critical of colonial capitalism. Often marketed under the headline "Let us guide our own destiny" in large, capitalized, and bold typeface, the shipping line signaled a loud rejection felt deeply from Trinidad to West Africa.[26] Even as the ships never made it to Africa, the economic destiny that was signified in the Black Star Line was useful to West African economic liberation from British colonial capitalism and spoke to a sense of greater African emancipation.[27]

Yet even as the Black Star Line engendered an intervention within Garvey's imperial rhetoric, it also converged with the masculine imaginary foundational to Garvey's vision through its employment of the ship as a symbolic reference to masculine power.[28] Indeed, Garvey and Garveyism have been heavily, and often correctly, questioned for their imagination of a Black empire that hinged on male leadership. The circulation of the ship within the symbolic lexicon of Garveyism continued to disappear Black women, placing itself within a lineage of rebellions aboard slave ships and the multiracial marronage of pirate ships wherein Black women's political impact is all but erased.[29] The association of ships with masculinity and its marriage to the persistent disavowal of Black women's labor is a critical oversight in the trafficking of the ship as a Black political symbol, especially as it emerges from a critique of white nation-building that hinged simultaneously on the construction of blackness as excessively raced and excessively gendered. Still, despite these failings, the use of the ship as a political icon carries with it a subversive force. While the advancement of heterosexual men over and above all others was not something unique to the Garvey movement, this hierarchical holdover occurs within the formation of the white West that expelled Black people from the proper confines of gender, where the constitution of white nations attempted to naturalize the link between whiteness and civilized masculinity. This does not excuse the patriarchal posturing, but it does resituate it and, even more so, seeks to unsettle how the ship comes to take up conceptual space within Black politics as a Black masculine expression that continues to shift away from the actual history of Black dissent aboard the ships of the Middle Passage. Bearing the significance of Black people aboard ships, as Carnegie has argued, its voyages recapitulated the primordial memory of the slave ship and the kinship ties it obliterated by using the ship to reconstitute the Black community.[30] Further, as a bold refusal to remain within the geographic strictures set by white authority, the Black ship challenged the white nation's hegemonic control.

White Nations

The letters from J. H. Wagner and James L. Houghteling, a chief administrative officer and the commissioner of the Department of Labor, state rather plainly that the voyages of the shipping line themselves had little bearing on Garvey's deportation proceedings. At the same time, the US government was particularly fearful of the movement's international dispersion caused by the "unregulated flow of information," which provoked their response to activate what Carnegie calls various "sedentarizing modes of containment."[31] One such mode was to formally restrict the travel of the UNIA leadership with the thought that such free movement would only stoke public interest and thus expand the movement.[32] Such travel troubled established state authorities in the United Kingdom, France, Belgium, and especially the United States, where the Bureau of Investigation, US Postal Service, military intelligence, immigration and passport officials, the State Department, and the US Shipping Board all carefully surveilled the Garvey movement. Despite the US government leading a plot to either imprison or deport Garvey, revealed in the correspondence between J. Edgar Hoover and his superiors, in no way did it act on its own. The alarmed government authorities of these various nations collaborated by sharing intelligence and coordinating their strategies of control. The collusion suggests the growing threat that the UNIA's movement and its ships posed to the West writ large in transgressing the established boundaries of the white sociogeographic landscape, but it also speaks to the synergetic development of white global dominion. Like the enslaved who encountered countless spatial strategies meant to avert the jump from the ship but could readily be thrown from it, the policing and punishment of Black travel at the turn of the twentieth century staged the elemental paradox of Black mobility in the white world as both the cause and the penalty of criminalization. Garvey himself noted this in one of his speeches delivered in Philadelphia in 1919 after intercepting communications between Washington and the Panama Canal Commission. Reflecting on the request by officials for the federal government not to issue a passport to Garvey to visit Panama, he stated in turn, "Some want me to go and some don't want me to go. What must I do?"[33] Ultimately, his travel, like all Black movement, was meant to occur only at the discretion of Western authority.

The West's vestibular reification of Black abjection, especially in the United States in the first quarter of the twentieth century, deeply hinged on the constraint of Black mobility. In the years following Reconstruction, the Black Codes were replaced by Jim Crow laws in the southern states.[34] Like its precursor, this new set of laws was meant to govern the spatial emplacement of Black life and formalize segregation, which commanded the color line and restricted Black people to substandard facilities and services. In the rest of the nation, the spatial violence enacted on Black people was not ushered by the same legislation overseeing public spaces of racial contact but developed as pervasively if not more covertly. Beyond domestic borders, the threat of an internationally dispersed Black dissent imagined as the correlate of Black mobility emerged from and reconsolidated whiteness at a global level, shedding the strict national affiliations of individual countries for a global white nationalism—the constitution of white nations—that unified the West. The charter of domestic whiteness thereby underpinned global whiteness, all of which occurred through the spatial repetitions that rendered Black abjection, consolidated white unity, and punctuated the very essence of the white nation-state.

The white nation serves a constitutive purpose that assembles white identity as an authority over the distinctions of peoples and places that conditions the possibility of conquest. In the United States, this founding conquest is the twinned enactment of Native genocide and Black enslavement. In the case of blackness and following emancipation, this conquest continues as spatial delineations that are productive of hierarchical differentiation, as reifications of white dominion over Black people. In this respect, Black populations were not simply restricted to other facilities and areas that were often unequal to the facilities and areas of whites. Such oversimplification of segregation is often an extension of a well-tread argument of ideological discrimination, an outcome of racist attitudes or racial ideologies that denigrate those of African descent. While attractive to US progress narratives and liberal democratic discourse, it rides on the assumption of ideological consciousness and maintains facile accounts of practices that exist in their absence. These spatial environments are indicative of much more than that. As I have continued to argue, these spatial practices that made up vestibular subjection were themselves productive of Black abjection and at the most quotidian level codified white sovereignty over space generally, far beyond those spaces that were under the jurisdiction of discriminatory laws. As such, the practices of Black segregation established white dominion over space on both sides of the Mason-Dixon line. My brief point here is twofold: that segregation practices helped to establish both North and South at once as part of a white nation and that reductions of segregation to repercussions of ideological racism are done in bad faith.

In the same way that we cannot reduce Black political practices to ideological intents, we cannot remain tied to an understanding of blackness that requires the evil intent of white constituents. To do so would be to misunderstand the positional power of the white socius, which requires no personal desire or hate to churn Black death and abjection; no ideological precursor is required to practice antiblack violence. The ideological delineation between the North and the South as progressive and backward or anti-racist and racist relies on this logic of obvious and determinable ideological racism preceding discriminatory practices. In turn, the constitutive practices of antiblackness are transmogrified into racism, which is more easily derided as a surmountable aberration in the national imaginary, and the North is absolved of its formative hand in Black precarity and gratuitous violence. Further, the assertion disaggregates the project of the Western world generally from the practices of the US South specifically. But practices are excessive, which explains in part how the Jim Crow practices of the South are indicative of a structural relation that shapes white nation-building as a whole. While Jim Crow was indeed its own objectionable system of oppression, requiring its own theoretical attention, when we understand the excessive quality of practices and spatial practices as reiterations of a structural relation, it becomes easier to think of the national, and global, reach beyond the geographic locales of the southern United States that institutes and maintains white dominion.

In the United States, while the Civil War was created by and produced intra-white tensions, the Black Codes and later Jim Crow laws issued shortly after the war's conclusion served to restore white unity via the spatial dominion over Black people. Put simply, where a countrywide debate over "what to do" with Black populations exacerbated division among whites, Black people were also used to heal this conflict through their segregated management.[35] Intra-white conflict was diminished with increased control of white Southerners over Black populations. At the same time, the segregation of the South brought great economic benefit to the North, through both the employment of cheap Black labor and the use of Black workers to break work strikes among poor white workers.[36] Even more crucial to the strengthening of white unity, the segregation of Black people in the South bolstered white social status everywhere across class and gender.[37] As such, the gulf between North and South created by the Civil War and Reconstruction was bridged in their aftermath by securing white belonging in the noosing of a Black populace into an ever precarious and exploitable space of nonbelonging; the union of the white nation depended on a violent spatializing of Black life, corralled as easily by the lynch mob as by the police wagon at the mere suggestion of blackness beyond its place. As a matter of course, the vestibular subjection across the North and South were not in any way identical. Where the South had strict repressive policies, the North often appeared "softer" with its various forms of Black deprivation. Yet the nation was consolidating on both sides, nationalizing a racial regime where Black people were not simply noncitizens but were reconstructed as anti-citizens whichever state they may have taken residence.[38]

The consolidation was marked by an ascription to what Du Bois had called "this new religion of whiteness" wherein whiteness is defined as "the ownership of the earth forever and ever."[39] Australian historians Marilyn Lake and Henry Reynolds refer to this ascription as the emergence of "white men's countries."[40] This was occurring globally, a phenomenon that was transnational in scale, but enacted through national practices and had nationalist outcomes to which border protection and sovereignty became decisive. We have known the policing of national borders to play a significant role in the production of global power dynamics that reinforce colonial relationships, racial taxonomies, and economic disparities. The show of strength at the national line has always been married to the thickening of the global color line.[41] Crucial to the divine right of white possession over the earth's entirety that draws this line is the intentional linkage between racial superiority and masculinity, where manhood was enmeshed with white strength and fulfilled masculinity was tied to free movement and self-government. In 1909, just a decade before the Black Star Line was to send out its first ship, US president Theodore Roosevelt was waiting for his Great White Fleet, a parade of sixteen US Navy battleships around the world in a show of military power, to return. Mighty in stature and number, and painted starkly white, it served as a reminder of white masculinity—Roosevelt's proverbial big stick—that policed the global seas. It is within such demonstrations of "glorious manhood" that maritime space was maintained for white dominion and on which Garvey's Black masculine imaginary attempted to cut in.[42] To subvert the national terms, and thus the global terms, of engendered race that foundationally exclude Black men, Black seafaring took on growing significance as a space for the expression of "masculine bravado," hewing the patriarchal politics of Black travel of the day.[43]

The Black Star Line waded in a sea that connected a globalized white manhood, a fellowship formed in the excision of blackness from the white body politic. When wanting to mend fences between the United States and Britain in the latter's newfound push for democratic government, such "fellow feeling" was established on a shared identification with whiteness and its survival of "the negro problem." British democrat James Bryce, author of *The American Commonwealth*, a canonical study in US politics, and the ambassador to the North American country, made it his life's mission to mend the disjuncture between the once warring nations, which depended on a cultivation of antiblackness and a deep deference to the US democratic project. Black people, according to Bryce, were an "alien element, unabsorbed and unabsorbable."[44] He declared them a threat to the white way of life that only grew as they become more educated and the deference of slave to master died off; in 1891, he predicted even greater threat in the next two to three decades.[45] He further argued that federal involvement to protect Black suffrage in the South would only create intramural white conflict and that "American history and European experience" have warned not to attempt to "overcome nature by force of law."[46] The problem of the multiracial democracy after the Civil War in the United States and at the articulation of Black and white would then pave the way for staunch protections against foreign immigration across the globe at the behest of Bryce's fondness and admiration for white Americans.[47] The emergence of white men's countries thus secured the premise that "multi-racial democracy was an impossibility," with the case of the newly free Black populations in the United States proffered as the primary evidence.[48] To Bryce, expulsion was not a viable option, as "it would be necessary to prevent their return by laws even stricter than those directed against the Chinese."[49] Coupled with a suggested "severe transport system," Bryce invoked the structural antagonism foundational to the management of other non-black immigration and illustrated the throughline connecting the slave and migrant ships. The antiblack practices of the United States would continue to prove as a kind of testing ground to promote other white nationalisms. In fact, the literacy tests that were used to disenfranchise Black people in the United States, both in the South and North, that Bryce so championed in his 1891 essay would serve as a model for literacy tests used by the British in the colonies and metropole to nullify the racial equality promised to all British subjects.[50]Antiblack laws in the United States also inspired policies in other countries like South Africa and Australia dealing with their own "race problems."[51]

This transmission did not just happen in one direction, as the rhetorical use of "alien" by James Bryce would eventually be recycled in the language used by J. Edgar Hoover. Perturbed by the international threat posed in places like Panama, in his correspondence with colleagues at the Bureau of Investigation Hoover complained that there was no federal grounds on which Garvey could be deported as an "undesirable alien."[52] Indeed, the proximity of blackness and the global reach of the "darker" races would prove to be too threatening post-emancipation, and segregation would come to be the main method of hierarchization that assembled racial difference and arranged the relationship of Black dependence on white resource management. In effect, the "negro problem" in the United States was imagined as a global problem, threatening the dominion of white democracy everywhere, and would strongly affect the production of the global color line and the establishment of white men's countries via their networks of intellectual exchange and white supremacist discourse. It evidences how practices that are used against those within the nation are also used to shore up these globalized racial boundaries. Jim Crow was terroristic, but no more or no less than the antiblack terror that occurred in places like Chicago and New York or Bristol and Algiers, indicative of what Christina Sharpe has called "the being out of place, and the noncitizen always available to and for death."[53] It is in the performativity of the democratic nation in the wake of slavery and at the institution of civil society, where white citizenship appositionally created Black anti-citizenship in precarity and policing—never achieved because it is always at risk of being removed—and governed by the "[white] instinct of self-preservation."[54] In and against this simultaneously national and global vestibule of the West inheres the political orientation of Black ships instantiating a collective that is as much an expression of Black diaspora as it is one of Black anarchism.

Black Diasporas

Katherine McKittrick has argued that Black political histories have long been rendered un-geographic by way of the spatial domination that has occurred ideologically and practically at the hands of white European colonial exploration and national expansion.[55] As the previous section has shown, Black populations have had to live against

Western geographies that "erase and despatialize their sense of place" and whose discursive machinations of landedness, fixity, and ownership ground the establishment of the white West as a collection of nation-states.[56] The voyages of the Black Star Line have sailed in opposition to this logos, instantiating a practice of movement that threatened the geographic authorization and arrangement of (white) nationalism and (white) nations. Instead of being relegated to an example of Garvey and the UNIA's failure, when we think diasporic rather than national, and anarchistic rather than imperialistic, the Black Star Line can teach us about disruption. The Black Star Line traveled even farther than it literally traveled on the ocean, making landfall in countries it never actually dropped anchor. By resisting the carceral control of white nation-building, the Black Star Line effected the jump from the slave ship through a ship of its own. It capitalized on Black resistance to white geographic authority, marking a global but non-Western mobilization that directly opposed Western control and ways of doing. It reflected, made use of, and functioned as a Black diaspora, signaling a shared, though not identical, political refusal toward Black liberation.

To situate the Black Star Line as a refusal of white nationalism, a reoriented understanding of diaspora as an analytic from which to understand the force of these oceanic expeditions is necessary. This reorientation does not attempt to operationalize diaspora as it has been typified to empirically study political participation. It also does not attempt to define a network of actors from which to understand diaspora. Instead, this reorientation offers a reconceptualization of Black diaspora to think about movement beyond the nation-state and its given framework for migration, displacement, wandering, and voyaging. Thinking Black anarchist movement as a Black diasporic movement not only further explains the concept of Black anarchism but also productively pushes the concept of Black diaspora beyond the conventional frames of nationalism. Two moves are necessary for explaining the reading suggested here, which are separate but overlapping, beginning with diaspora as anarchism and building to Black diaspora as Black anarchism.

Diaspora is typically understood through the "stem and seed" metaphor, which often relies on physical dislocation from an origin, and further implies a linear and unidirectional movement. Within these conceptual confines, there is little to no consideration of the in-between at all, depending solely on a consideration of experience at either the point of origin (homeland) or the location to which one has been displaced (new land). Such definition fails to account for the points of articulation, the "process of linking across gaps," and the expansive space in which linking occurs outside, or at least not restricted to, the social practices, norms, and expectations of a singular location.[57] Yet to think unconventionally is to think diasporically on a "spatial register" without a tie to the borders that work to delimit space, to consider people and place *across* space alongside the ways in which geographic space is constituted and tied to certain and distinct populations.[58] From this vantage, diaspora holds within it a non-nationalistic quality. The definitionally anarchistic approach to diaspora is thus meant to distinguish it from this seemingly necessary emphasis on a sense of homeland.

As referenced above, a primary achievement of the nation-state in the twentieth century has been the systematic establishment of heavily surveilled and acutely guarded borders the world over.[59] Opposition to such policed barriers and attendant privatization has been central to contemporary anarchist movements like Occupy in 2012 while also an extrapolation of opposition to the general repression of the nation-state that is distinctly foundational to classical Anarchist thought that concentrates its revolutionary energy on state authority. While the state preserves the principle of sovereignty, a principle of "absolute authority that stands above social relations," a diaspora in turn disrupts the sovereign function of the state to govern society and submit its people to political power through a "unifying principle of representation."[60] Although diaspora is understood and named by way of a single nation-state, rendered legible through its consolidation, diaspora is marked by an implicit disunity. The diasporic subject, being dislocated from their original homeland, is never fully assimilated to the new land. Loyalties are always questioned, barring the diasporic subject from full inclusion, although one may acquire legal citizenship. Considering a diaspora's inherent noncompliance to the containment of the nation-state as an interruption of the latter's premise reveals an immediately recognizable glimpse at the linkages between a diaspora and anarchism.

Diaspora is categorically opposed to the monolithic; at its very core, diaspora is about dispersal and diffusion. In other words, while diaspora often maintains its cogency through an ascription to the unifying force of origin, its incapacity to be strictly grouped and sorted readily sustains its anarchist inflection. Diaspora is inherently collectivist, engendering a break with vertical structures in its resistance to the top-down organization of homeland and new land that ascribes to the sovereignty of the nation-state; in doing so, it enacts a more horizontal perspective. It works toward the alternative, against constraint, restrictions, and borders, to foster new pathways and forms of connection that stand outside the nation-state model. It is in this way that the Black Star Line's assemblage of a collective Black power demands diaspora and also may grow beyond Garvey's imperial intentions.

A noted problem of the voyages of the Black Star Line for scholars attempting to measure their success and for Western governments seeking its outright control is that their navigation and movement is either inappropriately directionless and therefore ineffectual or intractably nomadic and thereby dangerous. Said another way, its wandering beyond and without the horizon of the Western political—what raises its Black anarchistic inflection—is often the reason it is absented political salience or deemed menacing. Accounts wedded to capitalistic convention and deriving the Black Star Line's locomotive meaning from the origin and destination of goods, where all other locations are either unnecessary or less important, are reductive. Relatedly, the US Bureau of Investigation's characterization of the political danger of these voyages limited to the countries and populations with which they had made contact is encumbered by a similar nation-state logic. Both interpretations misunderstand the critical import of this maritime roaming because of an adherence to the landed, linear, owned, and easily representable.

To speak differently about the Black Star Line is to speak differently about diaspora, and to render a Black anarchistic reading, as it were, is to challenge the nation-state model in its entirety, that is, at its foundation. Brent Hayes Edwards argues that a politics of diaspora rejects the Western notion that knowledge production is categorically linked to the nation.[61] While moving beyond nation has the potential of running headlong into a critique that the definition of diaspora is becoming too expansive, meaning everything and nothing simultaneously, this reconceptualization of Black diaspora maintains the major tenets of diaspora (trauma, dispersal, stigmatization, and memory) while shedding itself of the restrictive frame that requires a successful movement across geographic borders. As such, it urges political imaginaries cutting ties with the meaning-making of the nation-state, resisting consolidation, dispelling a hierarchical nature, attuned to the importance of movement itself, and understanding of the significance of collective determination against the confines of white spatial authority.

The globality of white dominion suggests that the relationship of people across the world, while historically tied to geographic locations, also happens beyond and through borders. In the establishment of these borders, their location is of less importance than that of the structural relationship of power that allows these lines to be drawn and the separations made between populations in the first place. To think diasporically, then, is to hold white dominion in view and realize the "artificiality of national boundaries" and to recognize them as a question of governance.[62] In this formulation, and with the evidence provided in the previous sections, it may be more useful to consider the West, as Edouard Glissant has argued, as more a project than a place.[63] Such a consideration would move us away from these artificial borders and toward an attention to the national project as the expansion of white dominion that governs, constitutes, and maintains race. A Black diasporic analysis necessarily emerging from a history of enslavement and colonialism, better allows us to understand this constitution through white dominion because it invites "juxtapositivity," allowing us "to put together the scattered pieces of the puzzle" and place modernity alongside coloniality to stimulate sharpened and more capacious critiques.[64] Indeed, diasporic thinking does not immediately bare a definition of race, but it does open up the possibility of thinking across and between seemingly disparate geographies and people as born from a connected history of colonial-racial domination. Diasporic thinking illustrates how national borders have situated hierarchies of difference that structure the world and take seriously how they have dictated life and death.[65]

Of course, these signifiers of difference cannot easily map onto national boundaries insomuch as they stretch across entire continents. And yet the common narration of national boundaries does aim to deny the sameness that can be seen from England to the United States to Australia in cultivating white dominion.[66] Using the Black Star Line to shape a diasporic lens generates a conceptualization of Black diaspora that challenges its conventional understanding as merely the geographic dispersion of people of African descent. Instead, the Black diaspora of the Black Star Line is ultimately an opposition of dispersion to the racial requirements that necessitate the nation-state. It takes up Iton's reconsideration of diaspora's "rediscursive" potential to "denaturalize the hegemonic representations of modernity as unencumbered and self-generating and bring into clear view its repressed, colonial subscript."[67] Inherent to this alternative understanding of Black diaspora is a removal of the resultant hegemonic and modern camouflage that papers over the violent sutures that link and delink Black populations across the globe. The voyages of the Black Star Line bring to the fore the sedentarizing practices of the Western state as processes of white reterritorialization, marking out the foundational undesirability of Black belonging within the white nation-state.

The epistemological policing of diaspora that privileges the nation-state also bears the erasure of oppositional sites and practices out of alternative links and communities.[68] Interrupting this tendency, Black diaspora resists the limit of politics housed in nations and is a means by which our normative ascriptions to this construal of politics can be denaturalized. This would mean rethinking geography and power, a politics irreducible to the discourse of citizenship and a suspicion of homeland narratives meant to authenticate geographies governed by fixity, property, and hierarchy, and ultimately, hegemony. As a heuristic of Black diaspora, the Black Star Line invokes the nation as that which "cannot sustain [Black] aspirations for emancipation" and offers an assemblage of developing a political community that expresses non-state horizons.[69] As a frame for the production of knowledge and theories of politics, the Black diaspora of the Black Star Line inaugurates a decentered way of understanding the routes of relation that resist and are in excess of the frameworks that rely on official borders and maps. The invocation of diaspora is not meant to overdetermine the Black community and assume its political affinities, interests or even its organization, but it is to claim that a Black anarchist resistance to order is also a resistance to the antiblack project of globalizing nation-states.

Black (Anarchist) Collectivities

Engaged in a Black diasporic practice or, maybe more correctly, a practice of establishing Black diaspora, the Black Star Line provoked Black liberating zones and engendered the formation of a "transnational community."[70] The importance of the ship in defiance of the nation-state is amplified in what Linebaugh and Rediker refer to as hydrarchy, a conceptualization of maritime relations that goes in two particular directions. The first is the "organization of the maritime state from above"; the second is the "self-organization of sailors from below."[71] The former can be used to understand the way white nationalism employs ships as "walls of the state," the conquering of land power through occupancies and conflicts fought on oceans. In the white nationalist hydrarchy, or what Linebaugh and Rediker refer to as "imperial hydrarchy," the ship was the "engine of commerce" and the "machine of empire."[72] Yet within this form of hydrarchy grew the other oppositional and subversive form, which functioned as an undercut of imperial authority and mercantilism.[73] The Black Star Line captures the essence of this bottom-emerging hydrarchy, a mobilization of the collective that oppugns white dominion that aims to know the world.

The Western governments' marked fear of international dispersion of political opposition foregrounds the geopolitical threat posed by the Black Star Line. The force of diasporic Black political dissent is the thrust of Black anarchist collectivity across and against the sovereignty of the United States and the West. In this, the Black anarchism of the Black Star Line is a distinctly non-Western anarchism. Where the modifier *Western* is not demonstrative of geographic region but instead a geographical project à la Glissant, the voyages of the Black Star Line interrupt. Mildly chaotic in practice (we cannot forget the rotting coconuts and the financial disruption of many families and individuals), the voyages were, more importantly, a practice of chaos itself. As I hope I have made clear, the West aims to organize the world, often through the production of discrete nation-states that render a racial hierarchy. While often expressing itself through geographic regions, productions, claims, and practices, the West is not simply located, but locating. The Black Star Line refused that desire to locate, to fix. This was not simply a reactionary refusal, though the refusal did come in response to the sedentarizing techniques indicative of the production of a white nation. To stage new Black cartographies against the West's geographic hold is not only anti-Western, but anti-order.

The nation-state issues a demand of nationalist comportment, that is, loyalty to the state and its project of white sovereignty. It additionally requires that meaning-making happen through territory and nation, but the Black ship moves in de-territorialized spaces, shaping and affecting land rather than becoming overdetermined by it. The Black Star Line indicated a structure of practice that was in and of itself a refusal of fixity. The voyages produced a relationship to the state that did not rely on Black national affiliation but suggested "different and dissident maps and geographies" that allow us to think about how blackness is instead an "oppositional force" that runs counter to white dominion.[74] The voyages further reflect a "geography of survival" in the midst of the racially constitutive segregation of the West as it mobilized "the black world's sense of itself as a global racial community."[75] It also mobilized a particular understanding of Black freedom, the unfettered movement of Black people.

Yet as an outgrowth of the UNIA and Garvey, it is necessary to detail how the Black Star Line's Black anarchist orientation, determined in part through its disruption of the nation-state, relates to established ideologies of Black nationalism and their intersection with Black anarchism. Lorenzo Kom'boa Ervin, former political prisoner and current organizer and theorist of Black anarchism writing during the 1980s, recapitulates Black diaspora through what he refers to as the necessity for "African intercommunalism."[76] He suggests that the history and legacy of slavery, as well as "economic neocolonialism," has dispersed Black people across every continent, making it possible, and arguably necessary, to "speak of black international revolutionary solidarity" that stands in direct opposition to the nation-state. It is defined by Ervin as the bringer of "war, tension, and national enmity," representing and enacting "dictatorship and oppression of the many over the few" no matter if their banner reads 'revolutionary' or 'socialist.'"[77] Ervin argues that Black anarchism requires a global perspective that opposes the overbearing authority of the nation-state. Here, Ervin is clear that he is not arguing against struggles for Black national liberation movements, especially within the context of Africa. In this vein, Black anarchists have long been critical of Anarchism's dismissal of Black nationalism where Anarchism stitches itself closed to what it determines to be ascription to the nation. Black anarchists have argued in return that in the case of Black radical politics, "nationalism can be anti-state."[78] Typically, Anarchism dangerously and incorrectly suggests, as argued by George Ciccariello-Maher, that "all nationalisms are the same," denying the "historical capacity [of Black nationalisms] to generate . . . other struggles."[79]

The African intercommunalism that Ervin's Black anarchism stands for indicates a support of these movements to the extent that they "struggle against a colonial or imperialist power" while warning of the dangers of dictatorship upon the achievement of state power.[80] Ervin's caution reflects the risk of taking up the Black Star Line, invariably tied to Marcus Garvey's nationalist project that imagines himself as "Emperor of the Kingdom of Africa," as a Black anarchist practice. However, Ervin's gesture also provides granularity to a debate that is too often easily dictated by white Anarchist command, as he introduces an important distinction between a universal opposition to state authority and an opposition to colonial-racial authority embodied in the state. Ervin's distinction is given even more texture when placed into dialogue with Georges Sorel's definition of the state proffered within his delineation of force and violence. Sorel argues that "the object of force is to impose a certain social order in which the minority governs, while violence tends to the destruction of that order."[81] Ciccariello-Maher argues that Sorel's definition of the state as the wielder of force provides more specificity to *what* about the state that is opposed, focusing our attention on *substance* rather than the unmarked institution itself.[82] He uses this focused attention to take Anarchism to task for its dismissal of Fanon, who he notes to have an anarchist orientation toward violence but is often claimed as too racially essentialist or "an apologist for nationalism" to be of value for Anarchist thought.[83] Contesting this claim, he suggests that both Sorel and Fanon place greater significance on content over form and what follows is a "view which is more about liberation from inequality than the literal elimination of institutions."[84] This is instructive as it invites a refocusing of our attention toward the specificity of Black anarchism that aids our new orientation toward the Black Star Line and Anarchism's Eurocentric universalism that can disavow the state without contesting racial antagonism. While acknowledging the potential, and arguably inescapable, pitfalls of some decolonial nationalist movements, both Ervin and Ciccariello-Maher demonstrate a closer look at Black nationalism than is normally permissible within an anarchist frame, suggesting that

Black anarchism's foundational attention to the colonial-racial project requires an understanding of nationalist struggle, especially those examples of "radical decolonial nationalism," that is different from that which should be given to Eurocentric movements because of a history of colonialism.[85]

Although the concern of this chapter has not been to recuperate Garvey's nationalism but instead to focus on the Black Star Line as practices beyond their given intents, it would be remiss to deny that his political agenda has been quickly marshaled as simply imperialist or nationalistic in a way that fractures this Black movement from its colonial-racial history. For example, Carnegie has argued, there has been an attempt in places like Jamaica to "re-root" Garvey, celebrating conventional notions of nationalism and territorial sovereignty while at the same time displacing imaginaries and transgressions enacted by the Black Star Line that vehemently "[supersede] the territorialized nation-state."[86] A Black anarchist frame, understood in relation to this reoriented understanding of Black diaspora, solicits more nuance, requiring that the antiblack context from which these practices emerge and that which these practices contest remain central to any analysis. This is of course not to hedge bets on the state or tether Black anarchist practices to Black nationalism. On the contrary; cognizant of "the risks that can cost us everything if we do not engage in reflective critique," Black anarchism is ultimately geared toward its abolishment.[87] Yet the state confronted and contested by Black anarchism is not the same state confronted by Anarchism, where the state often, if not always, goes unnamed. The state that Black anarchism contests is an antiblack state, antiblack not just in its mores but in its foundation. This is not the state that opened the previous section, the unmarked state that is put into contradistinction to an unmarked diaspora. That unmarkedness, that state that goes unnamed, is indeed part of Black anarchism's necessary critique of white Anarchist thought.

In parsing out the need for African intercommunalism as based in neocolonialism, Ervin bridges his analysis of Africa with his analysis of the conditions of African Americans through his use of the colony analytic. For Ervin, a Black anarchist politics requires the liberation of the Black colony, which then jettisons the socio-spatial relationship between white and Black through practices of self-determination, through steering one's own destiny as the ships of the Black Star Line aimed to do. This shared Black colonial frame is a new linking, one enabled by a Black diasporic sense, that frames how a Black anarchist politics can circulate mirrored in the movement(s) of the Black Star Line. It must then also be considered alongside the international networks of support of Garvey and Garveyism that stretch from the United States to Jamaica to Ghana, as well as the international dispersion of UNIA chapters, which speak to a decentralization of power, albeit bubbling under the surface of Garvey's claims to empire. To that end, even as the Black Star Line emerged from Garvey's imperialist vision, it was a subversion of white imperialism and white nationalist authority. As hydrarchy from the bottom, the Black Star Line attempted an interruption of order. Its practices of unfettered movement fueled a mass movement, mobilizing a Black collectivity in direct opposition to the national consolidations of white dominion.

3

Ruination

I've lived with repression every moment of my life, a repression so formidable that any movement on my part can only bring relief, the respite of a small victory or the release of death. In every sense of the term, in every sense that's real, I'm a slave to, and of, property.
—George Jackson, *Blood in My Eye*

The government, in its simplicity, offers itself as the absolute, necessary, sine qua non condition for order.
—Pierre-Joseph Proudhon, *General Idea of the Revolution in the Nineteenth Century*.

In 2015, to commemorate the Watts uprising, the *Los Angeles Times* published a series of op-eds and editorials reflecting on the watershed moment and its legacy. From the standpoint of the half a century passed, "WATTS: 50 YEARS LATER" in large part attempted to distance itself from their 1965 coverage that was grossly unsympathetic and unquestionably hazardous to Black Angelenos. At the same time, the semicentennial retrospect's very titling was careful to rescind any necessity to name the fierce confrontation with local, state, and federal forces a "riot" or a "rebellion." In the wider discourse for popular protest of increasingly gratuitous antiblack police violence, there remains a controversy of terms and a necessary resistance to sensationalized representations of such events. Historian Robin D. G. Kelley's *Times* op-ed echoes this in his opening warning to on this day expect crude reductions to gruesome statistics and violence, something readers were all too familiar with a year—to the day—from the severe police sup-

FIGURE 3.1: Overturned car, Watts, Los Angeles, California. Photograph by Harold Filan. Lehigh University Art Galleries, Bethlehem, Pennsylvania.

pression of the 2014 protests in Ferguson, Missouri. Still, Kelley's claim that "what they burned is less important than what they built" couched in the assessment that "a focus on violence and looting" fails to engage residents' actual confrontation with "social and economic catastrophe" begs the question, What if the opposite is true?[1]

In 1965, as six days of tempestuous confrontations with the state ensued, political officials and pundits decried random terror and lawlessness—and they were not referring to the police.[2] They emphatically called it a riot, a narration of protests to state-sponsored racial violence that was as common then as it is now. Like Kelley, many scholars have decisively troubled these accounts, explaining the inciting conditions and continued effects. This chapter gestures toward these questions but engages the indicia of rebellion's "insensate rage of destruction," like arson, theft, and vandalism, as a fundamentally germane set of spatial subversions allowing us to understand the communiqués of the conflagration differently.[3] Through this spatial refraction, rebellion's Black anarchist force reveals *cataclysmic critique*, a disruptive leap from white society's urban ghetto, antagonistic to both state and civil society. Pushing past the policed perimeter of where politics take place and how it is to be conducted, Watts residents confronted militarized forces and civilians cohered as a white panic. Further, despite characterizations running the gamut of desultory and reactionary to criminal and cathartic, these destructive practices abut the state's own propertied analysis and solutions by proposing questions of property itself and interrupting an ever-growing nexus paying fealty to law and order. Listening at the socio-spatial register allows us to hear the rebellion differently, where ruination counters the state fables of the common good and crime prevention told through environmental design that inalienably link property and the police.

Black Ghetto, White Society

During and after World War II, as part of the wider Great Migration, Black migrants arrived in Los Angeles in large numbers. Greeted by racially restrictive housing covenants, limited opportunities for employment, and the threat of violence, they were limited to small areas in South Central Los Angeles, chief among them being Watts.[4] When Watts was annexed by the city of Los Angeles in 1926, residents were predominantly Mexican and Mexican American rail workers, but as the neighborhood developed in the mid-twentieth century, it became, as historian Gerald Horne notes, a "black island in an otherwise white sea."[5] On the east, it was bordered by a number of white cities, including Lynwood, which was known as "the friendly Caucasian city" until the 1950s, and on the south it was hemmed in by Compton, which in 1930 had only one Black resident.[6] By 1960, some of Los Angeles's Black neighborhoods merged, resulting in a nearly forty square-mile ghettoized space with few jobs, poor mass transit, limited highway access, inadequate schools, high risk for disease, and little public housing.[7] With increasing white flight, the Black urban ghetto came to sign congestion, impoverishment, unpredictability, and immorality, which occurred coeval with the emergence of growing white suburbs as the affluent, sprawling beacon of "the good community."[8]

Ushered by alienation and municipal disinvestment, the urban ghetto meant to simultaneously confine and exploit Black Angelenos. Alongside the environmental landmarks of unpaved roads, old structures, and general dilapidation, the area was heavily policed. The nature of this policing was also exceedingly ordinary in Watts as it was in other Black parts of the city, state, and country. The police stop on Wednesday, August 11, 1965, that would be named the inciting incident for six days of violent unrest and millions of dollars in property damage was as stringent as it was routine.[9] A white California Highway Patrol (CHP) officer stopped two young Black men, Marquette Frye and his younger brother Ronald, for speeding and began to arrest the older Frye, the driver, under the claim of appearing intoxicated. Ronald then rushed to retrieve their mother knowing full well how quickly the arrest could turn even more violent. And it did. Mother Rena Price was struck by a police officer, and Marquette was forcibly subdued.[10] A watchful crowd grew quickly as Marquette's brother and mother were subsequently arrested, and soon a conflagratory conflict between Watts residents and local law enforcement from the CHP, the Los Angeles Police Department (LAPD), and the county took shape. Three days later, on Saturday, the local police would be supported by fourteen thousand members of the state's National Guard called in by the governor's office. Between August 11 and 17, there would be over thirty deaths, more than one thousand injured, and nearly four thousand arrested, almost all of whom were Black.[11]

Both local and national media alleged that the uprisings were made up of reveling rioters, expressed through the phrase "Burn, baby, burn!" that journalists reported hearing on the ground, a narrative buttressed by the official word from Washington that labeled Watts's Black residents terroristic. In his classic study on the rebellion, Horne puts the number of people called in to quell the insurrection at sixteen thousand.[12] While white spectators miles away envisioned a scene of carnage perpetrated by so-called rioters, the reality was that officers of the state were moving quickly through the streets of South Los Angeles firing at will.[13] For

Horne, the turning point that transformed a "community revolt against the police" into a "police revolt against the community" was the death of Deputy Sherriff Robert E. Ludlow.[14] Yet even as Horne could hardly be accused of suggesting that police were pushed into escalation in his estimation of the events and while the police action was in literal terms a response, it would be disingenuous to consider the police reactive. The nature of the police is such that vindication for antiblack violence is categorically unnecessary, absurdly blatant in the redundant nomenclature of "justifiable homicide" applied to the police deaths of Black Watts residents. Put differently, the sentiment of transformation shrouds the severity attendant to the quotidian in the antagonistic and antagonizing relation of society to its Black constituents.

Violence organizes, rather than simply expresses, the socio-spatial location of Black populations within and beyond the urban setting. While two moments of state-sponsored violence bookend the Watts rebellion and seem to be divided temporally (inciting and retaliatory) or by the size of the target (individuals and masses), in fact they indicate gratuitous violence and routine ignominy as the constitutive formation of the Black ghetto. They also illustrate the free ambit of the state. Marquette Frye's stop at the hands of the CHP was routine—it "occurred under rather ordinary circumstances" as the McCone commission confesses. So, too, were the beatings and militarized force that characterize the suppression of the uprising that followed. We know that violence is fundamental to policing; it is what the police represent. To be absent, inefficient, insensitive, brutal, and excessive in their force is to be doing their job effectively. As the embodiment of violence, they are also simply the "most direct" hand of the state, how it "imposes its will on the citizenry."[15] If the state has a monopoly on violence, then the police are simply its principal manifestation. Yet as Kristian Williams points out, this monopoly is what makes it often difficult to decipher the boundary between force and excessive force; indeed, it is what makes it sometimes impossible to even call force violence, because the state and protection of the state are the sole executor and reason of legitimate violence. As such, baring the rubric in its very execution, any difference between force and excessive force used on the Black body is merely discursive. Any conceptual coherence of excessive force against Black individuals or masses unravels just as easily as its badged practitioners are acquitted.

In South Central Los Angeles, between 1963 and 1965, sixty Black men were shot and killed by police officers; twenty-five of these Black men were unarmed, and twenty-seven of them were shot in the back. In many ways, while this represented a dramatic rise in police violence at the time, it also existed within the context of an accepted antagonism between Black populations and the state. This is clear in LAPD chief of police William Parker's 1965 television warning that the metropolitan Los Angeles area would be 45 percent Black in five years: "If you want any protection for your home and family, you're going to have to get in and support a strong police department. If you don't do that, come 1970, God help you!"[16] Parker's words clearly claim the police as the principal defense of the territory, invoking the divine in a manner that not only naturalizes white authority and power but names it God given. Bubbling just under the surface of a warning to white Angelenos is the threat to Black ones, where the police function to keep the population as small as possible and by recklessly unspecified means. The urgency of this function is meant to turn on the threat of a growing Black presence to white domiciles, reproduction, and ways of life.

Geographically, the antagonizing relation lends shape to what Dhanwant K. Rai and Barnor Hesse call white territoriality, where, in the case of Watts, state forces police and promote a white sense of "proprietorial relation to social space."[17] The antiblack violence that animates the policing of urban unrest in Los Angeles is an attempt to control the area to the extent that it is a manifestation of the territorial relationship. It is a relationship characterized by ever-increasing anxiety over Black populations resisting the right to control as much as it is an anxiety over the maintenance of whiteness as the right to control.[18] So while police brutality is not contingent on any Black resistance, the police activity during the Watts rebellion feeds off this very anxiety as a matter of defending the territory and the relation that conditions it. Policing while providing security for whiteness also gives it "a sense of place" and "identity," which is constitutively foreclosed to the Black urban populace.[19] Said differently, it is this policing violence that cuts the line of the relation, where it is the expression and constitution of white identity and by the same token, for Black people, the definitional expression of being out of place in the very neighborhoods in which they reside.

White territoriality is bound up with white sovereignty, directly linking racial policing[20] and the securitization of civil society to the maintenance of "the order of democracy's white citizenship" and thus through, rather than despite, liberal democracy.[21] Together, they propose a story of political order in the West different from that which we have traditionally been told is either a generally unraced history or a racial history that can be divorced from democratic ideals. The constitutive force that converges across these two terms does not simply emerge in the hands of governments, political thinkers, or badged officers but is reflected in the interaction of common residents. Dominion can and is expressed at the most quotidian and environmental levels. It is reductive to think of ghettoization as something enforced only by the police or produced only by governmental policy and legislation. It is more accurate to think of this territory as both a reflection and production of civil society that was indeed subject to the surveillance and enforcement by any man, woman, or child. The police "simply bear the impress of the institution of race."[22] Expressed through the police but produced in any everyday interaction, the violent spatial practices of the mid-to-late twentieth century and beyond are an assembling of blackness *through* practices of segregation, expulsion, disinvestment, and degradation. This is to say, spatial conquest was not simply state-expressed in the strict sense. As Patrice D. Douglass maintains, "The social is conditioned by a form of police power that deputizes the socius . . . to police the boundaries of Blackness"; with deputization comes the embodiment of the state and the capacity to enact state power over Black constituents.[23] This is the institutional and territorial power of antiblackness, not simply a case of white control over a single Black community. While focused on the physical territoriality at the edges of the western United States, this is restricted neither to the country, the continent, nor even the "flat cartographic map" but includes the "multidimensional expanse of the territory."[24] As Cecilio Cooper has argued, "the spatial limit of the colonial encounter" is taken to the cosmological and cosmographic level.[25] Housed in the environmental establishment of segregation and ghettoization, as just one example in infinitude, spatial conquest illustrates the sovereignty of whiteness dependent on the non-sovereignty of blackness.

White Panic

The boundary line of white dominion had been crossed, security had been breached, and very quickly the markers separating state and civil society were shown to have never truly existed. As the dust settled on Watts and immediately following Governor Pat Brown's formation of the McCone Commission to examine its causes and determine recommendations, those from all over the surrounding areas of California wrote to Sacramento, the state's capital. The state may have responded to the rebellion with more than double the strength necessary, but they were backed by white citizens in a frenzy, indicating the emergence of a moral panic. The sheer volume of letters submitted to the governor's office indicates a high level of alarm among whites, with many of their authors calling for "rioters" and Black people generally to be violently returned to their place, mass bloodshed notwithstanding. They reveal that the police, as the militant arm of the state, do not alone produce the vulnerability for Black populations inherent to any expression of white territoriality.[26] Demonstrating a consolidation of white power meting violence to exert Black nonbelonging, the letters show that what takes shape is a *white panic*.

The letters named the Black ghettoized population "lawless, hate-ridden hoodlums," ungrateful for everything they had in Los Angeles and coddled by the government.[27] Writing in droves, citizens attempted to disclose the uprising as criminal rather than political and directly opposed the reality described in the terms *rebellion, uprising,* and *self-defense*. Part of its purpose was to reverse victim and offender, placing white society under threat rather than the Black populations who were killed on the city's streets. It equally provoked and justified the exorbitantly violent suppression experienced by Watts residents because it conceived of them and their tactics as raging, uncontrollable, and altogether irrational. This is clearly indicated in the letter from concerned citizens in Long Beach, a city along the California coast and over fifteen miles from the inland Watts, who decried Governor Brown's public scolding of Los Angeles's chief of police as an invitation for rabbles of Black residents to invade neighboring cities. The spectral threat was one of contamination, where the uncontainable approach of blackness hinged on not only a fear of racial mixing generally, a transgression of the structural antagonism, but of the encroachment on white women's vulnerability specifically. The enclosed demand for Black people to be returned and contained to their place reflects the continued fear of Black sprawl that existed at the nexus of race and gender deployed by whiteness, and which often set the stage of white violence. Here, blackness is, as Douglass reminds us, "conditioned as a social contagion" that fortifies the "social and human body politic."[28]

While rumors of sexual assaults on white women did not directly provoke the police violence in ghettoized Los Angeles as they had in so many cases in the Jim Crow South decades prior, this figure did continue to shape the state and civil response. The trope of the Black rapist haunted Southern California as it did the rest of the country where the free movement of Black residents was indicative of the lurking danger of Black transience. White women and their progeny were considered the embodiment of white political power and in need of formidable protection. On the other hand, fear of Black men's sexuality, which figured prominently in white media accounts of the 1965 uprising, was deeply entangled with a fear of the power they could wield politically should their claims to manhood and citizenship be successful. As such, Black gender tropes that hinged on stereotypes of excess and immaturity saturated onlookers' perspectives of the urban uprisings and were weaved throughout their responses to the threat of a Black incursion on white territory. The letters swung from blatant fearmongering of blackness' spectral threat to shameless infantilization. One letter, simply signed "a citizen," called for Governor Brown to take the approach of a father who must "punish the child."[29] This infantilization is also present in the commission report as a metaphor: "Frustrated and disillusioned, the child becomes a discipline problem."[30] By invoking children, whites effectively posit punishment as a reminder of Black place and as what will benefit them in their maturation. They also name Black tactics juvenile and misguided, like teenagers in need of a firm hand. As such, white citizens effectively bait and switch the narrative, rhetorically gifting rights to a Black populace only to order the state to violently seize them.

Across the hundreds of letters sent to the governor emerged a deep-seated fear of a Black "anarchy" and "plain lawlessness," subsequently charging the state with being soft and offering unnecessary protection. The language is unmistakably plain that white residents saw no need for a police review board, believing the McCone Commission to be a farce and blaming Black people for their own impoverished conditions. The causes of the urban unrest were neither meaningful nor relevant to the actions that they saw as beyond the pale, so when letter writers were not calling on Black residents to comport themselves differently, their focus was celebrating the police. In the main, citizens took their cues from mainstream white news media that did not question police tactics except to call for a bigger and more unrelenting presence within Black enclaves.[31] Turning to these letters and media accounts as the cultural context in which the militarized police violence operated, one sees less a reaction to actual physical threat and more an attempt to allay white fear and anxiety. It is in this discrepancy "between threat and reaction" that there is an "ideological displacement" that Hall et al. call moral panic.[32] Similar to how 1970s British society figured "mugging" and "mugger" as a crime committed by working-class Black youth, the "rioter" and the "riot" in the 1960s United States were gathered as indicators of societal degradation. blackness, crime, and youth and converge into a narrative of anarchic chaos, initiating crisis, and instigating an "authoritarian consensus."[33] In the Watts rebellion, the moral panic was evidenced not simply by the exorbitant police response but also by the disproportionate media sensationalism and increased attention by white residents from all over the California area. Pulling on the racial fantasy of Los Angeles that ostensibly distanced it from the urban plight of metropolitan areas like Harlem or Chicago, political officials, journalists, and white citizens invent a hyperbolized rebel as thankless and self-centered, staged as justification for intemperate suppression and regulation. Appraised under the theoretical schema of the moral panic, the rebellion's frenzied white reaction exposes historically repressed conditions of "the riot," which in turn reveals something crucial about the nature of white dominion, the material and ideological linkages between crime, blackness, space, and politics, and the connected role of the police and the citizenry.

The general thesis of societal reaction theory and the specific logic behind the moral panic conceive of deviance as created from the interactions between narrators, audiences, and social control organizations.[34] The significance of the "Watts riots" as a narrative construction that laces state and civil response reveals a necessary uncoupling between the rebellion and its antiblack referent. Charging lawlessness, terrorism, and unbridled "white hate" ensconces the structural conditions, where the matter of facts exist as diminishing returns. In effect, the "riot" supplants the rebellion as a new ideological construction of reality, and within this reality, only a riot can make sense.[35] These new terms tautologically deploy new definitions and new understandings of Black tactics. Consequently, this rhetorically initiated reality lacks the capacity to initiate moral panic over antiblack violence.[36] For if indeed a moral panic arises because something is defined as a threat to societal values and interests, then it is imperative to note that police brutality enacted on Black flesh does not incite a moral panic, that it does not threaten social values.[37] In part, this is because the success of reaching a moral panic lies in the capacity to draw links between specific events and wider anxieties.[38] As society is not moved by any moral anxiety over Black death, especially in the way they are moved by anxiety over Black autonomy, no moral panic can emerge.

The moral panic that does materialize proximate to the events of the Watts rebellion indeed reveals a racial anxiety, but one that is significantly animated by a territorial crisis. This territorial anxiety is evidenced in the media, and citizen letters' use of the term *anarchy* to describe the events that unfolded on those hot August nights, which far from mirroring the tactics extolled under our rubric of Black anarchism are meant to invoke a mass of Watts's residents perilously encroaching on the social order. The claim is as much physically territorial over the geographic space as it is ideologically territorial over the space of politics. As such, there is a simultaneously discursive and material repetition of ritualistic policing of the rebellion's boundary transgressions, all and at once attempting to resolve threat to white dominion. These practices of policing clarify the ever-expanding territorial contours of white authority, and the defamation of the rebellion's body of work in the hands of concerned citizens and journalists becomes a discursive extension of the rebels' physical defilement at the hands of the police. Like the visual images of violence plastered across newspapers and flashing on television, the discursive explanations given of the Black people who died at the hands of the police or the narrations offered to describe Black actions as riotous terrorism were performing in the name of order. Together, they attempt to recalibrate the boundaries of the ghetto as the threat to white territorial control that signaled the disintegration of the city's, state's, and nation's white character. It is the threat to white territoriality, both physically and ideologically, that defines the white panic that emerged in and from the Watts rebellion. Rather than tell a different story, as it were, of the events, the theorem of white panic is proposed to glean from the narrative an overarching grammar that stake's its mobilizations. The white panic indexes the Black position as it extends the state of capture, but it also explains the entanglement of moral values and white identity as a territorial investment.

State Solutions

A 1968 study on white reactions to the Watts rebellion found that while some whites were sympathetic to its reasons linked to a history of injustice, the vast majority thought it "hurt the Negro's cause" and that it would only increase the social distance between the races.[39] It is unclear what the "Negro's cause" was believed to be, although the paradigm of race relations that seems to rear its head, as indicated by the reference to social distance, does offer some clues. Used in part as a barometer to determine political acceptability, this application of race relations is undergirded by two major assumptions. The first is the divine right of the state and civil society to decide the worthiness of Black people to exist in proximity. The second is that the "Negro's cause" is undoubtably a pursuit of assimilation, integration, and inclusion. As has been shown, white panic does not see any Black truth but responds to the imago of Black rage and conceives of Black incursion as the riot's content. Thus, as imperious as the white panic may be, its anxiety retains this assumptive logic. If a "riot" determines the narrative event, it does so inculcated in the larger schema of race relations.

On Tuesday, August 17, almost a week after the uprising in Watts began, Representative Adam Powell, chair of the House Education and Labor Committee and first Black representative to be elected to Congress from New York, issued into the Congressional Record an extension of remarks titled "Anatomy of a Riot."[40] In it, he argued that the recent series of events was caused by a deep-set anger in the Black community, stemming from "historical deprivations they have suffered at the hands of a largely callous and indifferent white society." This explanation was given in tandem with a sharp disavowal of the "riots" and praise of President Johnson for condemning the "inexcusable outbreak of violence." The underlying cause for Powell is not the racial structures of power per se but the white leadership that has soundly and repeatedly "rejected the efforts of black people to participate fully in the running of the total community." So while he clocked Watts as a "sociological detonation of unbelievable proportions," he also assailed it as an "orgy of purposeless annihilation" that vexed his American identity. In part, Powell was upset that Black residents in Los Angeles had given up the moral high ground that was earned in the early 1960s by the nonviolence of the civil rights movement. In the same move, he also invokes the state as the organ and channel of change, where state reforms were meant to mobilize Black populations pursuing the democratic promise of inclusion. As such, Powell, too, obfuscates the central antagonism of white sovereign will and Black liberation as he ushers the uprising through the narthex of race relations.

Powell is quite in step with the larger arguments and proposed solutions garnered in the various state and federal commissions from McCone to Kerner, the latter of which was called by President Johnson in response to a number of urban uprisings during the "long, hot summer of 1967." Both McCone's and Kerner's commissions resolutely call for improving Black living conditions, access to education, and the relations between the police and the Black community, categories understood as the underlying causes for the urban unrest and providing the commissions' legible shape of Black ghettoization. For the state, the Black ghetto that houses the Black family was both the reason and the evidence for "this spiral of failure" of race relations.[41] Under the cover of white democratic stories, the paradigmatic language intended to describe racial encounters without recourse to the reality of antiblack hierarchical segregation and was forwarded via efforts of "urban renewal" expected to remedy the ghetto quandary.

The theory, predominantly associated with the work of sociologist Robert E. Park on the late nineteenth century migration of Black Americans to Chicago, largely hailing from the Southern states, is illustrated through a cycle (of contact, conflict, accommodation, and assimilation).[42] Race relations' attendant logic is such that race enters the picture only with nonwhite peoples, and successful race relations are ones where nonwhites are able to properly assimilate. As such, in practice, race relations presupposes self-contained and separate races that should be kept apart but are otherwise brought together. It naturalizes the Western specification of white and Black sociality in spatial encounters and normalizes both white jurisdiction and Black assimilation to spaces of whiteness. This generalization stands by way of its narrative foreclosure of the antagonistic relation; an inoculated summation of cyclical contact that denies white dominion and its antiblack fulcrum, the longhand of the Black ghetto. In fact, by way of its presuppositions, the race relations paradigm preemptively excludes any possible referents of colonial or racial power. As such, race relations carries with it a segregated, or ghettoized, social form that forecloses any discussion of its antiblack formation, effectively dissimulating social regulation and spatial segregation by way of a discourse of assimilation and successful integration.

Although linked to Park, the idea of race relations has had a historically far reach in practice, buttressing the ways neighborhoods are policed, cities are planned, and populations are managed. Largely shaping the state's response to the Watts rebellion and "urban blight" long after it, it became central to questions of housing. Housing is offered here as emblematic, although not exhaustive, of a larger state story meant to solve, and fail, Black ghettoization through the shared Esperanto that laces race relations, environmental design, policing, and crime: property. As it can probably be gleaned, housing was a central issue in urban life for Black Angelenos with overcrowding, discriminatory policies and practices, and a lack of resources exacerbating the already isolating experience of living in a racially sequestered area. At the same time, Los Angeles's urban housing had been considered relatively decent when juxtaposed with other cities, with the McCone Commission plainly offering citation of a Black interviewee who stated, "There is no question about it, this is the best city in the world" as a comparative assessment of "housing for Negroes."[43] While it may not fulfill the urban nightmare of high-rise housing and congestion at increasing elevations as compared to places like Chicago or New York, the fantasy of Los Angeles as a racial paradise holds little weight.[44]

The 1949 Housing Act that was meant to provide affordable housing for workers, predominantly Black, after the war and all over the continental United States led by a white public's fear of Black intrusion meant that these housing projects were often contained in select parts of the city. A lack of preparation for an increasing number of residents coupled with a quick decline in federal funding accelerated the failure of these and marked a gut-wrenching blow to any chance for Black livability in the city. As such, the Watts rebellion only exacerbated an already existing anxiety over the housing for, and of, Los Angeles's Black population. The Housing Authority of the City of Los Angeles oversaw a series of public housing projects that was meant to resolve the tension of white society's fear of blackness and Black people's need for livable housing. Although it was heralded by the banner of welfare policy, through public housing the state initiated an extension of white territoriality while making use of a lexicon of assimilatory race relations, Black community empowerment, and self-help. In the 1960s and 1970s, as fears of crime continued to push both liberal and conservative political agendas, architects and urban planners were also emphasizing the need for their plans and suggestions to be taken on by groups like the city's housing authority, toting descriptions of violence in the streets and images of graffiti that conflated protests and street crime. This promoted and capitalized on a fear that was equally broad and specific in terms of its reach and in surreptitiously alluding to race and class.[45] While poor housing conditions were in desperate need of improvement, the designers, planners, and administrators in charge of housing utilized this fear and mobilized the ghetto as an unruly and crime-ridden rookery breeding protest and disorder. While the ghetto signified the degradation of society, this signification also professed that reconditioning the enclosure could prevent the possibility of further dissent.

The work of Oscar Newman and his concept "defensible space" capitalizes on this economy of fear and has had a far reach in urban planning, continuing to buttress much of the discussion on crime prevention through design well into the twenty-first century.[46] Coined in 1969, defensible space was representative of a more general push for the architectural expression and production of a law-and-order society in immediate response to the urban uprisings across the civil rights and Black Power eras.[47] Its predecessor, *The Death and Life of Great American Cities*, written by Jane Jacobs in 1961, was critical of urban renewal policies of the 1950s that were typified by the likes of Robert Moses but also claimed that the control of disorderly conduct and maintenance of order would be achieved by "eyes on the street," which linked the community and police in efforts to keep the public peace. While Jacobs made only passing reference to crime, defensible space's later contemporaries, including "broken windows" theory initiated by George L. Kelling and James Q. Wilson and "crime prevention through environmental design" proposed by criminologist C. Ray Jeffery, augmented Jacobs's interventions, further leaning on police to maintain community order and explicitly linking disorder and crime.[48] Emerging in the context of increasing police violence and loud exclamations of rapidly increasing urban depravity, defensible space is just one example of a wider logic of governance focused on crime prevention as the principal solution to social ills. It is within this logic that President Johnson discursively and materially converts his War on Poverty into a War on Crime and for which the Reagan administration would later cut funding for the US Department of Housing and Urban Development in all areas except in the case of security, which received a budgetary increase.[49] Developing the theory of defensible space, Newman argued that higher crime rates in high-rise apartment buildings were linked to a lack of ownership and responsibility by residents and illustrated that problems surrounding social control, crime, and public health could be solved by producing an environmentally informed self-defending community.

With architectural design, Newman could "create thresholds and transitions between public and private realms" and through this could establish "'turf' that residents can survey and defend."[50] Well into the 1990s, the US Department of Housing and Urban Development was still employing Newman's ideas, claiming that the use of technologies of defensible space "enable residents to take control of their neighborhoods, to reduce crime, and to stimulate private reinvestment."[51]

Rallied on the concept of defense—in ways meant to shield from abolitionist or anti-racist critique—the texture of these spatial paradigms systemize the axis of property in the intimacy of Black criminalization, policing, and carcerality.[52] According to Newman:

> *Defensible space* . . . inhibits crime by creating the physical expression of a social fabric that defends itself . . . an environment in which latent territoriality and sense of community in the inhabitants can be translated into responsibility for ensuring a safe, productive, and well-maintained living space. The potential criminal perceives such a space as controlled by its residents, leaving him an intruder easily recognized and dealt with.[53]

A later casebook portends the benefits of "mainstream life" and "upward mobility," claiming the empowerment of residents to better their communities. In this mobilization of self-help, safety and security, and community, Newman dilates the carceral logics. Policing and surveillance are diffused into the domestic environs under the guise of environmental autonomy and through the discourse of spatial privatization and individualism. Newman's theorizations purport the benign while entrenching the property relation and actualizing the penal state in the domestic sphere.

The casebooks of defensible space suggested that common grounds were unsafe because they function as unassigned space and claimed that space shared by fewer families is inherently better maintained. By Newman's estimation, the increasing number of people claiming a territory was proportional to a decrease in individual rights to the space, which meant a decrease in the chance for families to reach an "informal agreement" about "acceptable usage."[54] In a similar vein, the 1977 comprehensive security plan sponsored by HUD for Nickerson Gardens, a 1,066-unit public housing project in Watts, worked to combat residents' fears and, again, lower crime rates by recommending the reduction and ultimate eradication of unassigned space, calling instead for the creation of "clusters" or "mini-neighborhoods." These clusters, they argue, would need to be defined architecturally through "fencing, hedging, and the presence of entryways" and would "encourage territoriality" as well as involve residents in the maintenance of their own environments.⁵⁵ For example, the authors state:

> Front and rear yards should be defined with modest, symbolic demarcations so residents will be encouraged to take control of their yards. These improvements coupled with the others included in this plan, should reduce the amount of unassigned, anonymous space and suggest a hierarchy of space similar to that found in middle-class housing. Residents would have interior space, private open space—such as yards, semi-public space (in this case, the cluster), and finally, project or neighborhood space.⁵⁶

They also called for a redistribution of recreational space based on age, divided into elementary, teenage, and adult areas to reduce what they termed the competition over space.⁵⁷ The authors reasoned that the goal was to increase a sense of ownership, like that of the middle and upper classes, and so planners delineated spaces and established functionality. The rhetorical recourse to designation and functionality found throughout the Nickerson Garden's report signals the disruption of accessibility to public space and the eradication of ambiguity. This discourse also draws a clear correlation between ownership and safety. In marshaling the allegedly undeniable benefits of ownership, defensible space theory is able to fortify the state narrative and further establish crime and the criminal as culpable for structural inequalities for which the property relation is actually the culprit.

As it ascribes to privatization and self-empowerment, Newman's guide musters property as the solution to crime, disorder, and urban malaise. Private property is marked by the "right to exclude" and "founded on shared cultural values defining who can do what with the valued resources within a community,"⁵⁸ where these shared cultural values themselves support a logic of extraction and ownership that is foundational to colonial relations. Looking specifically at the urban ghettoization of Black communities characterized by increased surveillance and depletion of resources, Kwame Ture and Charles Hamilton name this process of alienation a production of the colony.[59] Under this colonial schema, the right to exclude and orient that characterizes white space-making is a racialization of both the terrain and those who are excluded. But this relationship between property and racialization can of course be traced much further back than the 1960s to origins of property rights in the United States in the colonial-racial domination of both Black and Native populations, where the former was enslaved as objects of property and the latter was eradicated or removed as they were thieved of their land for the benefit of white possession and occupation.[60] In both, as Cheryl Harris has argued, the racial line determined the relation to property; whiteness was a source of both privilege and protection, and the absence of whiteness meant being either an object of property or dispossessed of rights to property.[61] The privilege of whites became embedded in property's initial definition because "possession—the act necessary to lay the basis for rights in property—was defined to include only the cultural practices of whites," that is, of conquest.[62]

Private property under neoliberalism expands and maintains the dominion of whiteness under the rubrics of security and development, which are expressly carceral in nature as they draw borders, prescribe punishments, and promise violence for and against those found outside the bonds of property. As such, Newman's invocation of privatization and spatial ownership blurs the absurdity of Black residents' mimetic enactment of property ownership. Said another way, property relations, and the directive for Black people to mime property ownership is meant as a salve for the devastating effects of those same property relations that inequitably divide the city's inhabitants—that historically mark whiteness as human over blackness as nonbeing indelibly linked to its structural positioning as property rather than propertied. Newman's invocation of property endorses a US national fable that effectively shifts antagonism from view but also dematerializes the history of property that has created this structural inequality in the first place.

This is further shown across the over two hundred pages of text that make up the Nickerson Gardens report (and this is not to be understated), wherein ambiguity indexes the possibility of crime, crime is the given obstacle to be overcome, and ascendancy is possible only through ownership. But nowhere else is this specter of crime more present in the proposed housing guides than in the suggestion to reduce penetrability of the site. Far from shielding communities from state intrusion, the reduction was meant as a deterrence to factitious outside agitators, to assist resident and police surveillance, and increase thoroughfares that could serve as "an informal pathway to patrol and survey."[63] In short, the report advised the reduction of spatial ambiguity and the increase of spatial functionality that promised greater opportunity for trespassing and further justification for amplified surveillance. Not only does the underlying logic submit to the police and surveillance as crime deterrents, but it continues to locate the problem of ghettoization on criminal behavior. Furthermore, it demonstrates the constitutive coupling of the security project and the privatization of space, married in their efficiency to extend spatial confinement shrouded in a language of assistance. Descriptions of functionality that are meant to delineate proper activities within space and under surveillance, while seemingly benign, belie a security state that insinuates and conjures Black criminality. Thus, Newman's claim that in the projects, it becomes "impossible to tell resident from intruder" reflects not only a desire for identification but details a deep distrust for low-income communities and acutely normalizes the easy conflation of blackness and danger.[64]

While defensible space may have been conceived as a response to high crime within the inner city and an implicit critique of urban scapegoating, Newman's push for internal defense operationalized privatization in a manner not dissimilar from the impetus behind white gated communities, where the fear of encroachment by the stranger drives a desire for security.[65] So, while defensible space may appear as a justified and reciprocal response to ghettoized communities reeling from violence and degradation, the framework oversimplifies the racial antagonism and egregiously recycles white law-and-order responses to Black urban encroachment. The turn to insular inclusion that actively absents community beyond the "family living unit" or "territorial zone of the cluster of family units" eradicates public space and knits the community to police surveillance. It functions to disrupt the possibilities of mass political action, increase chances for antiblack state violence, and effectively conflates witnessing with surveillance.[66] While arguably offering a challenge to conservative urban fearmongering in his time, Newman's work traded in exactly that fear of crime to shore up white security from inside the Black enclave. The neatly defined and apportioned spaces proposed by Newman and taken up in Nickerson's plan for the largest public housing project west of the Mississippi elicit a solution to overcrowding, caused by the contracting hem of white territoriality, that is decidedly carceral in form.

Bringing the "urban grid"—what Mabel O. Wilson describes as the recalibrative technique of subtraction, addition, and reorganization well suited for capitalist development and most often seen at the level of city streets—inside, Nickerson and Newman pack buildings in a manner strikingly similar to the ship's hold and the prison's block. Urban renewal's public housing only underscores the vestibular subjection of blackness, the forms "continually renewed and strengthened by, and often complementary to, inescapable cycles of false assimilation and impoverishment."[67] As such, taking this cross-cut reveals what Dennis Childs calls the "concentric/accumulative view of history" that "discerns grim congruence in the very places that the liberal white supremacist state implants the socially seductive illusion of progress and the repressive ideological machinery of 'postracial' amnesia."[68]

Security, like crime, is racially coded, so amid an unraced lexicon, it "[places] the issue of inequality beyond any visible horizon."[69] Through the rhetoric of property and privatization, defensible space theory ushers in the Black ghettoized relation essential to the law-and-order society without the necessity of its conventional form. Here, the definitive demarcation of space is offered as the predecessor of safety but only in accordance with the exclusionary and protective efforts of white security.[70] Urban housing reveals a larger and comprehensive apparatus of security wherein the housing projects that were created for Black residents offer further evidence that for Black people, surveillance is constitutive to their socio-spatial location in the city. As Mike Davis has argued, "the neo-military syntax" that runs throughout both architectural designs and its criticisms is an insinuation of violence that imagines danger. In revealing the antiblack inflections of urban planning as an extension of the law-and-order society, the call for defensible space comes across "just about as subtle as a swaggering white cop."[71] The ghetto as a home, as a spatial environment that is recognized as owned by its residents—as a place—is emptied of meaning in Los Angeles as it is in other Black urban enclaves. From the inside, Newman's work was able to fortify the functions of ghettoization, producing order and disrupting disorder, and trading in the rhetoric of community. His projection of spatially privatizing ghettoized space legitimates coercion and mystifies carcerality under the specious logic of security.

The defensible ghetto is only a concrete slave ship by another name, maintaining the violent regulation of Black lives left adrift.[72] This reference to the slave ship is not merely rhetorical but is meant to refract the socio-spatial particularities of ghettoization and ghetto housing through the antiblack shape of the hold. Like the slave ship, ghettoization was meant to hold and force the movements of Black populations, deliberately producing conditions that gratuitously exacerbate Black mortality while simultaneously segregating them from nonblack citizens. The "concrete" modifier brings attention to movement in place, that is, slave ships that never move, marking how ghettoization propels Black life into the direction of death by the very practices of sedentarization and containment. The concrete also signifies the modern elaboration of this containment, that is, how the slave ship, as a vestibular subjection that works to determine Black life, has continued, but not unchanged. The ideology of defensible space is just one primary example of how the hold continues to develop in its attempt to maintain Black alienation. Intending to solve the problem of low-income public housing, the suggestions of those like Newman provide an entrée into the spatial paradigms that continue to steer the design of the city, a striking example of the rhetoric and practice of carcerality at the urban level.

Cataclysmic Vantage

Espousing property and extolling criminal culpability as the heartbeat of urban malaise and Black suffering, the discourse of urban renewal betrays a coherence of state and civil society under the aegis of law-and-order. State solutions explicitly proposed through housing development or implicitly issued by the fiat of political derision meant to adjudicate the alleged causes of the Watts uprising as a matter of propriety and the proprietary. A variegated conglomerate of state actors taking the order of society for granted, they are resolved in its maintenance as they propagate the narrative of race relations and its assumed logic of assimilatory objective. As Powell's ascriptions to the proper governmental channels prohibit the surfacing of alternative ways of doing that unsettle the fabled national promise of full citizenship, property destruction, taking a variety of forms including arson, theft, vandalism, and looting, extrapolates debates of this objective in the provocation of disorder.

Calling out the participants for wasting precious energy in "futility," citing misdirection as it was aimed "inwardly against ourselves," Powell's words illustrate many of the problems that violent urban uprisings raise for our political imaginaries structured by loyalty to state authority and lineal reformist transformation.[73] Its temporal and orientational grammar faithfully envisage state repair and ardently dismiss vandalism as no better than a "pernicious exercise."[74] Powell, or any other reformist, is not the obstacle, of course. Given the promise of violence and the "closures of politics" to the practices of the gratuitously disenfranchised, this spatial elaboration of urban uprising is not a romantic one and it does not portend obliteration of the state or, for that matter, any easy reflection.[75] What it is, however, is the query of the fire, a turn to the intellect of destructive disruption, or what Wilson, Sean Anderson, and the Black Reconstruction Collective term "unbuilding," as an aperture of the antagonism and interruption of state prescripts and prescriptions.[76] In the act of property destruction, we are struck with the suggestion that ghettoization is neither a state aberration nor an instantiated and established place but a "deliberative process."[77] Rather than a moment in which Black rights are simply being revoked or ignored, destruction as a method of "taking apart" in order to "understand how the built fabric came to be" reveals a non-habitation, where any claim of ownership ruefully initiated by the state cannot also be suspended at its behest.[78] While the popular admonishment of the urban revolt as "riot" deploys imagery of uncritical destruction that is pointlessly disruptive and generally ineffective, which turns on the sentiment of negation, destruction asks what it means to absent absence, to leave the ruins of failed Reconstruction in "utter ruination."[79]

As I have discussed elsewhere, creation and destruction are coeval to Black anarchist politics, not in a naive hope but with an understanding that practiced destruction and violence may provide constitutive thrusts summed by the belief that violence is necessary to the destruction of violence and the anticipation of alternatives.[80] This recognition of direct action is best conceptualized in the axiom the propaganda of the deed, first asserted by Italian revolutionary and socialist thinker Carlo Pisacane in his 1857 "Political Testament," where he argued "ideas spring from deeds and not the other way around. . . . The flash of Milano's bayonet was more effective propaganda than a thousand volumes by doctrinarians." Along these same lines, thirteen years later, in "Letters to a Frenchman on the Present Crisis," collectivist anarchist Mikhail Bakunin conceptualized, "We must spread our principles, not with words but with deeds, for this is the most popular, the most potent, and the most irresistible form of propaganda."[81] The deed of destruction is in this way communicative.[82] In his elaboration of Black anarchism, William C. Anderson conceptualizes ruination as a "revolutionary abolitionism" where the "bold confrontation" with the state requires the "process of destruction."[83]

In its concern with the disruption of Black death and the protection of Black life, the performative violence of the revolt communicates a different temporality than that which structures society. Whereas within the temporality of society revolts appear and exist as aberrations to social order incited by isolated though repeated practices of racial violence, the Black anarchist revolt as cataclysm initiates an opening to alternative futures in which a resistance to the neat closures of the state inheres. As one instance of an expansive constellation of discontent, the revolt troubles the temporal frames that structure state perspectives where political practices exist as engagements with representative and electoral politics assumed to move society forward in time. Black anarchists have long reflected on the necessity of *activity* in political action to disrupt state groundings. While in prison as a member of the Black Panther Party and Black Liberation Army, Kawasi Balagoon warned that Black people must take up actions because "inactivity creates a void that this police state with its reactionary press and definite goals are filling."[84] For Balagoon, Black activity is needed to interrupt and prohibit the antagonistic activity of antiblack society. Anarchist Panther Ashanti Alston issues a similar emphasis as he argues that the *Black* in Black anarchism has less to do with phenotype than of "someone who can resist, who can see differently when I am stuck, and thus live differently."[85] Creativity is emergent from the conditions of antiblack oppression, born of a need to survive in opposition to the comportments required by racial authority. It is a process of getting unstuck from the sedentarizing practices of the state's ghettoization and also a leap out. It pushes toward a future that can begin only at the conclusion of the antiblack state.

The destructive deed is also a deed of clearing. Ruination is itself "a bifurcation, a lawless deviation, an unstable condition that opens up a new field of the possible."[86] The Watts rebellion as cataclysm refers then not only to present disaster but appeals to its definition within the field of physical geography as producing change, an upheaval that alters. This clarification is important, as cataclysm is meant to encompass both presents and futures, destructions and creations; it invokes ruination as a process of refusal and transformation. As an opening up of the possible by destructive means, it does not close at the impress of retaliatory violence by the hands of the state but remains open as it continues to haunt white society, its residue appearing in the revolts that are sure to come after it. But if the Watts rebellion as cataclysm is speaking, what is it saying? Rather than provide declarations, destruction may be better understood as asking questions. By exploding in the fault lines of territoriality's antagonism, it asks, as Christina Sharpe does, "Where might the simultaneously carceral, freeing, and durational tensions of *the latitude and longitude of this place* shift, transform, break open, become unnecessary?"[87]

The uprising against property is the "peculiar force *of* (or, perhaps, *toward*) justice that emerges in the crisis of the system of the repressed-irrepressible, of the accepted-unacceptable" that animates the structural antagonism between Black populations and state authority.[88] Within this formulation, the revolt emerges from and critiques the antiblack conditions fundamental to state solutions of urban renewal packaged in housing plans and commission reports as repressions that occur in the practice and relations of property. If the societal valuation of property is based on shared understandings of who can do what with space and resources, then the destruction of property is a challenge and a rejoinder disrupting the propertied foundations of social life.[89] It is of no surprise then that property destruction is vilified in the media as ineffectual and juvenile, pathologies issued as indictments, imputations of communities who turn inward to destroy their own communities. Yet, such accusations fall on deaf ears that effectively issue their own scathing doubt: *Whose property? Whose destruction? How to ruin ruins?* In the privatization of property are the narratives of security and development used to etch the structural antagonism—materially felt, but seemingly visually undetectable—into the landscape. As this line drawn between the Black criminal and the white innocent becomes placed under further cover by neoliberal aphorisms, so too does the practice of property destruction within Black protest become less easily seen as political practice.

Despite its use as residence, the property of the ghetto was not the property of a Black populace. In the Watts rebellion, the physical buildings themselves "acquire[d] significance beyond their actual value," taking on symbolic economic value, as their destruction performs a deprivation of value and interrupts the space of capital, but also as physical markers of Black impoverished nonbelonging.[90] In this articulation, property destruction and theft challenge the structural foundations of (white) society expressed through practices of Black ghettoization that not only house Black populations but on whose accumulation and desire it depends. In listening to what the upheaval is speaking, the question of "Whose property?," expressed in the direct action of property destruction, is a multilayered critique, a leap *from* the ghetto, a leap *to* destructive alterity, a leap *against* white sovereignty. If property is the right to exclude, then property destruction far from indicating a desire for societal inclusion is instead a rejection of its system in sum.[91] While white society admonishes Black communities for having laid waste to their home and to their autonomy, the spatial actions of arson or vandalism may emphasize a form of critique punctuating that neither home nor autonomy was ever in hand. To use the words of George Jackson:

> Their line is "Ain't nobody but black folks gonna die in a revolution." This argument completely overlooks the fact that we always have done most of the dying, and still do: dying at the stake, through social neglect, or in U.S. foreign wars. The point is now to construct a situation where someone else will join in the dying. If it fails and we have to do most of the dying anyway, we're certainly no worse off than before.[92]

As Jackson invokes death as the conditions under which Black people in the ghetto are already forced to live, he does not intend for Black lives to be executed in vain but argues that the fight toward any alternative future may indeed come at the cost of violence against those who oppress, to destroy violence with violence. This assessment runs perpendicular to the lugubrious judgment offered by the McCone Commission that "the avenue of violence and lawlessness leads to a dead end."[93] This moralizing discourse used to dismiss the rebellion's destructive disruption is not of a different kind than the claims to morality used against those who jumped from slave ships to their deaths, similarly occluding these practices as failed modes of freedom.

Jackson's words are indeed jarring, and this dissonance is heard in the rebellion itself, much to the dismay of many who seek security rather than risk. This refuge is often disseminated in the search for demand, for clarity, and indeed for the propagandist's intention; where any legible answer to the search is subject to the safe vantage of state horizons. The question of demands is meant to obfuscate practices where often the "very content of the actions themselves, actions which go against their very ends [are] in turn overflowing their political forms."[94] The cataclysmic vantage of the Watts rebellion overflows on a narrative meant to mis/apprehend both the political subjectivity of Black people and their conditions of possibility, the narrative that maintains the "vote," electoral politics, or state-sponsored tactics as something that can properly represent Black interrogations. Demands, as Johann Kaspar argues, are simply "screens to interface between worlds of rage and worlds of law," which presume that interface is possible. They are meant to pull us to the perspective of the law as the significant effector of change rather than staged encounters of racial antagonism and the source of wanton degradation.[95] Powell's desire for the demand and disgust with what he calls a "riot" thus betrays his reliance on Western political proceduralism. This common turn to the systematic progression through electoral representation may serve the questions at the level of civil rights, but can it make sense of those, and for those, who have been rendered socially dead?

The disillusion with demand also reveals why the destructive refusals of Black anarchism may not correspond to a politics of prefiguration. As many across radical traditions adhere to prefiguration as a necessary tenet, where "learning by doing" generates the possibility to "reveal alternative logics of life," such an orientation can overdetermine what is transformative.[96] The danger of fitting these practices into this normative frame is that what is prefigured exists, by definition, within the dimensions of the known and may only provide contestations of the world that are "compatible with the reproduction of the existing world indefinitely into the future."[97] Similar to the inquiry for demand, prefiguration inhibits our understanding of the philosophical content of the revolt as it privileges questions of what is achieved by revolt rather than the questions that are asked *by* the revolt. The physically destructive revolt, like the enslaved who jumps the slave ship, holds no guarantees of what may come and, thankfully, has the potential of embodying possibilities of which we have no understanding. This is indeed the anticipatory power of the cataclysm as refusal and as erasure. Neither we nor those who generate revolt can know what those possibilities are. Indeed, the revolt does not remake the world. But in its interruptive questioning of our current world, it surely takes the first step in clearing ground for its anticipation.

4

Maneuvers

"What's going on?" I asked
"You're being moved."
"Where am I being moved to?"
"You'll find out when you get there."
—Assata Shakur, *Assata: An Autobiography*.

The judge denies our motion for a postponement. The judge denies all our motions. I want to scream.
—Assata Shakur, *Assata: An Autobiography*.

One must see what is not there, feel the trace of a form of power that cannot be named, and as Shakur demonstrates, remember what was never written down
—Stephen Dillon, "Possessed by Death: The Neoliberal-Carceral State, Black Feminism, and the Afterlife of Slavery."

Prisons are popularly thought of as spaces that lack movement, with images of hard steel defining carcerality and marrying unfreedom to stagnation. While the prison may indeed rest on a formula of stationary confinement, the rationales and practices used to maintain broader security and order can be said to be based crucially in movement. Central to this schema is the policing of Black populations, who are not only disproportionately affected but whose subjection to carceral modes of domination serves as the foundation for mass incarceration as we know it in the United States. The Black captive body has been and is punished for mobility and punished with mobility, reduced to a state of oscillation and often disoriented to its causes and manifestations. My aim here is to continue to scratch at the surface of incarceration's complexity, the intricate linkages between confinement and the burden of movement that emerge in Black social death in the modern world. This chapter is concerned with the US carceral landscape that emerges in the criminalization of Black people and Black politics through the legal concept of vagrancy and how, in turn, Black surreptitious movement contests practices and spaces of incarceration, focusing specifically on Black political prisoner Assata Shakur's transnational escape from incarceration in New York to exile in Cuba and its discursive omission in her 1987 autobiography.[1] Tracing her peripatetics within and beyond the scope of her self-authored text, we encounter vagrancy as an elaboration of how antiblackness materializes via vestibular subjection by way of displacement, disorientation, and en/forced movement.

In looking at the tension between Shakur's clandestine movement and these carceral forces, a Black anarchist inflection is elucidated, even as we are attuned to the political interval that remains shaped by the carceral conditions in which her practice resides. To keep both this inflection and interval in view, I present a reformulation of Shakur's escape as dis-incarceration, which takes seriously the flight toward Black liberation as one that is still meaningfully incomplete. This conceptual undertaking elaborates the significance of a continual absconding from the field of representation that has been constituted by discursive and material hegemonies of antiblackness. Shakur, both literally and textually, tunes an abolitionist politics and demonstrates a movement that must perpetually press against the carceral conditioning of the West. Incomplete and iterative, her insurgent transience contests, and at the same time incites, the West's carceral geographies. As the loudest echo of the slave's jump from the slave ship, the transient tactics of the incarcerated reveal a generative site for further study of the meaning of Black politics, and in particular the meaning of dis-incarceration as one modality of Black political (non)participation. But to even get to Shakur and her evasions of the West's carceral authority materially and literarily, we must first wrestle with the multiple genealogies of the prison and mass incarceration that have been developed and taken root in carceral studies with the aim of displacing some of the dangerous elisions that have come as a result.

Carceral Stories

In the United States, the Black subject—the epitomic racialized, sexualized and vilified body—is the primary prison subject. While others have been subject to the discriminatory presence and practices of the criminal justice system, Black populations have a specific, and historically foundational, relationship to the carceral system in the United States. Since the era of chattel slavery, the term *Black criminal* has emerged as a redundancy wrought by centuries of violence that began with the linking of the proclivity for crime with the enslaved. Today, blackness has become the territory on which the prison has founded itself as a technology of death, containment, repression, and gratuitous violence. Undoubtedly, the recent surge in scholarly approaches to criminalization and mass incarceration can be attributed to the fact that our current political landscape is still very much shaped by the disproportionate arrest and imprisonment of huge portions of the Black population, as well as the continued growth of the prison industrial complex more broadly.[2] Yet even major texts in carceral studies push origin stories for the prison and mass incarceration that either do not engage with this racial history or do so from a perspective that disentangles the institution from antiblackness as a structural antagonism. Two of these texts illustrate the risks of this ray—the infinite trajectory from a point of origin. Michel Foucault's 1975 *Discipline and Punish: The Birth of the Prison* outrightly aims to explain the development of the modern prison and claims Bentham's panopticon as central to its function. Written some thirty-five years later, Michelle Alexander's *The New Jim Crow: Mass Incarceration in the Age of Colorblindness* is less about detailing the evolution of the prison itself and more concerned with explaining the current crisis of mass incarceration, one that she characterizes through an understanding of a racialized caste system. What follows is a brief discussion of these texts that propose origin stories of mass incarceration and have assumed prominence through the erasure of antiblackness as a founding logic of carcerality.

Both texts have arguably become required reading for those interested in explaining contemporary carceral problems, aiming to make sense of the prison, both its purpose and its effects. The texts are each animated by their own impetus, in Foucault's case explaining the prison's development over time and in Alexander's case providing a historical analog to current institutions. With each, the theoretical beginnings affect their analytical destinations, meaning that the penal state and penal history that each proposes rests on who is imagined to be imprisoned. The task, then, is to bring these subjects to the fore and place the wider theoretical conceptualizations of the prison system in relief. *Discipline and Punish* implicitly centers an imprisoned body that is male, white, and heterosexual but whose transgression of social norms requires the prison system as a project of normalization and control. *The New Jim Crow* focuses instead on Black and Brown men and boys who have been racially profiled and overly surveilled, and ultimately argues that mass incarceration is at root a problem of policy that can be reformed.

Unlike Alexander's understanding of the prison system as flawed by racial discrimination, Foucault argues that disproportion is the basis of the carceral system. In this, there is no sense in asking moral questions of the prison—the carceral institution is already immoral. Biopolitically, as a project of control and power over life itself, the prison constitutes, not adulterates, the polity by drawing and normalizing lines of division between the deviant and the normal. Yet to assume that Foucault would contend with any racial disproportion would be generous. While Foucault pays considerable attention to the lines drawn between the inside and outside of the polity, that of the normal and abnormal, claiming that "all the authorities exercising individual control function according to a double mode; that of binary division and branding (mad/sane; dangerous/harmless; normal/abnormal)," he says nothing of the ways in which these designations are assembled racially as divisions that structure prison history.³ Said another way, if indeed "all the mechanisms of power" are "disposed around the abnormal individual, to brand him and to alter him," Foucault's constitution of abnormality is not tied to race-making. His examination of the prison and its origins revolves around the construction of an "unspecified body," that, as argued by Joy James, allows him to "sanitize state repression" and argue the historical undoing of spectacular violence.⁴

Foucault's racially unmarked account of the birth of the prison is particularly egregious given that, as Brady Heiner has argued, he came to his interest in the institution of the prison and was able to conceptualize institutional power through the analytic of war because of his intellectual contact with Black Americans, specifically the Black Panther Party and political prisoners George Jackson and Angela Davis, theorizing the relationship between Black populations and the state.⁵ That he makes not a single citation of these crucial interlocutors or any explicit reference to blackness given their impact on his now seminal work has been accurately described an "epistemic injustice."⁶ Alongside this, as Heiner, James, and Davis, among others, have shown, it also makes his account of the prison both incomplete and inaccurate at its most basal level. To pose his genealogy of discipline and punishment, Foucault turned away from the racialized violence committed, or sponsored, by the United States and ultimately privileged an unraced subject. Even with a generous reading that considers Foucault's account to be focused on French history, he has still turned away from the racial violence embodied in the French colonial prison. The underlying paradox in Foucault's work seems such that where his analyses would "seem particularly appropriate to the colonial area," still "colonialism itself does not figure."⁷

It is not simply that Foucault has turned a blind eye to a history that was very much within reach and arguably inspired his analyses but that his account of institutional power, especially as it relates to the prison, that is taken up almost universally places antiblackness under erasure. This seems to begin in his imagined epochs of the prison, where he argues that the spectacular and public violence of punishment gives way to rules of management in the early nineteenth century, an argument that he anchors in the claimed disappearance of the tortured and maimed body. Yet we know that when it comes to Black history and Black bodies, the tight hold of public spectacle did not loosen. The history of the United Stated post-emancipation is littered with nooses and murderous mobs, but these are sidestepped in Foucault's chronicle of carceral development. This is in part possible because his concern with the deviant body does not engage blackness as a mark of deviance, failing to recognize how black(ened) bodies matter differently.[8]

Foucault's timeline that claims that punishment will continue to become more hidden among the penal system only hides Black flesh and the history of antiblack punishment. This is a temporal claim that is corroborated through the suggestion that the locus of punishment transitioned from the body to the soul, a claim that makes particular use of late eighteenth–century English philosopher Jeremy Bentham's panopticon and its disciplinary exercise of power. For Foucault, Bentham's panopticon aimed to be the perfect system of control wherein all inmates could be surveilled by a single watchman, which hinged on the inability of inmates to know exactly who was being observed at one time and thus were all compelled to self-police out of the knowledge that anyone was always subject to observation.[9] Foucault emphasized the role of architecture in the transformation of subjects, to "make it possible to know them, to alter them," where the panoptical prison dependent on unceasing surveillance inserts individuals in a "fixed place, in which the slightest movements are supervised."[10] Specifically, the panopticon renders the inmate permanently visible, perfecting power so as to "render its actual exercise unnecessary," and evidenced the development of punishment towards the covert and discrete—where the fear of surveillance by one controls the actions of the many—supplanting the gruesome spectacles of sovereign power and turning punishment into a practice of transformation that occurred at the level of the soul.[11] But Davis has shown this line of thinking to be ineffective when we consider the enslaved who were understood as lacking the soul that was to be transformed.¹²

What Foucault tracks is a white prison, and a white prison subject, that was emerging in Europe at the same time as chattel slavery and functioned as a form of punishment that maintained white equality and the "racialized universality of liberty."¹³ Despite his accurate assertion of the power of surveillance and the importance of fixity, his narrative is inconsistent with the spectacular and covert distributions of power that happen together and at once for blackness, a fact that Simone Browne deftly illustrates in her side-by-side exploration of Bentham's panopticon and the slave ship *Brooks*.¹⁴ To use Foucault's genealogy to universally understand the contemporary prison is to disappear the explicit link that was drawn between slavery and punishment in the US Constitution's Thirteenth Amendment and the material penal practices that continue to produce the link between blackness and criminality, which have produced a prison system affecting Black populations more than any other. This disappearing act riddles his entire origin story, quite possibly because an attention would unrig his entire curriculum, and dangerously buttresses the erasure of blackness from the story of carcerality, where the punishment of Black flesh continues to "circulate everywhere" but "resonate nowhere."¹⁵

On the other hand, Alexander's work, which has won an NAACP award and been named one of the most influential books of the last twenty years by the *Chronicle of Higher Education*, puts forward an explicitly racial analysis, resting in the apperception of a racial caste system from Jim Crow to mass incarceration. Employing Jim Crow as a historical analog, Alexander argues that the contemporary penal system has been as effective in caging Black and Brown people into "permanent second-class citizenship" that extends beyond the physical prison structure.¹⁶ In drawing out this lineage, she locates chattel slavery as an original sin that was supposed to be rectified post-emancipation, understanding Jim Crow segregation as happening during a time in which rights should have been distributed (i.e., during Reconstruction) but were subsequently withheld. Mass incarceration is placed in a linear evolution whose distance from slavery is marked by the interval of Jim Crow and reduces both to a consequence of bad racial ideologies and inappropriate use of state power that continues to lock Black people into "an inferior position by law and custom."[17] As such, the framing advances a liberal understanding of the contemporary predicament of Black populations increasingly affected by incarceration, assuming the legitimacy of the law and the state as the protector of life and property. *The New Jim Crow* fashions no substantive critiques of any of mass incarceration's systemic issues, its foundational relationships, or even its most formative practices. An eye toward failed policies and backward politics, Alexander's explanation of the police, the government, or even the prison as an institution is principally galvanized by the impropriety of discrimination, where very little is said about the caste system she invokes at multiple points other than to say the prison functions more like it than a system of crime prevention or control.

While Alexander is able to steer us to a concern with the racialized subject, her reformist approach ends up hindering her ability to study the prison as a "racialized system of control" as she claims to do in the book's introduction.[18] Her analysis reasons that there is a mistaken idea of what blackness is, or who Black people are, that then informs the illegitimate application of said ideology to material relations. The solution set forth is not to abolish prisons but to abolish the elaboration of the prison-industrial complex that occurs as a result of this mistaken and misplaced ideology, betraying an appeal to norms and morality that imagines an idealized prison system as the proper institution of state punishment. As such, Alexander deals with mass incarceration as a problem separate from the structural integrity of antiblackness intrinsically tied to the production of the social. This stems from a failure to comprehend punishment for Black populations as "neither a breakdown of the strategies of containment . . . or an excess of entrenched power" but indicative of "the demarcation of [modernity's] most fundamental boundary."[19] As the previous chapters have shown, in this fundamental demarcation, punishment of and violence toward Black flesh are not reactive but are constitutive, evidenced from slavery to mass incarceration in the gratuitous violence that has served as a defining feature of Black subjectivity and etched the boundary line of the polity. The prison system is not actually broken, as Alexander postulates; on the contrary, it is flourishing in the hunt of its objective. Yet with a disproportionate emphasis on discrimination that papers over any theoretical attention to the structural foundations of either system in her analogy, Alexander's origin story leaves the prison's constitutive relationship to antiblackness dangerously unquestioned and misdirects any pursuit abolish our contemporary carceral problem. That is, by implying a misuse of the prison, the prison itself is sheltered from an abolitionist perspective, one that would take seriously an imagination beyond this state-sponsored institution of punishment "directed at all the social relations that support [its] permanence."[20]

So where do we go from here, within Foucault's conceptual stronghold of the panopticon and with Alexander's racial turn steeped in liberal rhetorics of reform? This question is posed for the benefit of an alternative origin story that may get us to a more capacious understanding of the function and formation of the penal state. Such an origin story turns toward the foundational entanglement of blackness and carcerality, but it does so slightly behind the conventional mainspring of these peculiar institutions. When blackness is considered, plantations often begin such explanations. Ships have largely been disregarded in the study of carceral geographies, in part because the carceral often invokes the land. But prisons were on the sea, and the sea has always been central to the history of antiblackness. Because the modern world emerged with the trade in enslaved Black flesh carried out on the ocean, the ocean is tuned to different architectures and subjects, ones that reorient and deepen our understanding of carcerality and the carceral conditioning of Black life.

The sea moves the world, and recent scholarship in carceral studies has begun to reckon with it. Most notable is the recent shift which wrestles the carceral away from the conceptual hold of the fixed, that slippage between carcerality and sedentarizing containment to which is briefly referred at the beginning of this chapter. In one example of this shift, scholars have turned to the eighteenth- and nineteenth-century ships that conveyed convicted individuals from Great Britain to British colonies as the originary precursor to the modern prison, recognizing the ways in which mobility is entangled with confinement. Kimberly Peters and Jennifer Turner's work on the convict ship has impressed upon us a need to think about "movement during moments of mobility" rather than thinking of the incarcerated as "passive, as moved" in the ways that the panopticon has produced and privileged.[21] This is not, of course, to relegate carceral mobilities to only ships. Rather, it is a push to consider how the prison has always been a moving architecture, to think about mobilities in different spaces and directions—that is, not only thinking of movement along a journey in terms of transport between places but also considering those movements that happen within a space, constantly and minutely, because it is in these movements when power is especially exercised.[22]

The convict ship is meant to bear right of the panopticon, which concretizes an emphasis on fixity of the gaze and the prisoners as the crux of the prison, by providing a more nuanced and "motionful" understanding of how punishment works.[23] However, the turn to the convict ship that produces a new origin story for the contemporary prison by "mobilizing carceral geographies" floats close but fails to come aboard a ship that existed even prior, ironic given the authors' passing reference to Marcus Rediker's work on the slave ship as an intervention on the history of transatlantic slavery which is meant to mirror their intervention in carceral studies.[24] While attuned to the ways that the moving architecture of prisons are crucial to the institution's discipline and constitution of positions, it remains settled on a method of analysis that, like Foucault, is devoid of the prison's racial history and mechanisms. The imprisoned subject of Peters and Turner's convict ship that sails from Britain to North America and Australia is suggested to be a British or Irish convict of "lesser felonies" and thus given the alternative punishment of penal transportation to the colony.[25] We are left to assume that only whitened subjects were aboard these convict ships or that race did not matter to their institution, to their movement within themselves and between locales, knowing that neither is probably true. Transportation as punishment, which the convict ship embodies, is offered by Peters and Turner as evidence of the Foucauldian thesis for punishment that argues the move away from spectacular torture on the body and thus offers the same theoretical lacunae.[26] When looking at the contemporary makeup of the prison, its disproportion of Black prisoners, it seems ill-fitting to center its lineage on a convict ship that denies its connection to blackness. This is reflective of a larger pitfall of carceral studies that is the hiding away of blackness and the constitution of whiteness where any conceptual attendance to, for example, racial capitalism or reference to uneven distribution of criminality along multiple axes of social position is assumed to fill in the gaps. Such assumption offers a conceptual Band-Aid that betrays an inattention to the constitutive accord of antiblackness with carcerality. Intending a better explanation of carcerality, the convict ship is offered as the exemplar of carceral (im)mobilities and paradoxical use of mobility within immobility in ways that expunge antiblackness from the history of carcerality and its deep entanglement with en/forced movement.

The slave ship proposes a different analytical concern even more necessary and exemplary than the convict ship to questions of carcerality. Rediker reminds us that the slave ship was "a mobile, seagoing prison at a time when the modern prison had not yet been established on land."[27] Rather than simply pulling blackness into the frame, Simone Browne's suggestion to reread the panopticon through the *Brookes* plan shines a light on the very practices and relations of chattel slavery that Bentham quite literally stands on to conceptualize power and with which she retheorizes surveillance.[28] Dennis Childs also points us in a direction in line with that of Browne's provocation in his proposition of the "Middle Passage Carceral Model," which shifts the historiography of the prison past the centering of a white subject and locates slavery's architectures in the center of European imperialism as it traces the advancement from the chain gang to the penitentiary.[29] Both Browne and Childs bring the slave ship to bear on carcerality, focusing necessary attention on their material and conceptual links.

As mechanisms of containment and separation, both the slave ship and the prison engender blackness through gratuitous violence and practices of political repression. Nowhere else is the Black necrotic function of the slave ship so directly repurposed and re-pursued as it is in the prison. The carceral geographies of the slave ship and the prison also both existed in part to keep the rebellious and dissenting under the control of white authority. For the slave ship, as discussed earlier, the enslaved were disciplined through shacklings, separations, nettings, and gratuitous punishments that categorically assumed and conjured dissent. In the case of the prison, as Black political prisoners like Assata Shakur, Angela Davis, and George Jackson, have argued, its primary function was to repress political dissidents as much as it was to "solve" social problems of race and class inequity.[30] It is, to use the words of Jackson, the "ultimate expression of the law."[31]

As such, placing the hold and the cell in vibrating tension with one another draws attention to the cyclical temporality of Black life, the simultaneity of ship and prison holds wherein "past, present, and future exist in constant interface."[32] The cycle is itself a movement bearing a different conception of time, one that indicates the recurrence of vestibular subjections, constantly evolving but persisting, while also underscoring the temporality of the hold's imprisonment itself. On the slave ship and in the prison, time was carefully and purposefully controlled. Time in the hold, time on the deck, time for feeding, time for cleaning, time to destination, time everywhere, time nowhere. The time was rarely if ever the time of the enslaved. Likewise, "punishment is time," and in prison, this translates to not only how much time is spent in prison but *how* one's time is spent.[33] Through the execution of daily timetables meant to sequence routines and destroy temporal autonomy, the prison perfects "time-discipline."[34] Regimented and repetitious, time for the entombed and incarcerated is intimately linked to the carcerality of space. It is in movement that the matters of time and space converge, and it is in the movement across space that time is measured; the disciplining of time and space happen simultaneously, equally producing the position of the prisoner and enslaved through their movement. This is clear in the excerpts of Shakur's autobiography that open this chapter; the imprisoned like the enslaved are denuded of any ownership over time and space, consistently disoriented and constantly moved. Together, the slave ship and the prison hew the history of containment, an absence of time, and the burden of mobility acutely charting the origins of the modern carceral state.

Vagrant Criminalities

Mobility as an affliction is readily apparent across the history of containment for Black populations. Historically, the expansive carceral state in the United States has hinged on a criminalization of blackness intimately tied to matters of locomotion, including idleness, itinerancy, and homelessness. This is directly reflected in the slave codes, the post-emancipation Black Codes, and segregation laws, and enforced through contemporary loitering laws and homelessness ordinances. Under the structural antagonism of antiblackness, Black people have always been made to move, and their movements have been materially coerced and ideologically fabricated. This is especially true in the prison, where the incarcerated are shuffled between prisons, within the prison, and from the prison to the outside and back again in cycles of "recidivism." But the prison is only a classic exemplar of the larger carceral reliance on and production of transience, or more aptly, vagrancy yoked to blackness. Shakur's seemingly life-long movement enunciates a vagrancy that etches Black life in the United States as a process of criminalization and a condition of Black criminality.

Assata Shakur, a former member of the Black Liberation Army, was convicted in 1977 for the killing of a state trooper during a 1973 shootout on the New Jersey turnpike. She was arrested and later found guilty of first-degree murder for aiding and abetting. During this time, she was shuffled throughout the US penal system, although she spent the majority of her incarceration in solitary confinement. On November 2, 1979, Shakur broke out of Clinton Correctional in New York with the help of three members of the Black Liberation Army and was then stamped a fugitive, subsequently fleeing to Cuba five years later, seeking and acquiring political asylum in 1984. In 2005, she was classified as a domestic terrorist by the Federal Bureau of Investigation (FBI) and a bounty of one million dollars was placed on her head. In 2013, the FBI named her a Most Wanted Terrorist, the first woman to be given such a designation. Her bounty was then doubled to $2 million and overnight billboards were raised in New Jersey to advertise these developments. Since she has been in Cuba, the US government has made numerous attempts to extradite her, with Donald Trump's most recent public demand for the return of the "cop killer" coming in June 2017. Her asylum, while always uncertain, is now made even more precarious as official relations between Cuba and the United States develop. Yet this Black carceral condition of vagrancy is hardly a story restricted to Shakur. While she is individually targeted by the state, her autobiography as a "mode of Black theorizing", as Patrice D. Douglass argues, "becomes the tale of the collective," describing the "interlocking nature between the history of enslavement, the current conditions of Black life, and the call for Black Revolutionary politics and actions."[35] Continuing with Douglass, the autobiography explores "the ways that Black life is structurally bound to conditions that precede, anticipate, and exceed" any individual life because it "interrogates how the paradigm of antiblackness operates without recourse to the locations, performances, and identifications of individual black people."[36] It is in this way that Shakur's life and her narrative is approached to provide an alternative understanding of our carceral state and its constitutive foundation of antiblackness in general.

In *Assata*, Shakur consistently refers to her forced movement, such as in this chapter's first epigraph that recites a common exchange between her and a prison guard and bespeaks a constant and intentional disorientation. The second epigraph, also taken from her autobiography, catches motion's double meaning, as a technical term of jurisprudence and as a denial of personhood. Together, the excerpts clarify how movement frames Shakur's story as she navigates her experience in the prison, as we shift back and forth from her present incarceration to her life before it, and as we pass from her time in the United States to her current exile in Cuba. We move across the prison, we move across time, we move across borders. What becomes increasingly apparent throughout the autobiography is not simply her movement—that is, the movement itself—but that she is always forced to move, that until Cuba, she is never still, and even in Cuba, she is never free; that her abrupt transfers between jails without any word to her lawyer or any explanation "was a scenario that would be repeated over and over again."[37] Shakur discloses herself as not simply located but locomotive, vagrant.

In the *Oxford English Dictionary*, the term *vagrant* is innocuously defined as a person who wanders or roams, one who is not fixed or settled but is constantly moving with no permanent home, or as unpredictable movement and behavior. It takes a more prejudicial tone in its definition as a person who "lives by begging" or, as per its use relative to the law, "relating to or living the life of a vagrant."[38] Given the West's political orientation toward property, the insipid characterization confesses a deleterious signification, especially as it renders meaning for a status or condition of life. Here, vagrant is politically and legally stressed, connoting class hierarchies that hinge on ownership, employment, and domicile and imply their proper environments. The term *vagrant* also marks and is marked by blackness, especially in the United States, where post-emancipation Black Codes were passed in Southern states to restrict the lives of free Black populations and whose defining feature was a broadly defined and broadly enforced vagrancy law. Under the Black Codes of 1865 and 1866, authorities would arrest free Black people for minor infractions and subsequently have them committed to involuntary labor under what came to be known as the convict lease system.[39]

Through the codes, the use of vagrancy was integral to the transition from chattel slavery to more clandestine forms of racialized incarceration. In other words, policing movement was often the way in which free Black people were returned to a condition of servitude at the command of whites. Vagrancy laws were directly tied to the criminalization of blackness and Black freedom, used as a catchall to ensnare all Black people in the act, in the act of doing or doing nothing, and ultimately in the act of moving. As such, vagrancy was always already the enunciation of Black movement.

In its legal uses, vagrancy presumes that one is moving between or among coherent places that provide substantive and subjective meaning, either the place of residence, the place of employment, or the place of consumer transaction. To be marked vagrant is to be interstitial, and thus be nowhere that is valued in the eyes of the state. Still, rather than exhibiting an absence of meaning, interstitiality is an inundation of meaning; it is to be excessively known in relation to one's movement. Because of one's movement, but also no matter one's movement, vagrancy orders and gathers the blackness at and as the position of the criminal, an enunciation of dispossession that cannot be recognized as such. As a charge, vagrancy names a collection of threats against property and order that is also a racial categorization of a problem population as threat. That is, the charge announces Du Bois's question of being a problem to be solved and a threat to be contained—the threat of rebellion and the threat to property and security of recognized political subjects. By calling out the danger of the threat, vagrancy encompasses a futurity, where neither the criminal act nor criminal intent is required. As such, the charge of vagrancy is, as Saidiya Hartman reminds, a "status, not a crime" meant to indicate the "prophetic power of the police to predict future crime."[40] In other words, through vagrancy, criminality invokes the possibility of the criminal as a guarantee.

The preoccupation with regulating and coercing Black movement bridges the visual rhyme of the methods and system of chattel slavery to the new carceral manifestations that come in its wake. Vagrancy thus furthers the expansion of carceral geographies that hinges on the spatial dislocations and discursive circulation of Black people coeval with the fabrication of the Black criminal. While vagrancy is a charge that is applied to Black people it is also how they are forced to move. This is to say that vagrancy is not only a status offense or indicative of one's status as a social problem but also the status of Black movement that is produced through the postbellum geography of emancipation and Reconstruction. Of course, the function of Black criminalization is not only the regulation of movement and Black criminalization does not only occur through vagrancy, but this theoretical redirection does elucidate these connections and further argues that Black criminalization actually has very little to do with actual crime and much more to do with the locomotive conditioning of Black life as an absence of capacity to fulfill the requirements of the liberal subject, the human, and the citizen.

Angela Davis has demonstrated that the conceptual distinction of Black and white imbricated in the criminal discourse is one of criminality versus crime. Frank B. Wilderson III has built on this by arguing that for Black people, there are only two manifestations, that of the prison slave and the prison-slave-in-waiting, which posits not only the criminality that is ascribed to Black people but the way in which this ascription comes to structure their very existence in the world.[41] Black criminality is not measured by physical proximity to the prison but bears an inescapable condition of criminalization and carcerality as movement toward the prison and its correlates of gratuitous violence and death. That is, the prison itself does not represent a separation from a discrete before and after of criminalization for punishment is a condition of Black existence. This is both a theoretical gesture away from discipline as a response to crime and evidence of a larger carceral system that produces as much as it maintains Black criminalization. This is evident in the vagrancy laws of the Black Codes that indicate the established threat Black people have been imagined to pose to national security not for the weapons they may wield "but for *being* such weapons and thus always in need of containment, surveillance, sanction, deportation, elimination."[42] Furthermore, surveillance has been constitutive, operative anywhere and anytime irrespective of class or subsequent spatiality, rendering not only the individual but productive of an entire criminal assemblage of people. In blackness, individual criminalization always diffuses across the collective, not unlike Sharkur's "Wanted" billboards that were made to cast themselves over low-income neighborhoods in New Jersey when the state knew full well she was not stateside.

As a Black indictment, vagrancy was also a gendered and sexually charged indictment, emphasizing the imminent incursion of unbridled Black sexuality and the necessity of white supervision. The profusion of surveillance was once again justified by the presumed threat that blackness posed to white morality. Historically, this has looked like the assumption of sexual transgression, spatially underscored by the fact that in urban areas, Black neighborhoods were often the ones strategically arranged as enclaves of sexual commerce and vice.[43] This immoral and sexually charged distortion was central to the "caricatured criminal protagonists," which became a mass-produced "vehicle for white fantasies and taboo desires."[44] Specifically, the trope of Black hypersexuality fueled fears of Black men's desire for white women and Black women's seduction of white men. Historian Kali Gross argues that the shift in the perception of Black women from the "ultimate submissive" of slavery to the "dangerous urban aggressor" post-Emancipation was a consequence of the subversion, at least in theory, of uninhibited white access to Black women's bodies.[45] As such, the trope of hypersexuality was crucial to the criminalization of blackness for the benefit of, and in opposition to, those holders of whiteness, where Black women have been historically figured as sexually lascivious and dangerous. In this vein, press accounts of Black women's crimes were meant to elicit the illicit, fashioning sexual and violent overtones to spectacularize acts for wide and mainstream distribution.[46]

The fascination with the spectacle of Black criminality and the fabrication of vagrant Black flesh pulled on proper notions of sexuality and reached into questions of gender itself. Nineteenth century Italian criminologist Cesare Lombroso claimed that an absence of a stark distinction of Black men from Black women factored centrally in Black female criminality such that criminality became tied to the proposition that Black women were not properly gendered and Black womanhood was inherently inferior to white womanhood.[47] In this formulation, Black womanhood was rendered dangerous because it was understood to be marked by excess—excess in body type, strength, behavior, and criminal abilities and desires—reflecting what Douglass calls the "coordinates of gender . . . undone" endemic to blackness.[48] Painting the "portrait of the ferocious Black woman" aggressively on the prowl was meant to demonstrate the active threat that was to validate the use of violence in the suppression of Black women's activities, a portrait that clearly continues to circulate in Shakur's contemporary billboards without historical break.[49]

To be sure, for women generally, prisons have historically been used to morally condemn behaviors that are seen as deviating from notions of proper womanhood. Yet as Douglass demonstrates, because of the "human/Black divide" constituted by enslavement and reiterated in each vestibular subjection, "the symbolic integrity of gender is lost, a priori . . . at the ontological level."[50] That is, again returning to Douglass, "Black gender" is definitively destabilized and "rendered formless by its fungible status."[51] In Shakur's autobiography, this is evidenced in the persistent absence of protections and limitations from and on violence that gender is supposed to afford.[52] Black depravity mobilized the belief that Black people cross lines, that they are excessive, and that they move beyond the constitutive borders of humanity's categories. As such, while white women's crimes could always be displaced or explained away through the impress of humanity, blackness as the human's counterpoint linked depravity and criminality in ways that made the trope of the "depraved Black woman" a narrative redundancy. That said, the redundancy was mobilized, tying Black women's criminality to representations of deviant and unchecked sexuality, fetishized as compulsive, uncontrollable, and roving. Crime and the danger of unchecked Black movement were exaggerated in such a way as to shore up traditional notions of both white masculinity and white female morality.

These representations galvanized and justified urban policies, heavily influencing state authority over Black urban life. By promoting fear, the rhetoric of criminalization that conflated criminality with blackness through strategic manipulations and omissions, has often been traded upon for political power, with a "tough on crime" attitude being the most profitable and risk-free way to secure support from any constituency without revealing racial bias. In effect, the US government, especially from Lyndon B. Johnson's presidency onward, has been able to chisel out ideological boundaries of middle-class social and cultural values that normalize white dominance and Black danger turning on the imminence of Black ambulation beyond their place. As Davis has argued, Black people, then and now, are always punished for practices that go unchecked when performed by whites.[53] Furthermore, the presumed level of danger posed by Black people to white dominion is often not represented in the crimes that get incarcerated Black women convicted and the socioeconomic conditions from which these crimes often emerge is conventionally disassociated from their practice by the courts and outside audiences.[54] In her own case, Shakur's alleged crimes against the state indicate how Black criminalization existed at the point of imagined Black threat to white dominion, and this articulation is historically rooted. The Black Codes—those collections of laws with broadly defined and broadly enforced rules about vagrancy—specifically outlaw runaways, the assembly of the free or enslaved, the disorderly, and those who neglect their calling. Vagrancy in relation to Black populations is always a declaration of permissible movements and always a repudiation of dissent. In that way, the charge of vagrancy paraphrases a critique and prohibition of Black political practice.

The writings of Black political prisoners like Shakur have brought this connection between criminalization, incarceration, and political dissent to the fore. Jackson, who was incarcerated in 1961 until he was killed during an escape attempt in 1971, and Davis, who was jailed for sixteen months from 1971 to 1972, were two of the major imprisoned intellectuals to conceptualize this relationship. Jackson's late 1960s and early 1970s prison writings, and those of Davis from the same time period, explain the correlative relationship of crime that is politicized and political activism that is criminalized.[55] In connection therewith, Joy James has argued that Black people are not only incarcerated at the highest rate for petty or violent crime but also constitute the highest percentage of those incarcerated for "political acts (including armed struggle) in opposition to repression."[56] The prison, according to political prisoners and contemporaries of Shakur, overwhelmingly, and at once, confined radical activists and racialized others.[57] But here, not only were Black people criminalized, but Black political practices were as well. This criminalization is utilized so as to deny the existence of the political prisoner within US prisons, which, as Davis argues, requires a double move, first to equate the "individual political act with the individual criminal act" and second to reduce the political event to the criminal event.[58]

The formation of the FBI's Counterintelligence Program (COINTELPRO) is archetypical evidence of the government's desire to criminalize and neutralize Black liberation movements, in particular the Black Panther Party and Black Liberation Army in which Jackson, Davis, and Shakur held membership. In a 1968 memo to FBI field offices, director J. Edgar Hoover explained that the purpose of COINTELPRO was to "expose, disrupt, misdirect, discredit, or otherwise neutralize" the political activity of Black political leaders by whatever means necessary including assassinations, frame-ups, and even the disruption of their service work.[59] When the latter was executed, like in the case of convincing Black community members that the Panthers' free breakfast program for children was serving poisoned food, government officials adjudicated members as criminals and the communities that might benefit from these programs as victims that required state protection.[60] This criminalized the Panthers' political work but also reiterates how this criminalization was intimately tied to the policing of the larger Black community.

Knowing intimately the criminalization of Black dissent, from their unique vantage point, political prisoners conceptualized the centrality of the prison movement to the larger struggle for Black liberation, especially the Black revolutionary movement of the 1960s and 1970s represented by groups like the Black Panther Party and the BLA. Like Jackson and Davis,[61] Shakur's escape mobilizes just as crucial a critique of the state, the prison, and antiblackness. Her act against the state was not an individualist act. Indeed, as James argues, she always invoked the people, the collective, as driving the need for anti-state action rather than simply being led by the movement.[62] That "revolutionary war was a people's war" was Shakur's understanding of both her part in the Black Panther Party as well as the Black Liberation Army and animated her escape as a critique that elaborates the Black masses against the carceral structure of antiblackness.[63] In rejecting the very validity of the state and its legitimacy to keep her incarcerated, Shakur's escape signals a full break with the system and is presented here as the obverse to reform. It exists in contradistinction to "law-abiding dissent," which often has broader social acceptance because of fidelity to accepted customs and credence in state power that make them more absorbable by liberal political philosophies.[64] In what follows, I will argue that the reform of the prison and even the eradication of specific forms of punishment are assimilable if they can maintain the aegis of the state and ensure carceral endurance. Counter to Shakur's dis-incarceration that enunciates order's carceral crux and disrupts state power by moving beyond its reach, reform chimes with liberalism in its fulfillment of the state's carceral cause.

Reformist Visions

Prison reform seems to be most deliberately in league with the state when it proselytizes prison development, which rather than work to gradually abolish the prison does the opposite, by ensuring a prison more expansive, durable, and impermeable to change.[65] Today, recent shifts in prison administration driven by what the *Atlantic* recently called "genuine human concern" have been made specifically to reduce the use of solitary confinement and increase the mobility of the incarcerated.[66] The underlying assumption has been that "modernizing" the prison away from pure immobilization and a greater concern to limit detrimental effects betters the conditions of the incarcerated, especially the Black incarcerated who are subject to increased solitary confinement and harsher restrictions.[67] Shakur herself has been used to signify the terrible conditions experienced by the imprisoned. *Assata*'s only footnote discusses the 1979 report initiated by her lawyer Lennox Hinds and carried out by the United Nations Commission on Human Rights documenting the treatment of political prisoners in the United States that uses Shakur's case to exemplify the unjustified use of solitary confinement to which she was subjected for over twenty months in the men's prisons and many more in women's and mixed prisons.[68] Hinds brought such brutalities to the attention of the UN seeking necessary intervention, but it also highlights how justification, inherent to the delineation of cruel and unusual, comes to bear on punishment. How is punishment justified? How is the prison imagined and reformulated so as to be a measured response? And how have shifts away from particular forms held space for new formulations of control?

In their study of prison architectures, Philip Hancock and Yvonne Jewkes draw out the paralleled transition of workplaces and prisons from highly aggressive and confined architectures to those promoting openness and flexibility, which have introduced a more underhanded method of controlling the imprisoned linked to the push for productivity.[69] In Europe and the United Kingdom between the twentieth and twenty-first centuries, pushes for reform have shifted prison architecture from utilitarian bastions of state authority to designs meant to mimic the flowing floor plans of a tech enterprise where a new aesthetic approach is thought to generate "organizationally desirable actions and identities" and increase rehabilitation.[70] In the United States, this looks like a similar shift from the telephone-pole design where rows of buildings would be connected by one or two main corridors to the more modern campus design with its many freestanding buildings surrounded by spaces of open land. While the former was known for the difficulty it caused for surveillance and riot control, the latter, originally designed for women and juveniles, increases patriarchal supervision and expands disciplinary policing.[71] As prisons move away from solitary confinement and promote the freer circulation of the incarcerated, prison administrators have begun to employ methods that are meant to maintain control while reducing the need for isolation. On the one hand, these architectural and administrative shifts may provide freer movement for the incarcerated on prison land and on the other hand may make even less visible the pernicious acts of violence that are perpetrated on and through Black bodies around corners and in back rooms.

A 2021 article in *Architectural Digest* debates the building of new prisons "boasting sunlight, air, greenery, and more programming space" in cities across the United States with some believing updated infrastructure to be an "antidote to mass incarceration" because it can increase rehabilitation and reduce recidivism.[72] The antidote's attendant mantra that "environment drives behavior" names the impact of spatial design but mislocates the problem to be solved.[73] Reaching a moment where formats encouraged by the tech boom have found their way into prison architecture, rehabilitation continues to circulate in reform discourse as if it is not a process meant to produce subjects who are deemed socially compatible, such that the antidote to mass incarceration is found in better behavior on the part of those who are the institution's targets. These architectural design innovations are not meant to, nor could they, redefine the deeper social relations constituted by the existence of the prison in the first place; rather, they reformat how these social relations are expressed and change how they are felt by the incarcerated. While one may argue that the prison looks different since Shakur made her escape, the changes to these prisons cannot be disentangled from the ever-increasing violence that conditions Black life both within and beyond the walls of the prison. These changes to the prison are meant to bear new citizens; they do not alter the dominant relationship of creation and creator and are remarkably absurd given that they are meant to promote a capacity to socialize that has no substantive purchase on the outside for Black people.

The dangerously uncritical turn to mobility within prison reform movements betrays the fact of mobility intrinsic to carcerality and its forms. Mobility has always been used by state forces as a means of discomfort, decreasing visibility, and increasing vulnerability of the incarcerated. Incontrovertibly, this has often been exemplified in images of unremitting labor or the constant shuffling of prisoners, but this does not tell the full story. Indeed, while the advancement of prisoner mobility in contrast to confinement to the cell and hypermanagement of the prison is justified by reformers as a move in the correct direction, in many ways the practice of affording limited freedom of mobility extends the space of confinement both within and outside of the prison. Outside, this can look like electronic monitoring, which has recently seen an upsurge in lieu of time inside because of overcrowding. On the inside, there is the growing use of "stepdown" or incentive programs that use increased recreation time or access to education and leisure materials to motivate the incarcerated to be, in effect, better prisoners.

Those who push for abolition do not advocate against reform in total but against a reformist framework that fails to keep the abolition of prison in focus.[74] Conceptually, prison abolition and Black anarchism are linked through their rejection of reformist politics and their drive to dismantle institutions that cohere by way of—and that embody—state authority. Given its very grounding in the abolition of slavery, the invocation of the term *abolition* or *abolitionist* to describe the anti-prison vision and anti-prison activist describes the prison's intimate connection to slavery, such that if you radically oppose one, you must also radically oppose the other.[75] The implication being that the structural antagonism forged in chattel slavery remains the animating condition of the prison as we know it. Along these lines, abolitionism maintains an anticipation of "a social landscape no longer dominated by the prison" while not yet having the answers to what the terrain may look like nor what may lie on the other side of the break. It is in this space that marks what Ernst Bloch calls the "not yet" and in which Shakur's dis-incarceration also floats.[76]

Dis-incarceration Nonrepresentation

Shakur's dis-incarceration provides its own intellectual analysis of the world, what Joy James has called "maroon philosophy at the borders reimagining freedom through flight."[77] Key to James's formulation is that the flight itself is the practice through which a philosophy of freedom can emerge. This line diverges from an understanding of freedom as a destination materialized, fully formed from Zeus's head. By this I mean attention is driven to consider the questions urged by Shakur's flight rather than the question of what is achieved by her break. To center this is not, however, an attempt to distill Shakur's political ideologies. Her thoughts and ideas are neither simple nor straightforward but are complex, and sometimes contradictory. To shift theoretical attention to (her) escapement is to garner a theorization of liberation that exceeds her personal ideologies, where, to borrow the words of Michel-Rolph Trouillot, "discourse always lagged behind practice" because "revolution was indeed at the limits of the thinkable."[78]

The escape of Assata Shakur is not limited to a moment where an individual was simply at her limit of being vulnerable to the machinations of the state. It was a break with a regime that structures Black being through gratuitous violence, wanton exploitation, fungibility, and surveilled (im)mobility. Yet dis-incarceration, rather than escape, is used to discuss Shakur's spatial interruption of the prison for several reasons. Although Shakur does jump the prison walls, her continued exile reflects the political interval in which her practice resides and demonstrates the necessary incompleteness of her action against the reterritorializing power of the state. Providing this alternative conceptual frame to understand her escape is to take up Barnor Hesse's call to consider the complexities of Black subversive freedoms or, rather, how Black anarchist practices "embody the meaning of freedom subversively."[79] Shakur must repeatedly elude Western control, of which the United States is in this case the biggest stakeholder, such that the secrecy of her whereabouts is sustained. Her dis-incarceration illustrates the continual, iterative, and processual nature of escape, and her evasions indicate an exertion of nonlinear trajectories of Black movement beyond the dominion of white authority. Her escape as dis-incarceral critique is one that continues to sharply challenge the state because of the very nature of fugitivity, the perpetuity of escape that is then a persistent rebuke of state authority.

Yet as they embody an insurgent transience against the spatial requirements of white dominion, they maintain a distance from the interpretations of completion that the word escape seems to stipulate, which fail to critically engage the carceral illimitability that limns Shakur's life specifically and Black non/being generally. Dis-incarceration reframes Black anarchism as a Black liberation*ist* politics, a gesture toward freedom that is not, and cannot yet be, achieved. Indexed by Shakur's outlaw status, her break from prison cannot be an achievement of freedom, because her flight does not free her from the carcerality of blackness. As I will argue in the following section, Shakur's dis-incarceral practice functions against the carceral geographies meant to contain her, but her own movement remains subject to its mechanisms of vagrancy. As such, it is a practice that occurs within the conceptual fields of both freedom and unfreedom. The prefix of dis-incarceration is also meant to describe her practice as a deed that precedes its demand, rejecting a linear trajectory and its coherent outcome from which we are to measure the accomplishment of her practice and realization of her claim. The rejection proposes that to be measured is to remain beholden to a horizon that shapes and dictates her act. In this way, Shakur's practice disrupts the horizons of the imaginable by refusing its own appraisal as much as it challenges the state's authority to keep her captive. It is an anticipatory abandonment of the prison as that ultimate expression of the law that does not yet have a destination; it is an anticipation of something else. Shakur forces one to reckon with flight as practice, the practice of the escape rather than its destination(s).

However, reckoning with this practice does not mean knowing this practice. This is clearest when we encounter her autobiography's transition from prison to Cuba as an absent chapter, as a fugitivity of the literature. Shakur never makes mention of how her actual escape happens, sounding an evasion of a system of representation that buttresses state authority; the textual omission of her practice pushes back on the very mechanisms for and desires of Western liberal horizons, its assimilations and appropriations. Her textual tactic is a challenge for both the processes of knowledge production and the production of knowledge itself. That is, even as "loss gives rise to longing," the omission questions our (archival) desires, challenging us to "respect what we cannot know."[80] By not narrating how she did it, she denies the pressures of the "reproductive economy" and demonstrates a necessity to work through the unknown as a productive space of politics.[81]

In the steps of Trouillot's study of the Haitian Revolution as a series of practices that exceed ideology, taking up Shakur's carceral evasions requires us to similarly think about how their very deed is "incompatible" with the West, subsequently undercut by a "failure of narration," a silencing through what Trouillot calls formulas of erasure and formulas of banalization.[82] The textual absence of Shakur's practice, the missing chapter as it were, walks the line of silence and secret. In his study of colonial Brazil, historian Greg Childs differentiates between the two on the matter of recovery, where the former is an omission that awaits revelation to ascribe value, often on the part of the historian, and the latter is more "commensurate with nonexistence."[83] As an attempt to keep things from the knowable, the secret is not an obstacle of understanding for Black anarchism but is fundamental to it. It is an indication of the nonrepresentational "possibility of revaluing that emptiness."[84] Shakur works against the temptation to "fill in the gaps" or "provide closure where there is none" and challenges our desire to know even as it provokes a necessity to study.[85] That is, her iterative escapement requires our theorization insomuch as a new approach to such practices is necessary, but it simultaneously indicates that we cannot approach these practices with an intent to know them with any certainty. It is at once a model of political praxis as well as a confession of the paradox of indexing the dis-incarceral tactic.

We know only *of* her deed, and of that, we actually know very little. So what can we begin to learn from, rather than about, these practices when we approach them through a different frame? What can these practices teach us about politics and the study of politics? In the case of Shakur's continuing story, the absent chapter reflects the necessity of that which is not yet finished, that which remains anticipatory and provisional, and as reflective of the very possibilities emergent in her practice that "clog the smooth machinery of the representation necessary to the circulation of capital."[86] The omission resists the reconciliation of recovery and perverts the representative requirements of political claim-making often necessary for the legal processes that have failed so many imprisoned Black people in the past. As such, it challenges the liberal underpinnings of some Black political practices that call for assimilation and representation as the route to liberation.

Assata mirrors the physical practice of dis-incarceration, where passage is both discursive and material, providing a textual mime to the ephemerality of Shakur's disappearing act. In other words, the absent presence of her flight in the text is itself an index of her flight, embodying its transient performance. This presence is signed by "The Tradition," the poem that connects the postscript and Shakur's final chapters in prison, where she names various modes and methods of dissent, refusal, and defiance that make up a long Black political history.[87] In using the poem in place of a narrative account of her own elopement, Shakur locates herself within this tradition of struggle, situating her practice among similar forms such as jumping the slave ship, running from the plantation, and the Underground Railroad, but also in killing the master and poisoning the mistress. In each stanza, she names practices within the Black radical tradition along with the steady repetition of carrying it on. Tunneling between the prison and the outside, the poem presents Shakur's migration from the US prison to Cuba as an underground and unseen practice, where the reader immediately recognizes that Shakur has made it out with the simple word *freedom* as an opening to the text's final pages.[88] Her own practice is an unmarked and unknown passage, augmenting an evasion of state authority and naming the political inflection of abscondence outside the legislative and the electoral, while reiterating the necessity of its persistence.

To employ Hartman and Stephen Best's evocative conceptualization, the textual tunnel beneath the surveillance of the West demarcates the fugitive space that is between the complaint and the "extralinguistic mode of black noise that exists outside the parameters of any strategy or plan for remedy."[89] Shakur exerts a racial chaos that is inaudible to the human project and represents the "political interval," which elaborates the distance "between the destruction of the old world and the awaited hour of deliverance."[90] It is in those moments of inaudibility, as Sarah Cervenak argues, where one bucks the attempt of scripted translation by the state that Black movement "aligns with the free."[91] Yet the inaudibility or invisibility that indicates the break with legibility as imaginings beyond our comprehension also gleam a governing order of antiblackness that is dependent on their repression. Dis-incarceration as an opacity works against the "instinct for possession," which is driven by a desire for integration, where "imperialism is a search for security." The secrecy of the chapter, then, does not properly function with and for the bourgeois demand of "guarantees in the present against the future," because it "introduces unknowns into those solved problems" from which antiblackness lives.[92] The secrecy both announces the threat as a threat and is also a threat in itself. Shakur's physical escape threatens the pervasive violence of carceral geographies, and her continued existence beyond the knowledge of the state remains threatening to order, requiring her continued evasions of the carceral conditions that lie in the prison's wake.

Exiles

If the entanglement of movement and punishment have been at all instructive, it has illustrated that carcerality has existed before the prison and is always expanding beyond it. As such, not only must carceral egress be a repeated practice, but it also runs up against the dislocations and disorientations inherent in the conditions of exile. Shakur makes her way out of a draconian penal architecture that is meant to contain her for the court-appointed duration and receives political asylum in Cuba where she is able to move, not only beyond the concrete walls of Clinton Correctional Facility but also past the borders of the United States and into a communist nation meant to represent all things exceeding US control and influence. However, while her locomotion across US national borders and relative mobility in Cuba mark out a new experience for Shakur that is reasonably different from that of her life inside the prison edifice, this change does not overcome the carceral geographies that produce her position as always already subject to the violence of the state. In her words, she had achieved her dream; she was elated and ecstatic, and she was also "completely disoriented" where "everything was the same, yet everything was different."[93] Often, when the story is told of Shakur, it is her unfreedom both within and beyond the cell in the United States that is highlighted, and in contrast, her exile in Cuba encapsulates her escape from white dominion. This discrepancy, while sometimes unintentional, trades in a long-standing and now much maligned dichotomy between the racial oppression of the United States and the imagined racial democracy of Latin America and misrepresents the complicated status of what it means to be a modern day maroon.[94] To be in exile is indeed to live a different condition of containment that remains under the watchful eye of the surveilling West, but one where Shakur's "fugitive flesh" continues to signify a criminal, a "commodity on the run," and the Black body evading capture.[95]

Marronage, to run away, to jump the slave ship, is to practice a sort of transience. It is both transitional and ephemeral; it is more passage than destination. Yet it also speaks of a kind of impermanence, for better and for worse. Shakur's transience continues to work against and within the vagrancy that names criminality qua blackness. While her movements oppose the movement of vagrancy manufactured through various mechanisms of criminalization, they also remain subject to it. Shakur is a maroon, no doubt, but like the maroons, she has not yet found freedom, or more precisely, has not yet escaped unfreedom. Parenti's 1997 interview with her is ripe with this tenuous, or transient, existence; she is simultaneously a resident of the "ultimate Palenque" and must "keep a low profile" because "security is still a big concern."[96] As a political refugee in exile in Cuba, Shakur is forced to lay low because her movements continue to be determined by the surveillance of the West, the US government in particular, and those it deputizes. In Cuba, she remains restricted to lands that are at once beyond the reach of the West and its US handmaidens and established by those very forces. Indeed, "there exist no fixed sites" of freedom and the reach of the West is hardly contained by geographic boundaries.[97]

Her exile focuses attention on the constitution of national borders by the virulent policing in and of antiblackness. As a fugitive, she ensures a displacement and diffusion of carcerality that reveals itself in a new form that supposedly softer in appearance remains materially significant as she stays subject to incessant desires of the state. In this new diffusion, US surveillance simultaneously plays on an othering *of* Cuba while subsequently demonizing her political refugee status that is made manifest through a constructed resonance *with* Cuba's communist, and undemocratic, subsistence. This begins to bare the construction of her identity as most wanted terrorist, one that reimagines a McCarthyist trajectory that claims a confluence of any dissent from the state with presuppositions of being pro-communist and un-American. Cuba's anti-imperialist commitments and public support for the struggle of African Americans, such as Shakur, has endeared it to those identifying with Black liberation while also angering the US government.[98] Indeed, this small nation had come to "symbolize a resistance to a state constructed as an imperial behemoth" that runs counter to the United States' ever-growing desire for control that dates back to the Cuban Revolution's challenge of the Monroe Doctrine.[99] As such, the policing of Shakur accommodates and makes further possible the policing of Cuba, where Shakur bears both the desire for the FBI to capture a Black fugitive and the United States' attempt to invade the sanctuary space for dissidents that Castro's racialized Cuba had come to represent.

Shakur's political asylum in Cuba causes many problems for the United States, one being that her migration confronts and reverses the Western narrative of the United States as that which takes in the refugees of Cuba. The US imagination of the refugee in the mid- to late twentieth century in relation to Cuba is typified by the shift from "freedom fighters" fleeing communism in the 1960s when refugees were often middle-class professionals, racialized as white, and relatively welcome by the United States government, to the 1980s with the Muriel boat crisis and the advance of Black Cubans, who were fleeing social and economic crisis in Cuba largely driven by the United States' blockade. In both ways, Cuba itself was racialized as a "dark" nation, and as such, the refugees, welcomed or not, were always figured as in need of US aid.[100] The case of Shakur and other political asylum seekers in search of refuge in Cuba turns this narrative on its head.

However, any claim that her asylum is indeed a critique of the US state goes unheard as divergent noise among the chorus of citizens and government agencies calling for her head, remaining largely irrelevant to her construction as terrorist within the US imaginary. These calls that name her a most wanted terrorist stake out the borders that obstruct her path and produce the nation-state, hinging on its power over its dissenters, the racialization of its borders, and the unmitigated capture of Black flesh. While a post-9/11 consciousness would have us believe that the terrorist remains the sole provenance of the racialized Muslim or Arab, the case of Shakur clarifies the necessary constitution of the Black abject (woman) to the production of a national security essential to the formation and organization of the West. This formation and organization make compulsory her excessive punishment at the hand of the state that simultaneously requires her presence in the United States for incarceration and her existence outside of its borders as rebar.

Vagrancy is made plain once again. Shakur is displaced, forced to come to terms with "the fact that you may never go back to where you come from" and reflecting the expansion of carceral geographies where the runaway must adjust to separation from home and loved ones.[101] As it has before, the state's continued hunt to capture Black flesh and pronounce Black criminality places a target on her back. But expanding carceral geographies also determine everyone for whom she becomes a proxy. This is pronounced through the billboards that are raised in New Jersey, hundreds and hundreds of miles from the Cuban coast. The large "WANTED" in white script on a red background, plastered with her image in black and white alongside the words "TERRORIST JOANNE CHESIMARD A/K/A ASSATA SHAKUR" that sit atop the subheading "MURDER OF A LAW ENFORCEMENT OFFICER" and signed by the phone number and website of the FBI listed at the bottom, the billboards are loud and governmental. The "A/K/A" gestures toward her name as if it were a criminal alias, which seems both redundant and excessive given that the label terrorist sits above it in a large and capitalized typeface. These billboards work to announce a political and social agenda, which reflect the public's perception of Shakur's criminality and link it to the intersection of her race, gender, and sexuality. They become literal signposts of Black female depravity that underpin a larger cultural narrative that shames and warns those who may take up causes and practices of Black dissent. For James, the accusation of "cop killer" today functions in the same way that the charge of rape did during the era of the lynch mob, that regardless of verity or substantiation mobilizes antiblack rage and excessive punitive force at the hands of both the formal criminal justice system and the deputized citizenry as a means of retribution.[102]

Rendered a "cop killer," Shakur is also fetishized as the terrorizing transgression of liberal boundaries that place political change within the hands of the state and the bounds of the law, which is offered as justifi-

FIGURE 4.1: Wanted poster, Federal Bureau of Investigation.

cation for the severity of sanctions threatened against anyone who may offer her aid.[103] Shakur, here, is both a "political embarrassment" for the US police state and a "political inspiration for radicals and revolutionaries," which makes her particularly dangerous for white national authority.[104] As a matter of course, the US government presents a narrative of her crimes that erases white culpability while subverting Black transgressions of white dominion that are then replaced by the re-inscription of myths of Black female immorality. As Douglass has argued, "at the symbolic and libidinal level, there remains value in reanimating the image of the dangerous, threatening, and infectious Black Revolutionary Woman."[105] Shakur herself discusses this fabricated public image while she is still incarcerated in the United States, sarcastically amused by the surprise of many inmates upon their first meeting that she is not "bigger, blacker, and uglier" or not "six feet tall, two hundred pounds, and very dark and wild looking;" the conflation of a dark complexion and criminality or danger not lost on her.[106] This conjuring of JoAnne Chesimard continues to circulate not only as a common reminder of her crimes against the state but also as a reflection of surveillance that extends the carceral landscape that conditions her and the Black position writ large. Through these billboards and the abject that they synthesize, Shakur as Chesimard becomes the exemplary figure through which the entirety of Black life can be policed and a whole Cuban nation can be breached.

In naming the emergent critique of her practice as the act of a terrorist, the billboards also evacuate her of political meaning through and by the conceptual acuity of the West's liberal lexicon. Rendering the fraught conditions of Black life invisible, to name Shakur a terrorist is to constitutively foreclose the terror wrought by the West on Black life. As noted earlier, these bilboards advance a constitutive surveillance, simultaneously fixing an entire population into position while also compelling vagrancy, a forced movement or hiding from the watchful eye that conditions blackness. They also illustrate how the popular consumptions of political action, in particular the narration of dis-incarceral possibilities and other modalities of nonparticipation, are shaped by and shape the assumption of the proper domicile of politics. The billboards are the state's narration of Black movement as dangerous and criminal, filling in the space that Shakur leaves vacant in her textual omission. In this, while drawing out the carceral landscape, the billboards simultaneously signpost the borders of the Western liberal political tradition.

In a 2014 statement, FBI special agent Barbara Woodruff did not shy away from the fact that Shakur's addition to the list of most wanted terrorists was not because she posed a bigger threat than when she held the designation of domestic terrorist but concerned a desire to bring national attention to the case that had supposedly faded from memory after forty years. That the desire to "bring the public's attention to the case" was meant to mitigate accusations that this was an extreme response illustrates both the quotidian nature of extremity for antiblackness and vestibular subjection's necessity of marking out the territory. It names an excision of Black populations from national belonging and a disavowal of their Black political presence. The billboards also name the threat of Shakur's Black anarchist practice as one that undermines the carceral geography of order and the socio-spatial location—that is, the home—of politics. Repression is thus meant not to punish the crime or even target particular acts but to terrorize the movement, to police Black abolitionist politics.[107] The billboards are just one part of a continuum of repression of Black liberation, coming after COINTELPRO and FBI director J. Edgar Hoover named the Black Panther Party the greatest threat to US security and only a few years before the Black Lives Matter movement would be labeled a "Black Identity Extremist" group by a leaked report from the FBI's counter-terrorism division.[108] Contemporary Black politics that fail to abide by the nonviolence mantra once heralded by the civil rights movement or which directly question and oppose the very foundations of antiblackness to state authority have long been criminalized through the rhetoric of terrorism.

In placing these billboards within US national borders and within the inner city of New Jersey especially, the signage functions as a mapping, physical signals that mark Black vagrancy as extant and warranting policing. Along with the fliers and calls to arms by federal forces, they ink the continued and extended absenting of place, of home, for Black people beyond the physical confines of the prison. If home denotes belonging, then a crux of blackness as a social relationality is the absence of home, a position of displacement and dispossession born of practices of containment and alienation. The absence of a formal haven formed by national belonging and the paradigmatic unavailability of protection that is meant to be afforded in the domicile site is constitutive to the Black position outside the socius, demarcating a paradoxical existence as both resident insider and sociopolitical outsider. Shakur and the billboards demonstrate this tension of home for Black populations, how home is both an object of desire and a mechanism of violence, how home is both a place for dwelling and a dwelling where one is always out of place. The prison, exile, and the Western nation-state are sites of home that are not only meant to house Black populations, that is, to sequester, but are spatial practices that constitute as much as they maintain Black life as alienated, gratuitously policed, and transient. While the prison signals the most resonant slave ship since they last sailed, the carceral topography that traces Black existence outside is the wake.

A reflection on the perpetuity of Shakur's long escapement, her dis-incarceration, as a Black anarchist practice does not mean to traffic in romantic notions of resistance, because often conceptualizations of resistance also fall within the confines of their liberal genealogies that march toward completion and attempt closure for stories that are exceedingly and excessively beyond closure. To observe the political impact of this practice through the revelatory frame of Black anarchism does not work to clear space on the yardstick of "heroic rebellion" alongside ship uprisings.[109] Like the enslaved who jump, dis-incarceration rejects the premise of this lexicon. It flags challenge through refusal and laced to abolition on the ground, unmoved by Foucault's raceless analysis and Alexander's reformist liberalism, hews new understanding. Abreast of the inextricability of carcerality and antiblackness, of vagrancy and unfreedom, dis-incarceration abolition bucks dependence on what comes next, unbeholden to questions to prove its worth as if there has been any burden on the institution being abolished to do the same. This Black anarchist abolition may be better understood as one unwedded to the prefiguration that is often dictated by the imagination of a world fitting the needs of the state, of liberalism, of the political *comme il faut*. Black anarchist abolition is the work to "destroy the gears," as William C. Anderson reminds us, but "it is not the revolution itself."[110] As the iterative tactic rejecting the premise of the state and its spatial emplacement, Shakur's praxis teaches us that abolition can be the jump from the slave ship, the refusal of representation, and the pursuit of opacity.

Conclusion

Parsing Paradox, Escaping the Inescapable

When I was a graduate student, newly forming a dissertation project and having to discuss my own work with senior scholars, an older professor asked me how I had the audacity to fashion a political lens around the death of the enslaved. She wanted to ensure that I understood that there was a difference between the enslaved who jump from the slave ship and those who lived to fight. While I stuttered something that I can no longer remember, I think back often to that evening. Now that years separate us, I realize that the answer to her question is less concerned with defending an alternative political orientation and more focused on shedding light on how the politics we do affirm retain a commitment to repair and restore in ways that deny uncomfortable questions about what abolition and radicality might mean. As I finish the project that I was just beginning then, I grasp now that what made me uncomfortable about her probing was her insinuation that I was fabricating, pulling at what she understood to be absence to create sum, to create thing. In reality, it was she who was asking me to fabricate, to provide a fictive closure where one did not and could not exist, to navigate a narrative map that would guide her from action to result and to assure her that there was a qualitative difference between revolt and abstention, between politics and whatever it was that I seemed to be so interested in.

Like Ishmael who uses Pip to reflect back to himself a sense of what he already believed to be true, my professor looked to the enslaved to confirm her own understanding of resistance, rebellion, and the proper locus of politics. But the enslaved could not be assimilated into the normative of the political as she understood it.[1] To jump the slave ship often meant immediately seizing an unexpected opportunity, navigating through the regulative space of the boat, and laying down a new cartography by slipping through the latticework of the "house" and finding a way past the netting. Once inside the slave ship, the jump was a seemingly insurmountable task. It was an escape that guaranteed nothing other than no longer being bound by the ship, pushing off the wooden structure and taking flight into a boundless ocean. The jump aroused a chaos aboard the ship as crew members quickly struggled to reacquire the enslaved and reassert their containment. These jumps elicited descriptions in the logs of captains and ship surgeons that attributed the behavior to madness. Linking the act to insanity was the only way of making sense of such a disarranging leap while maintaining the discursive coherence of the existing world. At the same time, this recourse to madness casts light on the threat of the jump to the existing order of the ship.

Through death, mobility, and destruction, the jump communicates criticisms of the existing antiblack world. In its other forms, the jumps elaborate collectivity, ruination, and maneuver. In chapter 2, the collective emerges in Black mobility as the critique of white nationalism that inheres within the project of the West; cataclysm erupts in chapter 3 as a ruinous questioning of the carcerality that works to condition everyday Black life; and in chapter 4, evasion surfaces in the dis-incarceration that attempts to maneuver the modern system that conjures the criminality of both Black people and Black politics. The salience of Black anarchist orientations is evident in the connectedness of these three modalities and the spaces of vestibular subjection from which they emerge. The constitutive relationships among Black confinement, white nation-building, and the state's political imagination, demonstrate that state spaces are not neutral and not all political practices are visible. Each of these sites exhibit a jump beyond the boundaries for where Black people can and cannot be and the ways they can and cannot live. They are methods of living beyond the "petrified zone," those immobilized spaces regulated by antiblack authority.[2] These three cases are different iterations of the jump from the slave ship—Black mobility within, against, and beyond the order of antiblackness. They, like the enslaved jumping from the slave ship, enact radical lines of flight that disarrange the boundaries of regulation but often, if not always, precipitate a violently depoliticizing response.

Said another way, as much as Western vestibular subjection establishes excessively raced and gendered bodies, Western political traditions equally repress the antagonisms and referents of Black anarchist practices. By arguing for a conceptualization of Black anarchism as a spatial praxis of anti-authoritarianism and an interruption of the reproduction of antiblack hegemonic structures, my aim has been to expand the purview of the Black radical tradition in bringing cohesive theoretical attention to practices conventionally dismissed and rarely thought together. These are practices precariously located in our political imaginaries often because of the very logics that structured my professor's audacious interrogation. The repulsion is rooted in the overreliance on state-centered politics alongside the raced and gendered renderings of the polity and its practices. That is, our conventional political orientations that adhere to state formations and liberal progression are not intended to question worlds. As such, they can make no sense of those practices that question; nor, for that matter, can they make sense of the questions these practices pose. It is thus unsurprising that my professor of history spoke from the integrationist framework that celebrates inclusion, citizenship, and individual rights and denigrates everything else, as Steven Hahn names it, as "somehow lacking in integrity."[3] Yet my professor's question was also rooted in fear. The fear of a politics "too radical to be formulated in advance of its deeds."[4]

The propaganda of the deed, or the deed that exceeds the demand, is foundational to Anarchism. So, too, is the desire to be "more than mere negation," and to live the imagined world.[5] The practices discussed across this book are indeed moments of rupture that have been obscured, illegible as world-questioning politics because our conventional political orientations operate within the horizons of this world. Yet the jump presses on this paradox of Black anarchist philosophies, the definitive ungovernability that refuses the meaning-making of the political itself encapsulated in the arresting question "What are your demands?" and the equally definitive commitment to prefiguration and the harmony of means and ends. While I have made plain that the theory offered here, originating in the jump of the enslaved, does not adhere to prefiguration, this decision is not meant to draw a line in the sand with other theorizations of Black anarchism. To do so would only concretize a typology of Black anarchism and Black anarchist practices that would tautologically fall back on prefiguration. It is, however, to caution us of the traps that may exist in a shared logic of outcomes. While not the same, there are resonances between the measurements of success based on outcomes and the "ethos of unity between means and ends" defined as prefigurative politics.[6]

It is also not the intention of this text to smooth conflicting emphases or to make definitive claims about what Black anarchism is and is not. As Uri Gordon, an activist-scholar at the forefront of Anarchist theory's relationship to prefiguration and a proponent of means-ends unity, cheekily suggests in his own Twitter bio, "If it's not paradoxical you're doing it wrong."[7] Paradox is necessary. Paradox is an insistent part of the Black anarchism introduced by the jumps of the enslaved. The jump asks, in part, of the Black radical tradition itself, how does one escape the inescapable? In a recent interview, held in close temporal proximity to the Black Lives Matter protests of June 2020 and within the confines of the global COVID-19 pandemic, Black anarchist Lorenzo Kom'boa Ervin advises that we must "make ourselves and our communities ungovernable." He notes that *ungovernable* is a term with which we are familiar and can mean many things to many people, but he loosely defines it through a series of applications: "It means the kind of tactics you engage in in the street, it means how the community is organized that they don't have to depend on these politicians, it means a mass boycott of capitalist corporations, a new transitional economy, and many others things as part of a resistance."[8] Black anarchist theory is expectedly and understandably concerned with means and ends, arguably more so than Anarchist theory writ large. Those seeking Black liberation are all too familiar with Black movements being hijacked for different ends. They are also well versed in the ways exploitative practices eat away at liberatory agendas.

A primary intervention of *Jump*, but more importantly of the jump that steers it, is that ungovernability questions governing as both practice and philosophy. The jump loosens the hold of vision, which so often can impose limits on the inherent possibility of practice. The jump is not limited by outcomes. It is indeed a negation. It is an abolition that "could only ever begin with degeneration, decline, or dissolution."[9] The enslaved who jump the slave ship disclose a mobilization of total refusal, one that neither begins nor ends with radical redistribution but poses questions of sovereignty itself. While outright not a celebration of agency or indicative of a faith in political prognostication, this is also not a dismal surrender to impossibility. It is about how the practice of refusal is entangled with tactics of survival. But it is also about the requirement of facing how the entanglement occurs under the auspices of a white dominion that functions on Black death. It is an abolition that in part functions to ask what does abolitionism mean? What is a politics of refusal or, for that matter, negation? What does it mean to think beyond restoration and instead face "the unimaginable loss of that all too imaginable loss itself (nothing for no one)?"[10]

To trace Pip's antecedents and begin with Black women on slave ships, to follow their jumps, has led us to oceans rather than lands. Like the Igbo who walked into water, or took flight, from the Georgia coast knowing exactly what it held, the enslaved who jump unsettle the seemingly settled dreams of freedom. They invite a new perspective that turns its back on the search for landedness for an answer that can root for us a prescription of the way forward, that place where ocean meets land, the horizon. They turn their back on property, the liberal subject, the nonblack subject. They turn their back on those political orientations and schools of thought that begin with and for these subjects in mind.

To return to the ocean is to engage the analytic Sharpe calls "wake work," where instead of proposing solutions that imagine a closure of the gaping hole created by slavery and ever-expanding carceral geographies based in rights-based claims and state-sponsored transformations, the jump from the slave ship signifies both a floating in and creation of that "interval between the no longer and not yet."[11] Within that created interval is a rejection of the horizon set forth by a Western liberal or even Western Anarchist tradition—that which is not yet an alternative but a negation—embodied in Black anarchist practices of anticipation.

ACKNOWLEDGMENTS

In countless ways, this book is a product of the collective labor of my interlocutors, mentors, colleagues, students, friends, and family. There is no way I could thank them all or in all the ways they should be in this space here, but I extend my deepest gratitude nonetheless and hope for your forgiveness if your name has been left out.

As first books often are, this one was born of an idea developed as a graduate student and as such would not have come to fruition without the many who inspired me, created opportunities for me, and otherwise assisted me throughout my doctoral studies at Northwestern University. My thanks to Sherwin Bryant, Suzette Denose, Mary G. Dietz, Bonnie Honig, Jasmine Johnson, Sylvester A. Johnson, Marjorie McDonald, and Alexander Weheliye. I am eternally grateful to the late Richard Iton for guiding me in independent study and giving me the room to explore anarchist questions alongside the Black Fantastic. To the students of my very first course, The Spatial Practices of Race, I share my gratitude for your intellectual verve and dedication and for your aid during one of the toughest quarters of my life. You know who you are. For those friends who thought with me and coupled every necessary challenge with steadfast encouragement, my deepest thanks go to Savina Balasubramanian, Tiffany Barber, Cecilio Cooper, Patrice D. Douglass, Christine Goding, Chad Infante, Kevin Levay, Tyrone Palmer, Brittnay Proctor, and Jared Rodriguez.

As a student, I was blessed with the guidance of a brilliant adviser who has now become a friend. For always being simply a text message away and bringing invaluable wisdom and critical analytical care to a project he always believed in, I am forever grateful for the mentorship and intellectual rigor of Barnor Hesse. It has been—and continues to beautifully be—emotional.

Thank you to the staff at NYU Press, especially Eric Zinner, Furqan Sayeed, and Ainee Jeong, for bringing *Jump* into the world. In addition, I want to acknowledge that the manuscript would not have found its publishing home without the editorial care and encouragement of Natasha Gordon-Chipembere.

Archival research and conference presentations of chapters were both generously funded by the Marcus Garvey Memorial Foundation, the Graduate School at Northwestern, and the Buffett Institute. For their time and effort answering my countless questions and assisting in my research, my appreciation goes to the library staffs at University of California Berkeley's Bancroft Library, Emory University's Stuart A. Rose Manuscript, Archives, and Rare Book Library, the Schomburg Center for Research in Black Culture, the New York Public Library's Manuscripts and Archives Division, the Los Angeles Public Library, and the Northwestern University Library. A portion of chapter 4 was originally published as "Assata's Escape as Disincarceral Practice" in *Cultural Dynamics* (2021). I thank the editors and those in the Transient Performance working group for giving this essay its first home. Parts of this project have also been presented to audiences at Cornell University, Brandeis University, Bucknell University, California State University Fullerton, and University of Massachusetts Amherst. I am thankful for the thoughtful questions and comments I have received at each of these campuses. I have also benefited from the scholarly spaces of the School of Criticism and Theory in 2014, as well as from my time at the Africana Research Center at Penn State University as a postdoctoral fellow in 2018.

Special gratitude to Christina Sharpe, Shatema Threadcraft, Jonathan Eburne, Alicia Decker, and Cynthia Young for their critical and incisive feedback on the manuscript and to Amira Rose Davis, J. Marlena Edwards, and Dara Walker for their significant insights. The support of my colleagues in the departments of African American Studies and Women's, Gender, and Sexuality Studies at Penn State has been invaluable. A special word of thanks must be extended to Hil Malatino and C. Libby, who took me under their collective wing from the second I stepped foot on Penn State's campus and opened their home to me in ways I will never be able to adequately repay.

While maybe not directly tied to the words that make up this book, I have learned some of the deepest lessons from my family. They have taught me about faith, dedication, and love and will eternally have my most heartfelt appreciation. My grandparents, aunts, uncles, cousins, nieces, and nephews of the Tenorio and Teves clans both living and gone have stood by me, prayed for me, and otherwise been the greatest cheer squad anyone could ever ask for since I began my educational expedition at age five. Special thanks must be given to my grandmothers, Frances Lucille Wester Teves and Maria Clara Cipres Tenorio, who have now both passed on but without whom I would not have had the spiritual and material strength to finish this long-standing project. They reminded me every day that this project could not have been possible save for the grace of God.

My parents, Susan and Eugene Tenorio, have made innumerable sacrifices to get me here—not least of which was letting me pursue a PhD program when they had definitely signed up for law school—and for that I will be forever indebted. There will never be enough words to acknowledge the interminable love and support I have received from my siblings, Nichole and Eric, which was always graciously suffused with humor and the ardent desire for me to never get too big-headed.

Finally, I extend my appreciation to the newest but nonetheless most encouraging member of this intellectual odyssey that is thought-to-book. To my partner, Elizabeth Aviles, I will never forget how you sat endlessly with me on those nights I cried in frustration when those thoughts refused to become sentences. As I shuffled paragraphs and the doubts crept in, you let me think out loud and always asked the questions that got me where I needed to go. Thank you for making certain I was fed, ensuring that I was caffeinated but not too caffeinated, and for lovingly ignoring the piles of books strewn about every possible surface in our house. Thank you for taking care of both my heart and my mind.

NOTES

INTRODUCTION

Epigraphs: Coogler, *Black Panther*; Melville, *Moby-Dick*, 452; Kanor, *Humus*, 29.

1. Sharpe, *In the Wake*, 19.
2. Frank, "Pathologies of Freedom," 436.
3. Frank, "Pathologies of Freedom," 454; Pease, "From the Camp," 19.
4. Melville, *Moby-Dick*, 453.
5. Melville, *Moby-Dick*, 453.
6. Melville, *Moby-Dick*, 523, 567.
7. Hartman, *Scenes of Subjection*, 3.
8. Such as that of Jason Frank, Donald Pease, and C. L. R. James.
9. Hartman, *Scenes of Subjection*, 3.
10. Wilderson, "Black Liberation Army," 200.
11. Melville, *Moby-Dick*, 453.
12. Pease, "From the Camp," 15.
13. Frank, "Pathologies of Freedom," 452 ; Hartman, *Scenes of Subjection*, 20.
14. Melville, *Moby-Dick*, 454.
15. Hartman, *Scenes of Subjection*, 18–19.
16. Melville, *Moby-Dick*, 6.
17. Frank, "Pathologies of Freedom," 437.
18. James, *Mariners, Renegades, Castaways*, 19–20.
19. James, *Mariners, Renegades, Castaways*, 54.
20. James, *Mariners, Renegades, Castaways*, 56–57.
21. James, *Mariners, Renegades, Castaways*, 58.
22. James, *Mariners, Renegades, Castaways*, 53–54.
23. Newman, "Anarchism."
24. Campt, "Visual Frequency," 80.
25. Hesse and Thompson, "Antiblackness," 457; Jung and Costa Vargas, *Antiblackness*, 8–9.
26. Hesse and Thompson, "Antiblackness," 457–58.
27. Kanor, *Humus*, 29.
28. Wilderson, "Black Liberation Army," 198.
29. See Jung and Costa Vargas, *Antiblackness*; Wilderson, *Red, White & Black*; Jackson, *Becoming Human*.
30. Black Rose Anarchist Federation, "Introduction," 2.
31. Ciccariello-Maher, "Anarchist Imperialism."

32 Evren, "Ain't No Black," 301.
33 Goldman, *Anarchism and Other Essays*, 2.
34 Robinson, *Terms of Order*, 212.
35 This is indeed what spurs George Ciccariello-Maher's scathing critique of Anarchism's dismissal of Black thinkers like Fanon and what has historically caused friction between Black anarchist thinkers like Ashanti Alston, Kuwasi Balagoon, and Lorenzo Kom'boa Ervin and white Anarchist camps in the latter's inattention to and contempt for Black nationalist politics.
36 Iton, *Black Fantastic*, 17, 289.
37 Iton, *Black Fantastic*, 17.
38 Proudhon, *Revolution*, 294.
39 Iton, *Black Fantastic*, 290.
40 Ervin, *Anarchism and the Black Revolution*; Alston, *Black Anarchism*.
41 Sharpe, *In the Wake*, 14.
42 Proctor, "Something Wonderful," 42.
43 Bey, *Anarcho-Blackness*, 26.
44 Anderson, *Nation on No Map*, 160; Bey, *Anarcho-Blackness*, 6–7; Hartman, *Wayward Lives*.
45 Wallace, "Gordon Matta-Clark's *Anarchitecture*."
46 Browne, *Dark Matters*; Childs *Slaves of the State*.
47 Spillers, "Mama's Baby," 47.
48 Sharpe, *In the Wake*, 21.
49 Jung and Costa Vargas, *Antiblackness*, 9.
50 Story, *Prison Land*, 168.
51 Tenorio, "White Carceral Geographies," 519.
52 Alston, *Black Anarchism*, 8.
53 Thrift, *Nonrepresentational Theory*, 22.
54 The *Leusden* was a slave ship of the Dutch West India Company that after becoming caught in a terrible storm in 1738, locked the enslaved Africans in the hold and let the ship run aground for fear that the enslaved would attempt to use the lifeboats. Over 650 enslaved Africans died by drowning or suffocation while the crew escaped. The 1781 *Zong* massacre is the second largest known killing of the enslaved during the Atlantic slave trade, wherein 133 enslaved Africans were thrown from the British-owned ship in the hopes of claiming insurance money.
55 Tiqqun, *Civil War*, 216.

1. REFUSAL

Epigraph: James, *Some Problems of Philosophy*, 230.
1 Abraham Dumaresq, log of the ship *Lawrance*, 1730–31. ZL-234. MssCol 1699, Manuscripts and Archives Division, New York Public Library.
2 Morgan, *Reckoning with Slavery*, 159.
3 Morgan, *Reckoning with Slavery*, 212.

4   See Ryan, "Revolutionary Suicide"; Bly, "Crossing the Lake"; Johnson, "Contesting the Myth."
5   Bell, "Slave Suicide," 526.
6   Bly, "Crossing the Lake"; Aptheker, *Slave Revolts*.
7   Taylor, *If We Must Die*, 12.
8   Hartman, "Two Acts," 3.
9   Samudzi and Anderson, *Black as Resistance*, 13.
10 Samudzi and Anderson, *Black as Resistance*, 19.
11 Browne, *Dark Matters*; Childs, *Slaves of the State*.
12 Malatesta, "Revolution and Reaction," 4; Browne, *Dark Matters*, 48.
13 Wilderson, "Black Liberation Army," 176.
14 Fanon, *Wretched of the Earth*, 2.
15 Equiano, *Interesting Narrative*.
16 Falconbridge, *Slave Trade*.
17 Rediker, *Slave Ship*.
18 Kanor, *Humus*.
19 Dow, *Slave Ships and Slaving*, xxix, 236.
20 Rediker, *Slave Ship*.
21 Lefebvre, *Production of Space*, 27–28.
22 Certeau, *Everyday Life*, 98.
23 McKittrick and Woods, *Black Geographies*, 4.
24 Lefebvre, *Production of Space*, 27.
25 Lefebvre, *Production of Space*, 26, 27.
26 Certeau, *Everyday Life*, 117.
27 Mendieta, "Land and Sea," 265.
28 Paul Gilroy, *Black Atlantic*, 4.
29 Smallwood, *Saltwater Slavery*, 73.
30 Smallwood, *Saltwater Slavery*, 73.
31 Dow, *Slave Ships and Slaving*, 134.
32 Rediker, *Slave Ship*, 169.
33 Camp, *Closer to Freedom*, 12.
34 Rediker, *Slave Ship*, 70.
35 Rediker, *Slave Ship*, 70; Dow, *Slave Ships and Slaving*, 133.
36 Spillers, "Mama's Baby," 218.
37 Lambert, "An Operative Architecture."
38 Sharpe, *In the Wake*, 74.
39 Hesse, "Racialized Modernity"; Hartman, *Scenes of Subjection*, 57–59.
40 Spillers, "Mama's Baby," 215.
41 Marchart, *Post-Foundational*, 146.
42 The concept of engendering race is borrowed from Saidiya Hartman's conceptualization of the relationship between gender and the slave where she argues, "The en-gendering of race, as it is refracted through Cobb's scale of subjective value, entails

the denial of sexual violation as a form of injury while asserting the prevalence of sexual violence due to the rapacity of the Negro" (*Scenes of Subjection*, 96).
43   Spillers, "Mama's Baby," 214.
44   Browne, *Dark Matters*, 47.
45   Lambert, "Overpopulated Space."
46   Morgan, *Reckoning with Slavery*, 213.
47   Rediker, *Slave Ship*, 243.
48   Sharpe, *Monstrous Intimacies*, 2.
49   Morgan, *Reckoning with Slavery*, 163.
50   Foster, *Rethinking Rufus*; Foster, "Sexual Abuse of Black Men."
51   Cobb, *Inquiry*, 90.
52   Hartman, *Scenes of Subjection*, 96.
53   Hartman, *Scenes of Subjection*, 99–101.
54   Douglass, "Assata Is Here," 91.
55   Here I am referring to the greater mobility experienced by enslaved men on plantations due to the nature of their labors that often authorized them to travel beyond their master's property, whereas women were more often restricted to the plantation during laboring hours and expected to keep to the slave quarters because of domestic labor outside of those hours. See Camp, *Closer to Freedom*, 28.
56   Hartman, *Scenes of Subjection*, 63.
57   Taylor, *If We Must Die*, 106.
58   Taylor, *If We Must Die*, 135, 122, emphasis added.
59   Taylor, *If We Must Die*, 122.
60   Taylor's work is not shy about its celebration of an outcome model for the study (and proper appreciation) of shipboard revolts and he builds much of his argument from this premise.
61   Oldham "Insurance Litigation," 300.
62   Walvin, *Zong*, 27; Smallwood, *Saltwater Slavery*, 72.
63   Walvin, *Zong*, 1.
64   The legal hearings later accepted a figure of 122 murdered, along with the ten who had jumped to their death (Walvin, *Zong*, 98).
65   Walvin, *Zong*, 101.
66   Walvin, *Zong*, 138, 147.
67   Transcript commissioned by Granville Sharpe. National Maritime Museum, Greenwich: Documents Relating to the Ship Zong, 1783, REC/19. Hereafter referred to as Sharpe Transcript 1783.
68   Walvin, *Zong*, 144.
69   Sharpe Transcript 1783, 52; Walvin, *Zong*, 146.
70   Rupprecht, "Excessive Memories, 12.
71   Lobban "Slavery, Insurance and the Law," 325.
72   Lobban "Slavery, Insurance and the Law," 327.
73   Lobban "Slavery, Insurance and the Law," 327.

74 Bell, "Slave Suicide," 534.
75 Higgonet, "Female Suicide," 232.
76 Iton, *Black Fantastic*, 18.
77 See Gomez, *Our Country Marks*; Rediker, *The Slave Ship*; Genovese, *Roll, Jordan, Roll*; Blassingame, *The Slave Community*.
78 Morgan, *Reckoning with Slavery*, 209.
79 See work by Lucy Parsons, Kuwasi Balagoon, Lorenzo Komboa'Ervin, and Ashanti Alson. For contemporary examples, see work by Zoé Sazmudi, William C. Anderson, and Marquis Bey.
80 Bey, *Anarcho-Blackness*, 7. Sazmudi and Anderson argue that the anarchism of blackness "describes a condition that might lend itself to a form of organization reflecting that tendency. Blackness itself is anarchistic as a result of Black exclusion from the social contract (and thus non-assimilation into the state)" (*Black as Resistance*, 109).
81 Morgan, *Reckoning with Slavery*, 218.
82 Higgonet, "Female Suicide," 229.
83 Higgonet, "Female Suicide," 229.
84 Tiqqun, *Not a Program*, 55.
85 Tiqqun, *Civil War*, 171; Scott, *Art of Not Being Governed*.
86 Tiqqun, *Civil War*, 207; Lefebvre, *Production of Space*, 59.
87 Parsons, "Principles of Anarchism," 3.
88 Iton, *Black Fantastic*, 16; Alston, *Black Anarchism*, 8.
89 Iton, *Black Fantastic*, 16.
90 Hartman, *Scenes of Subjection*, 55.
91 Taylor, *If We Must Die*, 138.
92 Kotef, *Ordering of Freedom*, 3.
93 Tocqueville, *Democracy in America*, 318.
94 Wilderson, "Black Liberation Army," 183.
95 See Smallwood, *Saltwater Slavery*; and Mustakeem, *Slavery at Sea*.
96 Rediker, *The Slave Ship*, 39; Bosman, *Coast of Guinea*, 282.
97 Hartman, *Scenes of Subjection*, 9; Tocqueville, *Democracy in America*, 318.
98 Sharpe, *Monstrous Intimacies*, 50.
99 Sharpe, *Monstrous Intimacies*, 59.
100 Bataille, *Absence of Myth*, 56.
101 Parsons, "Principles of Anarchism," 3.
102 Morgan, *Reckoning with Slavery*, 210; Ahmed, *Queer Phenomenology*, 7, 14–15.
103 Hartman, *Scenes of Subjection*, 109.
104 Hartman, *Scenes of Subjection*, 110.
105 Iton, *Black Fantastic*, 17.

2. COLLECTIVITY

Epigraph: Garvey, *Selected Writings and Speeches of Marcus Garvey*, 10.
1 Jagmohan, "Between Race and Nation."

2. Garvey, "Greatest Enemy," 3.
3. Garvey, "Greatest Enemy," 3.
4. See Cronon, *Black Moses*; Martin, *Race First*; Tillery, *Between Homeland and Motherland*. Also see Hancock, "The Black Star Line," for an alternative perspective on its economic potential. Less known, but similarly encumbered in the historical record albeit partly due to Garvey's own disavowal, is the Chief Sam Back-to-Africa movement. Unlike Garvey's ships however, Chief Sam's *Liberia* did make landfall on the African coast after travelling from Texas in 1914, with most of its passengers hailing from Oklahoma. The voyages put into motion by Chief Alfred Sam, a West African merchant who ended up forging a movement of mostly former enslaved people seeking a new life on the Gold Coast, are even less understood than those of the Black Star Line because they are relatively unheard of. While this is set to change in light of recent work by Kendra Field and Ebony Coletu, what we do know is that these emigration voyages have been similarly depoliticized as failures and fraud. Field and Coletu, "Chief Sam," 109.
5. Moses, *The Golden Age*.
6. Stephens, *Black Empire*, 111; Charles Carnegie argues that on a large scale, the Black Star Line was a show of black modern power that worked within what he calls Garvey's hybrid nationalism that, unlike traditional nationalism, was "decidedly ambivalent on the question of territorial integrity" and instead privileged "transterritorial claims." Garvey, according to Carnegie, coupled race and nation and decoupled nation and territory, endorsing a kind of "transnation" (Carnegie, *Black Transnation*, 52–53).
7. Jagmohan, "Between Race and Nation," 281–3.
8. Samudzi and Anderson, *Black as Resistance*, 25–31.
9. Alston, "Beyond Nationalism."
10. This is not to say that Garvey's political agenda does not matter or does not impact these voyages, but it is to argue that to remain tied to intentionalities privileges the prefigurative in a manner that prevents deeper theoretical engagement with practices as that which can and will always exceed the best laid plans.
11. Howison, "Destiny," 46–47.
12. Bandele, "Understanding African Diaspora," 748–49.
13. Howison, "Destiny," 30.
14. Bandele, "Understanding African Diaspora," 750.
15. Bandele, "Understanding African Diaspora," 755–56.
16. Howison, "Destiny," 30, 33.
17. Stein, "The World of Garvey" 93; Mulzac 1963.
18. Mulzac, "Star to Steer By," 84–85.
19. Garvey, "What We Believe."
20. Garvey, "What We Believe."
21. Clarke, "The Harlem Years," 17.
22. Carnegie, *Black Transnation*, 53.

23 Carnegie, *Black Transnation*, 60–61.
24 Mulzac, "Star to Steer By," 79.
25 Carnegie, *Black Transnation*, 63.
26 Ironically, often understood within a messianic frame, the Black Star Line was meant to be the rod of the Moses-figure Garvey, anticipating a deliverance of continental Africans from the chains of European colonialism (see Howison, "Destiny," 46), even though Garvey ultimately wished for it be under the control of diasporic Africans.
27 Howison, "Destiny," 41.
28 Stephens, *Black Empire*, 110.
29 Sale, *Slumbering Volcano*, 6; Linebaugh and Rediker, *Many-Headed Hydra*, 167.
30 Carnegie, *Black Transnation*, 63.
31 Carnegie, *Black Transnation*, 67.
32 Carnegie, *Black Transnation*, 68.
33 Hill, *Garvey Papers*, 91.
34 After the Civil War, Black Codes were laws that were employed in the Southern states meant to limit the freedom of Black people after slavery was formally abolished. The first codes were instituted in 1865 in Mississippi and South Carolina and included the requirement of written evidence of employment as well as limitations on activity and movement. If Black Codes were transgressed, Black people could be punished with arrests, beatings, and forced or unpaid labor.
35 Marx, "Race-Making," 182.
36 Marx, "Race-Making," 190.
37 Marx, "Race-Making," 191.
38 Singh, *Black Is a Country*, 23.
39 Du Bois, "Souls of White Folk."
40 Lake and Reynolds, *Global Colour Line*, 3.
41 Lake and Reynolds, *Global Colour Line*, 4–5.
42 Lake and Reynolds, *Global Colour Line*, 7; Stephens, *Black Empire*, 82.
43 Brown, *Dropping Anchor*, 301; Bolster, *Black Jacks*, 182; Stephens, *Black Empire*, 104.
44 Bolster, *Black Jacks*, 75; Bryce, "Negro Problem," 652.
45 Bryce, "Negro Problem," 651
46 Bryce, "Negro Problem," 653–54.
47 Lake and Reynolds, *Global Colour Line*, 57.
48 Lake and Reynolds, *Global Colour Line*, 6.
49 Bryce, "Negro Problem," 652.
50 Lake and Reynolds, *Global Colour Line*, 63.
51 Lake and Reynolds, *Global Colour Line*, 72; Bryce, "Negro Problem," 655.
52 The Bureau of Investigation, later named the United States Bureau of Investigation, was the predecessor of today's Federal Bureau of Investigation. Hill, *Garvey Papers*, 72.
53 Sharpe, *In the Wake*, 86.
54 Bryce, "Negro Problem," 649.

55 McKittrick, *Demonic Grounds*, x.
56 McKittrick, *Demonic Grounds*, xiii.
57 Edwards, *Practice of Diaspora*, 11.
58 Iton, *Black Fantastic*, 202.
59 Graeber, "New Anarchists," 65.
60 Newman, "Voluntary Servitude," 261.
61 Edwards, "Uses of Diaspora," 56–57.
62 Iton, *Black Fantastic*, 28.
63 Glissant, *Caribbean Discourse*, 2.
64 Iton, *Black Fantastic*, 202.
65 Iton argues that coloniality is "the means by which "Europe' imagines, makes, and manages itself and its others; or, more broadly, as the shifting processes through and by which identities are ascribed, hierarchically and spatially arranged, and consequently options, choices, and life-chances, are determined and dictated" (Iton, *Black Fantastic*, 199). This aligns well with Hesse's own remarks about the logic of race, believing "the formative signifier of *Europeanness*, [is] a defining logic of race in the process of *colonially* constituting itself and its designations of *non-Europeanness*, materially, discursively and extra-corporeally" (Hesse, "Racialized Modernity" 646).
66 Hesse, "Racialized Modernity," 652.
67 Iton, *Black Fantastic*, 201.
68 Iton, *Black Fantastic*, 256–7.
69 Iton, *Black Fantastic*, 196.
70 Carnegie, *Black Transnation*, 6.
71 Linebaugh and Rediker, *Many-Headed Hydra*, 144.
72 Linebaugh and Rediker, *Many-Headed Hydra*, 150.
73 Linebaugh and Rediker, *Many-Headed Hydra*, 156.
74 Iton, *Black Fantastic*, 200; Alston, "Black Anarchism."
75 Heynen and Rhodes, "Organizing for Survival," 396; Stephens, *Black Empire*, 112.
76 Ervin, *Black Revolution*, 40.
77 Ervin, *Black Revolution*, 40–41.
78 Alston, "Beyond Nationalism."
79 Ciccariello-Maher, "Anarchist Imperialism," 24.
80 Ervin, *Black Revolution*, 40.
81 Sorel, *Reflections*, 32–33.
82 Ciccariello-Maher, "Anarchist Imperialism," 29.
83 Ciccariello-Maher, "Anarchist Imperialism," 28.
84 Ciccariello-Maher, "Anarchist Imperialism," 29.
85 Ciccariello-Maher, "Anarchist Imperialism," 40.
86 Carnegie, *Black Transnation*, 69.
87 Anderson, *Nation on No Map*, 152.

3. RUINATION

Epigraphs: Jackson, *Blood in My Eye*, 7; Proudhon, *General Idea of the Revolution in the Nineteenth Century*, 70.

1. Kelley, "Inside the unrest."
2. The narrative of "anarchy" that continues to circulate and be recycled in contemporary popular discourse (from the 1992 LA Rebellion to the twenty-first century Black Lives Matter protests) on unrest is largely what Kelley is referring to.
3. McCone, *Violence in the City*, 1.
4. Vargas, *Never Meant to Survive*, 49.
5. Horne, *Fire this Time*, 26.
6. Horne, *Fire this Time*, 27.
7. Clark, *Dark Ghetto*.
8. Vargas, *Never Meant to Survive*, 45–48.
9. Kerner, *Civil Disorders*.
10. Abu-Lughod, *Race, Space, and Riots*.
11. Horne, *Fire this Time*, 3.
12. Horne, *Fire this Time*, 3.
13. Horne, *Fire this Time*, 75.
14. Horne, *Fire this Time*, 73.
15. Williams, *Our Enemies in Blue*, 20.
16. Cited in Vargas, *Never Meant to Survive*, 62.
17. Rai and Hesse, "Racial Victimization," 217.
18. The white anxiety over the authority of whiteness as authority (dominion) is what largely foments the white panic that is discussed in the following section.
19. Rai and Hesse, "Racial Victimization," 270.
20. Racial policing is so defined here as the "routine racial profiling and racial problematization of the black presence, in whatever form, that is aligned with obliging or coercing black social and political assimilation and conformity" (Hesse, "White Sovereignty," 582).
21. Hesse, "White Sovereignty," 583.
22. Hesse, "White Sovereignty," 586.
23. Douglass, "Unnatural Causes," 258.
24. Cooper, "Fallen."
25. Cooper, "Fallen."
26. Hall, *Policing the Crisis*.
27. Letters to Governor Brown.
28. Douglass, "Unnatural Causes," 258.
29. Letters to Governor Brown.
30. McCone, *Violence in the City*, 5.
31. Williams, "The View From Watts."
32. Hall, *Policing the Crisis*, 29.
33. Hall, *Policing the Crisis*, viii.

34 Cohen, *Folk Devils*.
35 Hall, *Policing the Crisis*, 29.
36 Hall, *Policing the Crisis*, 29.
37 Cohen, *Folk Devils*, xlii–xliii.
38 Cohen, *Folk Devils*, xxxvii.
39 According to this study of white reactions to the Watts rebellion, 74 percent thought it was detrimental to the "Negro's cause," while 19 percent thought it was helpful. This was listed alongside additional results that said approximately 70 percent of whites "felt the outbreak would increase the gap between the races," and 13 percent thought it would lessen it. See Morris and Jeffries, "Violence Next Door."
40 Powell, "Anatomy of a Riot."
41 McCone, *Violence in the City*, 4–6.
42 Park, *Race Relations*.
43 McCone, *Violence in the City*, 3.
44 See Shabazz, *Spatializing Blackness*; Duck, *No Way Out*; Lipsitz, *Racism*.
45 Knoblauch, "Economy of Fear," 347.
46 Reynald and Elffers, "Future of Newman"; Low, "Urban Fear"; Clarke, "Ideal of Community"; Knoblauch, "Economy of Fear."
47 The ideology of a "law and order" society developed most prominently during the 1960s with conservatives like Richard Nixon and George Wallace (and later Ronald Reagan) drawing a direct correlation between the policing of crime and the increasing of order, developing directly out of reports of increased urban street crime and the prevalence of racial unrest figured as "rioting." The point was to emphasize the necessity of law and policing for the maintenance of a properly functioning social order. See Dan T. Carter, *The Politics of Rage*; and Michael Kazin, *The Populist Persuasion*.
48 Jacobs, *American Cities*; Kelling and Wilson, "Broken Windows"; and Jeffery, *Crime Prevention*.
49 Shabazz, *Spatializing Blackness*, 64–66.
50 Clarke, "Ideal of Community," 49.
51 Newman, *Creating Defensible Space*.
52 See Walcott, *On Property*.
53 Newman, *Defensible Space*, 264.
54 Newman, *Creating Defensible Space*, 17.
55 Brill Associates, "Comprehensive Security Planning," ii.
56 Brill Associates, "Comprehensive Security Planning," 67.
57 Brill Associates, "Comprehensive Security Planning," 64.
58 Harris, "Whiteness as Property," 1714; Ray, "Shame and the City," 130.
59 Ture and Hamilton, *Black Power*, 23.
60 Harris, "Whiteness as Property," 1717.
61 Harris, "Whiteness as Property," 1721.

62 Harris, "Whiteness as Property," 1721.
63 Brill Associates, *Comprehensive Security Planning*, ix.
64 Newman, *Creating Defensible Space*, 12.
65 Low, "Urban Fear."
66 Newman, *Creating Defensible Space*, 51.
67 Wilson, "Multicultural City," 61; Anderson and Wilson, *Reconstructions*.
68 Childs, *Slaves of the State*, 11.
69 Clarke *Slaves of the State*, 49.
70 While often used interchangeably or as extensions of one another, such as in the assertion that security is the process by which safety is ensured, the difference between safety and security can be defined as the difference between the absence of harm and the prohibition of threat/danger. In the assertion that security leads to safety is the implication that safety comes as a result of prohibitions, in particular those that increase distance from subjective dangers or community heterogeneity, which in this case means racial others.
71 Davis, "Fortress L. A.," 215.
72 This concept is derived from two musical references, Aswad's "Concrete Slaveship" (1976) and Ice Cube's (O'Shea Jackson Sr.) "The N***a Trap" (2006).
73 Powell, "Anatomy of a Riot."
74 Powell, "Anatomy of a Riot."
75 Hartman, *Scenes of Subjection*, 65.
76 Anderson and Wilson, *Reconstructions*, 19.
77 Anderson and Wilson, *Reconstructions*, 19.
78 J. Yolande Daniels, cited in Hernandez, "Reimagining Blackness and Architecture."
79 Anderson, *Nation on No Map*, 185.
80 See Tenorio, "White Carceral Geographies."
81 Bakunin, *Bakunin on Anarchy*, 195–96.
82 Gilman-Opalsky, *Specters of Revolt*, 26.
83 Anderson, *Nation on No Map*, 160–62.
84 Balagoon, "Can't Fight Alone," 75.
85 Alston, "Black Anarchism," 8.
86 Deleuze and Guattari, "May '68."
87 Sharpe "Black Gathering," 26.
88 Gilman-Opalsky, *Specters of Revolt*, 12.
89 Truong, "Total Rioting."
90 Ray, "Shame and the City," 132.
91 Harris, "Whiteness as Property," 1714.
92 Jackson, *Blood in My Eye*, 6.
93 McCone, *Violence in the City*, 9.
94 Kaspar, "We Demand Nothing," 17.

95 Kaspar, "We Demand Nothing," 17.
96 Gilman-Opalsky, *Specters of Revolt*, 231–33.
97 Gilman-Opalsky, *Specters of Revolt*, 233.

4. MANEUVERS

Epigraphs: Shakur, *Assata*, 45 and 89; Dillon, "Possessed by Death," 121.

1   While I am focusing primarily on Black movement in and from the United States, my concern with the racialized policing of movement, the moral panic concerning Black sexuality and gender, and the criminalization of black political practices is a global one.
2   While this list is not exhaustive, such titles include Sarah Haley's *No Mercy Here: Gender, Punishment, and the Making of Jim Crow Modernity* (2019); Brett Story's *Prison Land: Mapping Carceral Power across Neoliberal America* (2019); Brian Jefferson's *Digitize and Punish: Racial Criminalization in the Digital Age* (2020); Carl Sudder's *Presumed Criminal: Black Youth and the Justice System in Postwar New York* (2021); and Ruha Benjamin's edited volume *Captivating Technology: Race, Carceral Technoscience, and Liberatory Imagination in Everyday Life* (2019).
3   Foucault, *Discipline and Punish*, 199.
4   James, *Resisting State Violence*, 28.
5   Heiner, "Foucault," 321.
6   Heiner, "Foucault," 343–44.
7   Young, "Foucault."
8   James, *Resisting State Violence*, 35.
9   Bentham, *Panopticon*.
10 Foucault, *Discipline and Punish*, 172, 197.
11 Foucault, *Discipline and Punish*, 201.
12 Davis, "Racialized Punishment," 99.
13 Davis, "Racialized Punishment," 99.
14 Browne, *Dark Matters*, 35–42.
15 Sexton and Lee, "Figuring the Prison," 1012.
16 Alexander, *New Jim Crow*, 12.
17 Alexander, *New Jim Crow*, 195, 12.
18 Alexander, *New Jim Crow*, 14.
19 Sexton, "Captivity," 198; Wacquant, "Race Question," 2002; and Davis, *Are Prisons Obsolete?*
20 Davis, *Are Prisons Obsolete?*
21 Peters and Turner, "Crime and Colony," 849.
22 Peters and Turner, "Rethinking Mobility."
23 Peters and Turner, "Crime and Colony," 849.
24 Peters and Turner, "Crime and Colony," 847, 849.
25 Peters and Turner, "Crime and Colony," 851

26 Peters and Turner, "Crime and Colony," 851
27 Rediker, *Slave Ship*, 45.
28 Browne, *Dark Matters*, 31–62.
29 Childs, *Slaves of the State*, 28.
30 Jackson, *Blood in My Eye*; Davis and Rodriguez, "Prison Abolition."
31 Jackson, *Blood in My Eye*, 99.
32 Childs, *Slaves of the State*, 39.
33 Hardt, "Prison Time," 65.
34 Thompson, "Time," 90–93.
35 Douglass, "Assata Is Here," 90.
36 Douglass, "Assata Is Here," 91.
37 Shakur, *Autobiography*, 80.
38 *Oxford English Dictionary Online*, s.v. "vagrant," accessed February 11, 2018, https://www.oed.com/dictionary/vagrant_n?tab=meaning_and_use.
39 Convict leasing was a system of penal labor in the southern United States that was prominent after the Civil War to recruit and control Black labor for private means, such as farms, plantations, or other businesses. Leasing out Black prison labor was used to replace the labor that was lost in these establishments with the abolition of slavery. See Alex Lichtenstein *Twice the Work of Free Labor* (1996).
40 Hartman, "Anarchy of Colored Girls," 474.
41 Wilderson, "Prison Slave," 18.
42 Sexton and Lee, "Figuring the Prison," 1014.
43 Blair, "Got to Make My Livin,'" 90.
44 Gross, *Colored Amazons*, 110.
45 Gross, *Colored Amazons*, 105.
46 Gross, *Colored Amazons*, 115.
47 Gross, *Colored Amazons*, 134.
48 Douglass, "Assata Is Here," 91.
49 Blair, *Colored Amazons*, 96, 105.
50 Douglass, "Assata Is Here," 93.
51 Douglass, "Assata Is Here," 95.
52 Douglass, "Assata Is Here," 93.
53 Davis, "Racialized Punishment," 100.
54 Shakur lists some of the crimes that Black women were often "in" for in the 1970s: "Jostling was pickpocketing; boosting was shoplifting; juggling paper was writing bad checks and dragging or playing drag was conning" (*Autobiography*, 87).
55 Heiner, "Foucault," 319.
56 James, "Prison Notebooks," 41.
57 James, "Prison Notebooks," 41.
58 Davis, "Racialized Punishment," 43.
59 Church and Wall, *COINTELPRO Papers*.

60 James, *Shadowboxing*; Heiner, "Foucault," 330.
61 Jackson named the conditions in which Black communities were presently living colonial and also conceptualized the central and strategic role of the prison in decolonization. Months before he was assassinated in prison, Jackson argued that the function of the prison was to "[serve] the needs of the totalitarian state," one of which was "to isolate, eliminate, liquidate the dynamic sections of the overall movement" especially its "protagonists" like himself and Davis. In response, he called for the interruption of this function by "[turning] the prison into just another front of the struggle" by those on the inside of it (see "Remembering the Real Dragon—An Interview with George Jackson, May 16 and June 29, 1971," *History Is a Weapon*, https://www.historyisaweapon.com/defcon1/jacksoninterview.html). Davis, for her part, in calling for community support of political prisoners, also argued for this political and conceptual connection, claiming that the support would provide an occasion "to link the immediate needs of the Black community with a forceful fight to break the fascist stronghold in the prisons and therefore to abolish the prison system in its present form." To her, because of the intimate ties between "poverty, police courts, and prison" as "imposed patterns" within Black urban life as opposed to white life, there was an "instinctive affinity" that bound "the mass of black people to the political prisoners" (see Davis "Racialized Punishment," 48–50). Because of this bind, Davis and others began to champion calls for prison abolition and not just the freedom of political prisoners.
62 James, *Shadowboxing*, 115.
63 Shakur, *Autobiography*, 242.
64 James, "Prison Notebooks," 44.
65 Davis and Rodriguez, "Prison Abolition."
66 Chammah, "Solitary Confinement."
67 Mincke and Lemonne, "Prison and (Im)mobility."
68 Shakur, *Assata*, 66.
69 Hancock and Jewkes, "Spatial Pains."
70 Hancock and Jewkes, "Spatial Pains," 620.
71 Morris and Worrall, "Prison Architecture," 1086–87.
72 Fedderly "New Prison Design."
73 Fedderly "New Prison Design."
74 In Dylan Rodriguez's 2000 interview of Angela Davis, she states that the most difficult problem for abolitionists is "how to establish a balance between reforms that are clearly necessary to safeguard the lives of prisoners and those strategies designed to promote the eventual abolition of prisons as the dominant mode of punishment." Some have called this "[exploring] the possibility of 'non-reformist reform'" (see Oparah, "Maroon Abolitionists").
75 Oparah, "Maroon Abolitionists," 394.

76 Bloch, *Principle of Hope*.
77 James, "Maroon Philosophy," 124.
78 Trouillot, *Silencing the Past*, 89–90.
79 Hesse, "Escaping Liberty," 308.
80 Hartman, "Two Acts," 3-4.
81 Phelan, *Unmarked*, 146, 148.
82 Trouillot, *Silencing the Past*, 95–96.
83 Childs, "Secrecy," 38.
84 Phelan, *Unmarked*, 148.
85 Hartman, "Two Acts," 8.
86 Phelan, *Unmarked*, 148.
87 Shakur, *Assata*, 263–65.
88 Shakur, *Assata*, 266.
89 Best and Hartman, "Fugitive Justice," 3.
90 Best and Hartman, "Fugitive Justice," 3.
91 Cervenak, *Wandering*, 14.
92 Levinas, *On Escape*, 50.
93 Shakur, *Assata*, 266.
94 Fuente and Andrews, *Afro-Latin*, 8.
95 Dillon, "Possessed by Death," 118.
96 Parenti, "Postmodern Maroon," 420.
97 James, *Shadowboxing*, 113.
98 James, *Shadowboxing*, 100–2.
99 Gilliam, "Conscience," 170; James, *Shadowboxing*, 103.
100 Ong, *Buddha Is Hiding*, 78–83; James, *Shadowboxing*, 84–105.
101 Parenti, "Postmodern Maroon," 421.
102 James, *Shadowboxing*, 113.
103 James, *Shadowboxing*, 113.
104 James, *Shadowboxing*, 114.
105 Douglass, "Assata Is Here," 97.
106 Shakur, *Assata*, 87.
107 Davis, "Racialized Punishment," 42.
108 Federal Bureau of Investigation, 2017.
109 Taylor, *If We Must Die*, 164.
110 Anderson, *Nation on No Map*, 160.

CONCLUSION
1 Hartman, *Scenes of Subjection*, 65.
2 Fanon, *Wretched of the Earth*.
3 Hahn, "On History."
4 Trouillot, *Silencing the Past*, 88.
5 Bey, *Anarcho-Blackness*, 95.

6 Gordon, "Prefigurative Politics," 522.
7 Twitter bio @anarchyalive (Uri Gordon), retrieved June 7, 2022, https://twitter.com/anarchyalive?lang=en.
8 William C. Anderson, "Ungovernable: An Interview with Lorenzo Kom'boa Ervin," Black Rose Anarchist Federation, September 11, 2020, https://blackrosefed.org/ungovernable-interview-lorenzo-komboa-ervin-anderson/.
9 Sexton, "*Vel* of Slavery," 593.
10 Sexton, "*Vel* of Slavery," 593.
11 Sharpe, *In the Wake*; Best and Hartman, "Fugitive Justice," 3.

BIBLIOGRAPHY

Abu-Lughod, Janet. *Race, Space, and Riots in Chicago, New York and Los Angeles*. Oxford: Oxford University Press, 2007.
Ahmed, Sara. *Queer Phenomenology: Orientations, Objects, Others*. Durham, NC: Duke University Press, 2006.
Alexander, Michelle. *The New Jim Crow: Mass Incarceration in the Age of Colorblindness*. New York: New Press, 2010.
Alston, Ashanti. "Black Anarchism." *Perspectives on Anarchist Theory* 8, no. 1 (2004): 6–9.
———. "Beyond Nationalism but Not without It." In *Black Anarchism: A Reader*, by the Black Rose Anarchist Federation, 72–75. Black Rose Anarchist Federation, 2016.
Anderson, Sean, and Mabel O. Wilson. *Reconstructions: Architecture and Blackness in America*. New York: Museum of Modern Art, 2021.
Anderson, William C. *The Nation on No Map: Black Anarchism and Abolition*. Chico, CA: AK Press, 2021.
Aptheker, Herbert. *American Negro Slave Revolts*. New York: Columbia University Press, 1943.
Bakunin, Mikhail. *Bakunin on Anarchy: Selected Works by the Activist-Founder of World Anarchism*. Edited by Sam Dolgoff. New York: Vintage, 1971.
Balagoon, Kuwasi. "Anarchy Can't Fight Alone." In *Black Anarchism: A Reader*, by the Black Rose Anarchist Federation. Black Rose Anarchist Federation, 2016.
———. *A Soldier's Story: Writings by a Revolutionary New Afrikan Anarchist*. Montréal: Kersplebedeb, 2003.
Bandele, Ramla. "Understanding African Diaspora Political Activism: The Rise and Fall of the Black Star Line." *Journal of Black Studies* 40, no. 4 (2010): 745–61.
Bataille, Georges. *The Absence of Myth: Writings on Surrealism*. Edited by Michael Richardson. London: Verso, 2006.
Bell, Richard. "Slave Suicide, Abolition and the Problem of Resistance." *Slavery & Abolition* 33, no. 4 (2012): 525–49.
Bentham, Jeremy. *The Panopticon Writings*. London: Verso, 1995.
Best, Stephen, and Saidiya V. Hartman. "Fugitive Justice." *Representations* 92, no. 1 (2005): 1–15.
Bey, Marquis. *Anarcho-Blackness: Notes toward a Black Anarchism*. Chico, CA: AK Press, 2020.
Black Rose Anarchist Federation. *Black Anarchism: A Reader*. Black Rose Anarchist Federation, 2016. https://blackrosefed.org.

Blair, Cynthia M. *I've Got to Make My Livin': Black Women's Sex Work in Turn-of-the-Century Chicago*. Chicago: University of Chicago Press, 2010.

Blassingame, John. *The Slave Community: Plantation Life in the Antebellum South*. Oxford: Oxford University Press, 1979.

Bloch, Ernst. *The Principle of Hope*. Vol. 1. Translated by Neville Plaice, Stephen Plaice, and Paul Knight. Cambridge, MA: MIT Press, 1995. First published 1954.

Bly, Antonio T. "Crossing the Lake of Fire: Slave Resistance during the Middle Passage, 1720–1842." *Journal of Negro History* 83, no. 3 (1998): 178–86.

Bolster, W. Jeffrey. *Black Jacks: African American Seamen in the Age of Sail*. Cambridge, MA: Harvard University Press, 1997.

Bosman, William. *A New and Accurate Description of the Coast of Guinea*. London, 1705.

Brill Associates. *Comprehensive Security Planning: A Program for William Nickerson Jr. Gardens, Los Angeles, CA, Prepared for Department of Housing and Urban Development*. Office of Policy Development and Research, 1977.

Brown, Edmund G. Papers, 1907–1996. Letters to Governor Brown. BANC MSS 68/90c. Carton 502: 29. Bancroft Library. University of California Berkeley, Berkeley, CA.

Brown, Jacqueline Nassy. *Dropping Anchor, Setting Sail: Geographies of Race in Black Liverpool*. Princeton, NJ: Princeton University Press, 2005.

Browne, Simone. *Dark Matters: On the Surveillance of Blackness*. Durham, NC: Duke University Press, 2015.

Bryce, James. "Thoughts on the Negro Problem." *North American Review*, December 1891.

Bush, George H. W. "Address to the Nation on the Civil Disturbances in Los Angeles, California." May 1, 1992. https://www.presidency.ucsb.edu.

Camp, Stephanie. *Closer to Freedom: Enslaved Women and Everyday Resistance in the Plantation South*. Chapel Hill: University of North Carolina Press, 2004.

Campt, Tina M. "The Visual Frequency of Black Life: Love, Labor, and the Practice of Refusal." *Social Text* 37, no. 3 (September 2019): 25–46.

Canot, Theodore. *Memoirs of a Slave Trader*. London: George Newnes, 1854.

Carnegie, Charles V. "Garvey and the Black Transnation." *Small Axe* (1999): 48–71.

Certeau, Michel de. *The Practice of Everyday Life*. Berkeley: University of California Press, 1984.

Cervenak, Sarah Jane. *Wandering: Philosophical Performances of Racial and Sexual Freedom*. Durham, NC: Duke University Press, 2014.

Chammah, Maurice. "Stepping down from Solitary Confinement." *Atlantic*, January 7, 2016.

Childs, Dennis. *Slaves of the State Black Incarceration from the Chain Gang to the Penitentiary*. Minneapolis: University of Minnesota Press, 2015.

Childs, Greg L. "Secret and Spectral Torture and Secrecy in the Archives of Slave Conspiracies." *Social Text* 33, no. 4 (2015): 35–57.

Church, Ward, and Jim Vander Wall. *The COINTELPRO Papers: Documents from the FBI's Secret Wars against Dissent in the United States*. Boston: South End Press, 1990.

Ciccariello-Maher, George. "An Anarchism That Is Not Anarchism: Notes toward a Critique of Anarchist Imperialism." In *How Not to Be Governed: Readings and Interpretations from a Critical Anarchist Left*, edited by Jimmy Casas Klausen and James Martel, 19–46. Lanham, MD: Lexington, 2011.

Clark, Kenneth B. *Dark Ghetto: Dilemmas of Social Power*. New York: Harper & Row, 1965.

Clarke, John Henrik. "Marcus Garvey: The Harlem Years." *Transition* 46 (1974): 14–19.

Clarke, Paul Walker. "The Ideal of Community and Its Counterfeit Construction." *Journal of Architectural Education* 58, no. 3 (2005): 43–52.

Cobb, Thomas. *Inquiry into the Law of Negro Slavery*. Philadelphia, 1858.

Cohen, Stanley. *Folk Devils and Moral Panics: The Creation of the Mods and Rockers*. New York: Routledge, 2002.

Coogler, Ryan, dir. *Black Panther*. Walt Disney Motion Pictures, Burbank, CA. 2018.

Cooper, Cecilio M. "Fallen: Generation, Postlapsarian Verticality + the Black Chthonic." *Rhizomes* 38 (2022).

Crang, Mike, and Nigel Thrift. *Thinking Space*. London: Routledge, 2000.

Cronon, E. David. *Black Moses: The Story of Marcus Garvey and the Universal Negro Improvement Association*. Madison: University of Wisconsin Press, 1969. First published 1955.

Da Silva, Denise Ferreira. *Toward a Global Idea of Race*. Minneapolis: University of Minnesota Press, 2007.

Davis, Angela Y. *Are Prisons Obsolete?* New York: Seven Stories, 2003.

———. "Racialized Punishment and Prison Abolition." In *The Angela Y. Davis Reader*, edited by Joy James, 96–107. Hoboken, NJ: Blackwell, 1998.

Davis, Angela Y., and Dylan Rodriguez. "'The Challenge of Prison Abolition: A Conversation': A Dialog between Angela Y. Davis and Dylan Rodriguez." *Social Justice* 27, no. 3 (2000).

Davis, Mike. "Fortress L.A." In *The City Reader*, edited by Richard T. LeGates, and Frederick Stout, 212–17. New York: Routledge, 2016.

Deleuze, Gilles, and Felix Guattari. "May '68 Did Not Take Place." In *Two Regimes of Madness*, edited by David Lapoujade, translated by Ames Hodges and Mike Taormina, 233–36. Semiotext(e), 2007.

Dillon, Stephen. "Possessed by Death: The Neoliberal-Carceral State, Black Feminism, and the Afterlife of Slavery." *Radical History Review*, no. 112 (Winter 2012): 113–25.

Douglass, Patrice D. "Assata Is Here: (Dis)Locating Gender in Black Studies." *Souls* 22, no. 1 (January–March 2020): 89–103.

———. "Unnatural Causes: Racial Taxonomies, Pandemic, and Social Contagion." *Prism: Theory and Modern Chinese Literature* 18, no. 1 (March 2021): 256–70.

Dow, George Francis. *Slave Ships and Slaving*. Salem, MA: Marine Research Society Press, 1927.

Du Bois, W. E. B. "The Souls of White Folk." In *Darkwater: Voices from within the Veil*, 29–52. New York: Harcourt, Brace, 1920.

Duck, Waverly. *No Way Out: Precarious Living in the Shadow of Poverty and Drug Dealing*. Chicago: University of Chicago Press, 2015.

Dumaresq, Abraham. Log of the Ship *Lawrance*, 1730–1731. ZL-234. MssCol 1699, Manuscripts and Archives Division, New York Public Library.

Edwards, Brent Hayes. *The Practice of Diaspora: Literature, Translation, and the Rise of Black Internationalism*. Cambridge, MA: Harvard University Press, 2003.

———. "The Uses of Diaspora." *Social Text* 19, no. 1 (2001): 45–73.

Equiano, Olaudah. *The Interesting Narrative of the Life of Olaudah Equiano, or Gustavus Vassa, The African*. New York: Modern Library Classics, 2004. First published 1879 by G. Vassa (London).

Ervin, Lorenzo Kom'boa. *Anarchism and the Black Revolution*. 1993. https://theanarchistlibrary.org.

Evren, Süreyyya. "There Ain't No Black in the Anarchist Flag! Race, Ethnicity and Anarchism." In *The Continuum Companion to Anarchism*, edited by Ruth Kinna, 299–314. London: Continuum, 2012.

Falconbridge, Alexander. *Account of the Slave Trade on the Coast of Africa*. United Kingdom: J. Phillips, 1788.

Fanon, Frantz. *The Wretched of the Earth*. New York: Grove, 1963.

Fedderly, Eva. "Can New Prison Design Help America's Mass Incarceration Problem?" *Architectural Digest*, April 1, 2021.

Federal Bureau of Investigation. "Black Identity Extremists Likely Motivated to Target Law Enforcement Officers." *Intelligence Assessment for Department of Homeland Security*. Washington, DC: Federal Bureau of Investigation, August 3, 2017.

Field, Kendra, and Ebony Coletu. "The Chief Sam Movement, A Century Later." *Transition* 114 (2014): 108–30.

Foster, Thomas A. *Rethinking Rufus: The Sexual Abuse of Enslaved Men*. Athens: University of Georgia Press, 2019.

———. "The Sexual Abuse of Black Men under American Slavery." *Journal of the History of Sexuality* 20, no. 3 (September 2011): 445–64.

Foucault, Michel. *Discipline and Punish: The Birth of the Prison*. Translated by Alan Sheridan. New York: Vintage, 1995.

Frank, Jason. "Pathologies of Freedom in Melville's America." In *Radical Future Pasts: Untimely Political Theory*, edited by Romand Coles, Mark Reinhardt, and George Shulman, 435–58, Lexington: University Press of Kentucky, 2014.

Fuente, Alejandro de la, and George Reid Andrews. *Afro-Latin American Studies: An Introduction*. Cambridge, UK: Cambridge University Press, 2018.

Garvey, Marcus. "Great Ideals Know No Nationality." In *Selected Writings and Speeches of Marcus Garvey*, edited by Bob Blaisdell, 10. Mineola, NY: Dover, 2004.

———. "The Negro's Greatest Enemy." In *Selected Writings and Speeches of Marcus Garvey*, edited by Bob Blaisdell, 1–9. Mineola, NY: Dover, 2004.

———. "What We Believe." In *Selected Writings and Speeches of Marcus Garvey*, edited by Bob Blaisdell, 164. Mineola, NY: Dover, 2004.
Genovese, Eugene. *Roll, Jordan, Roll: The World the Slaves Made*. New York: Vintage, 1976.
Gilliam, Angela M. "Confluence: Conscience, Color, and Cuba." *Latin American Perspectives* 41, no. 4 (2014): 164–83.
Gilman-Opalsky, Richard. *Specters of Revolt: On the Intellect of Insurrection and Philosophy from Below*. London: Repeater, 2016.
Gilroy, Paul. *The Black Atlantic: Modernity and Double Consciousness*. Cambridge, MA: Harvard University Press, 1993.
Glissant, Édouard. *Caribbean Discourse*. Charlottesville: University of Virginia Press, 1999.
Goldman, Emma. *Anarchism and Other Essays*. New York: Dover, 1969. First published 1910 by Mother Earth Publishing Association (New York).
Gomez, Michael A. *Exchanging Our Country Marks*. Chapel Hill: University of North Carolina Press, 1998.
Gooden, Mario. *Dark Space: Architecture, Representation, Black Identity*. New York: Columbia University Press, 2016.
Gordon, Uri. "Prefigurative Politics between Ethical Practice and Absent Promise." *Political Studies* 66, no. 2 (2018): 521–37.
Graeber, David. "The New Anarchists." *New Left Review* 1, no. 3 (2002).
Gross, Kali N. *Colored Amazons: Crime, Violence, and Black Women in the City of Brotherly Love, 1880–1910*. Durham, NC: Duke University Press, 2006.
Hahn, Steven. "On History: A Rebellious Take on African-American History." *Chronicle of Higher Education*, August 3, 2009.
Hall, Stuart, Chas Critcher, Tony Jefferson, John Clark, and Brian Roberts. *Policing the Crisis: Mugging, The State, Law and Order*. New York: Palgrave, 1978.
Hancock, Brittany. "Marcus Garvey's The Black Star Line: Hopes, Dreams, and the S. S. Yarmouth." *Journal of Caribbean History* 52, no. 2: 68–104.
Hancock, Philip, and Yvonne Jewkes. "Architectures of Incarceration: The Spatial Pains of Imprisonment." *Punishment & Society* 13, no. 5 (2011): 611–29.
Hardt, Michael. "Prison Time." *Yale French Studies*, no. 91 (1997): 64–79.
Harris, Cheryl. "Whiteness as Property." *Harvard Law Review* 106, no. 8 (1993): 1707–91.
Hartman, Saidiya V. "The Anarchy of Colored Girls Assembled in a Riotous Manner." *South Atlantic Quarterly* 117, no. 3 (July 2018): 465–90.
———. *Scenes of Subjection: Terror, Slavery, and Self-Making in Nineteenth-Century America*. New York: Oxford University Press, 1997.
———. "Venus in Two Acts." *Small Axe* 12, no. 2 (2008).
———. *Wayward Lives, Beautiful Experiments: Intimate Histories of Riotous Black Girls, Troublesome Women, and Queer Radicals*. New York: W. W. Norton, 2019.
Harvey, David. *Justice, Nature and the Geography of Difference*. Cambridge, UK: Blackwell, 1996.

Heimert, Alan. "Moby-Dick and American Political Symbolism." *American Quarterly* 15 (1963): 498–534.
Heiner, Brady T. "Foucault and the Black Panthers." *City* 11, no. 3 (2007): 313–56.
Hernandez, Arlette. "Reimagining Blackness and Architecture." New York: Museum of Modern Art, February 25, 2021: https://www.moma.org.
Hesse, Barnor. "Escaping Liberty: White Hegemony, Black Fugitivity." *Political Theory* 42, no. 3 (2014): 288–313.
——. "Marked Unmarked: Black Politics and the Western Political." *South Atlantic Quarterly* 110, no. 4 (2011): 974–84.
——. "Racialized Modernity: An Analytics of White Mythologies." *Ethnic and Racial Studies* 30, no. 4 (2007): 643–63.
——. "White Sovereignty (. . .), Black Life Politics: "The N****r They Couldn't Kill." *South Atlantic Quarterly* 116, no. 3 (2017): 581–604.
Hesse, Barnor, and Debra Thompson. "Introduction: Antiblackness—Dispatches from Black Political Thought." *South Atlantic Quarterly* 121, no 3 (July 2022): 447–75.
Heynen, Nik, and Jason Rhodes. "Organizing for Survival: From the Civil Rights Movement to Black Anarchism through the Life of Lorenzo Kom'boa Ervin." *ACME* 11, no. 3 (2012): 393–412.
Higgonet, Margaret. "Frames of Female Suicide." *Studies in the Novel* 32, no. 2 (2000): 229–42.
Hill, Robert A. *The Marcus Garvey and Universal Negro Improvement Association Papers*. Berkeley: University of California Press, 1983.
Holland, Sharon. *Raising the Dead: Readings of Death and (Black) Subjectivity*. Durham, NC: Duke University Press, 2000.
Horne, Gerald. *Fire this Time: Watts Uprising and the 1960s*. Charlottesville: University of Virginia, 1995.
Howison, Jeffrey D. "'Let Us Guide Our Own Destiny': Rethinking the History of the Black Star Line." *Review* 28, no. 1 (2005): 29–49.
Iton, Richard. *In Search of the Black Fantastic: Politics and Popular Culture in the Post-Civil Rights Era*. Oxford: Oxford University Press, 2008.
Jackson, George. *Blood in My Eye*. London: Penguin, 1971.
Jackson, Zakiyyah Iman. *Becoming Human: Matter and Meaning in an Antiblack World*. New York: New York University Press, 2020.
Jacobs, Jane. *The Death and Life of American Cities*. New York: Random House, 1961.
Jagmohan, Desmond. "Between Race and Nation: Marcus Garvey and the Politics of Self-Determination." *Political Theory* 48, no. 3 (2020): 271–302.
James, C. L. R. *Mariners, Renegades, and Castaways; the Story of Herman Melville and the World We Live In*. Lebanon, NH: Dartmouth College Press, 1953.
James, Joy. "Afrarealism and the Black Matrix: Maroon Philosophy at Democracy's Border." *Black Scholar* 43, no. 4 (Winter 2013): 124–31.
——. "American 'Prison Potebooks.'" *Race & Class* 45, no. 3 (2004): 35–47.

———. *Resisting State Violence: Radicalism, Gender, and Race in U.S. Culture*. Minneapolis: University of Minnesota Press, 1996.

———. *Shadowboxing: Representations of Black Feminist Politics*. New York: St. Martin's, 1999.

James, William. *Some Problems of Philosophy*. Cambridge, MA: Harvard University Press, 1999. First published 1911 by Longmans Green (New York).

Jeffery, C. Ray. *Crime Prevention Through Environmental Design*. Beverly Hills, CA: Sage Publications, 1971.

Johnson, Lynn R. "Contesting the Myth of National Compassion: The Leap from the Long Bridge into Trans-Atlantic History in Clotel or the President's Daughter (1853)." *Journal of Pan African Studies* 6, no. 8 (2014).

Jonas, Andrew, and Aidan While. "Governance." In *Cultural Geography*, edited by David Atkinson, 72–79. New York: I. B. Tauris, 2007.

Jung, Moon-Kie, and João H. Costa Vargas, ed. *Antiblackness*. Durham, NC: Duke University Press, 2021.

Kanor, Fabienne. *Humus*. Translated by Lynn E. Palermo. Charlottesville: University of Virginia Press, 2020.

Kaspar, Johann. "We Demand Nothing." *Fire to the Prisons*, no. 7 (2009).

Kelley, Robin D. G. "Watts, 50 Years Later; Inside the Unrest; Remember the Society They Built, Not What They Burned." *Los Angeles Times*, August 11, 2015.

Kelling, George L., and James Q. Wilson. "Broken Windows: The Police and Neighborhood Safety." *Atlantic*, March 1982.

Knoblauch, Joy. "The Economy of Fear: Oscar Newman Launches Crime Prevention through Urban Design (1969–197x)." *Architectural Theory Review* 19, no. 3 (2014): 336–54.

Kotef, Hagar. *Movement and the Ordering of Freedom: On Liberal Governances of Mobility*. Durham, NC: Duke University Press, 2015.

Laclau, Ernesto. *New Reflections on the Revolution of Our Time*. New York: Verso, 1990.

Lake, Marilyn, and Henry Reynolds. *Drawing the Global Colour Line White Men's Countries and the International Challenge of Racial Equality*. Cambridge, UK: Cambridge University Press, 2008.

Lambert, Léopold. "The Politics of Overpopulated Space." *Funambulist*, February 12, 2015. https://thefunambulist.net.

———. "The Slave Ship: An Operative Architecture Responsible for the Abysmal Atlantic Crossing." *Funambulist*, January 8, 2016. https://thefunambulist.net.

Lefebvre, Henri. *The Production of Space*. Translated by Donald Nicholson-Smith. Hoboken, NJ: Wiley Blackwell, 1991.

———. *State, Space, World*. Edited by Neil Brenner and Stuart Elden. Minneapolis: University of Minnesota Press, 2009.

Levinas, Emmanuel. *On Escape*. Stanford, CA: Stanford University Press, 2003.

Linebaugh, Peter, and Marcus Rediker. *The Many-Headed Hydra: Sailors, Slaves, Commoners, and the Hidden History of the Revolutionary Atlantic*. Boston: Beacon Press, 2013.

Lipsitz, George. *How Racism Takes Place*. Philadelphia: Temple University Press, 2011.
Lobban, Michael. "Slavery, Insurance and the Law." *Journal of Legal History* 28, no. 3 (2007).
Los Angeles Times. "Understanding the Riots: Los Angeles before and after the Rodney King Case." Los Angeles: Los Angeles Times Syndicate Books, 1992.
Low, Setha. "Urban Fear: Building the Fortress City." *City and Society Annual Review*, 1997: 53–72.
Malatesta, Errico. "Revolution and Reaction." In *No Gods, No Masters: An Anthology of Anarchism*, edited by Daniel Guérin, translated by Paul Sharkey, 352–54. Oakland, CA: AK Press, 2005.
———. "The Revolutionary 'Haste.'" *Umanitá Nova*, no. 125 (September 6, 1921). Available at *The Anarchist Library*.
Marchart, Oliver. *Post-Foundational Political Thought: Political Difference in Nancy, Lefort, Badiou, and Laclau*. Edinburgh: Edinburgh University Press, 2007.
Marcuse, Herbert. *An Essay on Liberation*. Boston: Beacon Press, 1969.
Martin, Tony. *Race First: The Ideological and Organizational Struggles of Marcus Garvey and the Universal Negro Improvement Association*. Dover, NH: Majority Press, 1976.
Marx, Anthony W. "Race-Making and the Nation-State." *World Politics* 48, no. 2 (1996): 180–208.
Massey, Doreen. "Politics and Space/Time." In *Place and Politics of Identity*, edited by Michael Keith and Steve Pile, 141–61. London: Routledge, 1993.
McClintock, Anne. *Imperial Leather: Race, Gender, and Sexuality in the Colonial Contest*. New York: Routledge, 1995.
McCone, John A. *Violence in the City—An End or a Beginning?: A Report by the Governor's Commission on the Los Angeles Riots*. Sacramento, CA: Governor's Commission on the Los Angeles Riots, 1965.
McKittrick, Katherine. *Demonic Grounds: Black Women and the Cartographies of Struggle*. Minneapolis: University of Minnesota Press, 2006.
McKittrick, Katherine, and Clyde Woods. *Black Geographies and the Politics of Space*. Cambridge, MA: South End Press, 2007.
Melville, Herman. *Moby-Dick or, The Whale*. New York: Penguin, 1992. First published 1851 by Harper Brothers (New York).
Mendieta, Eduardo. "Land and Sea." In *Spatiality, Sovereignty and Carl Schmitt: Geographies of the Nomos*, edited by Stephen Legg, 260–67. New York: Routledge, 2011.
Mincke, Christophe, and Anne Lemonne. "Prison and (Im)mobility. What about Foucault?" *Mobilities* 9, no. 4 (2014): 528–49.
Morgan, Jennifer. *Reckoning with Slavery: Gender, Kingship, and Capitalism in the Early Black Atlantic*. Durham, NC: Duke University Press: 2021.
Morris, Richard T., and Vincent Jeffries. "Violence Next Door." *Social Forces* 46, no. 3 (March 1968): 352–58.
Morris, Robert G., and John L. Worrall. "Prison Architecture and Inmate Misconduct: A Multilevel Assessment." *Crime & Delinquency* 60, no 7 (2010): 1083–1109.

Moses, Wilson J. *The Golden Age of Black Nationalism, 1850–1925*. Oxford: Oxford University Press, 1978.
Mulzac, Hugh. *A Star to Steer By*. New York: International Publishers, 1963.
Mustakeem, Sowande' M. *Slavery at Sea: Terror, Sex, and Sickness in the Middle Passage*. Urbana: University of Illinois Press, 2016.
National Advisory Commission on Civil Disorders. *Report of the National Advisory Commission on Civil Disorders*. Washington, DC: US Department of Justice, 1968.
National Maritime Museum. Documents Relating to the Ship Zong. Transcript commissioned by Granville Sharpe. Greenwich, CT: National Maritime Museum, 1783, REC/19.
Newman, Oscar. *Creating Defensible Space, Prepared for Department of Housing and Urban Development*. Washington, DC: Office of Policy Development and Research, 1996.
———. *Defensible Space: Crime Prevention through Urban Design*. New York: MacMillan, 1973.
Newman, Saul. "Anarchism and the Politics of Ressentiment." *Theory and Event* 4, no. 3 (2000).
———. "Voluntary Servitude Reconsidered: Radical Politics and the Problem of Self-Domination." *Anarchist Developments in Cultural Studies* 1 (2010).
Noor, Miski. Interview with Carol Costello about the Black Lives Matter protest planned for the Mall of America. *CNN*, December 12, 2015. http://archives.cnn.com.
Oldham, James. "Insurance Litigation Involving the Zong and Other British Slave Ships, 1780–1807." *Journal of Legal History* 28, no. 3 (2007).
Olson, Joel. *The Abolition of White Democracy*. Minneapolis: University of Minnesota Press, 2004.
Ong, Aihwa. *Buddha Is Hiding: Refugees, Citizenship, the New America*. Oakland: University of California Press, 2003.
Oparah, Julia C. "Maroon Abolitionists: Black Gender-Oppressed Activists in the Anti-prison Movement in the U.S. and Canada." In *Captive Genders: Trans Embodiment and the Prison Industrial Complex*, 2nd ed., edited by Eric A. Stanley and Nat Smith, 327–56. Oakland, CA: AK Press, 2015.
Parenti, Christian. "Postmodern Maroon in the Ultimate Palenque." *Peace Review* 10, no. 3 (1998): 419–26.
Park, Robert E. *Race Relations and the Race Problem: A Definition and an Analysis*. Durham, NC: Duke University Press, 1939.
Parsons, Lucy. "The Principles of Anarchism." In *Black Anarchism: A Reader*, by the Black Rose Anarchist Federation, 3–9. Black Rose Anarchist Federation, 2016. First published 1905.
Pease, Donald E. "From the Camp to the Commons: Biopolitical Alter-geographies in Douglass and Melville." *Arizona Quarterly* 27, no. 3 (Autumn 2016): 1–23.
Phelan, Peggy. *Unmarked: The Politics of Performance*. New York: Routledge, 1993.

Powell, Adam. "Anatomy of a Riot." Remarks of Hon. Adam C. Powell of New York in the House of Representatives, Tuesday, August 17, 1965. Congressional Record—Senate.

Proctor, Brittnay. "'Something Wonderful': Undisciplinarity and the Future of Black Studies." *ASAP* 7, no.1 (January 2022): 40–43.

Proudhon, Pierre-Joseph. *General Idea of the Revolution in the Nineteenth Century*. Translated by J. B. Robinson. London, 1923.

Rai, Dhanwant K., and Barnor Hesse. "Racial Victimization: An Experiential Analysis." In *Ethnicity and Crime: A Reader*, edited by Basia Spalek, 204–37. Berkshire: Open University Press, 2008.

Ray, Larry. "Shame and the City—'Looting,' Emotions and Social Structure." *Sociological Review* 62 (2014): 117–36.

Rediker, Marcus. *The Slave Ship: A Human History*. New York: Penguin, 2007.

———. "Teaching the 'Slave Ship' to Prisoners: Inside Auburn Prison." *Trans-Scripts* 3 (2013).

Reynald, Danielle M., and Henk Elffers. "The Future of Newman's Defensible Space Theory Linking Defensible Space and the Routine Activities of Place." *European Journal of Criminology* 6, no. 1 (2009).

Robinson, Cedric J. *The Terms of Order: Political Science and the Myth of Leadership*. Chapel Hill: University of North Carolina Press, 2016.

Rupprecht, Anita. "Excessive Memories: Slavery, Insurance and Resistance." *History Workshop Journal* 64 (2007): 6–28.

Ryan, Katy. "Revolutionary Suicide in Toni Morrison's Fiction." *African American Review* 34, no. 3 (2000).

Sale, Maggie Montesinos. *The Slumbering Volcano: American Slave Ship Revolts and the Production of Rebellious Masculinity*. Durham, NC: Duke University Press, 1997.

Samudzi, Zoé, and William C. Anderson. *As Black as Resistance: Finding the Conditions for Liberation*. Chico, CA: AK Press, 2018.

Saxton, Alexander. *The Rise and Fall of the White Republic: Class Politics and Mass Culture in Nineteenth-Century America*. London: Verso, 2003.

Scott, James C. *The Art of Not Being Governed: An Anarchist History of Upland Southeast Asia*. New Haven, CT: Yale University Press, 2009.

Sexton, Jared. "Captivity, by Turns: A Comment on the Work of Ashley Hunt." *Art Journal*, 2007.

———. "The *Vel* of Slavery: Tracking the Figure of the Unsovereign." *Critical Sociology* 42, no. 4–5 (2016): 583–97.

Sexton, Jared, and Elizabeth Lee. "Figuring the Prison: Prerequisites of Torture at Abu Ghraib." *Antipode* 38, no. 5 (2006): 1005–22.

Shabazz, Rashad. *Spatializing Blackness: Architectures of Confinement and Black Masculinity in Chicago*. Champaign: University of Illinois Press, 2015.

Shakur, Assata. *Assata: An Autobiography*. Chicago: Lawrence Hill, 2001.

Sharpe, Christina. "Black Gathering: An Assembly in Three Parts." In *Reconstructions: Architecture and Blackness in America*, 25–29. New York: Museum of Modern Art, 2021.
———. *In the Wake: On Blackness and Being*. Durham, NC: Duke University Press, 2016.
———. *Monstrous Intimacies: Making Post-Slavery Subjects*. Durham, NC: Duke University Press, 2010.
Sheehan, Seán. *Anarchism*. Chicago: University of Chicago Press, 2004.
Singh, Nikhil. *Black Is a Country: Race and the Unfinished Struggle for Democracy*. Cambridge, MA: Harvard University Press, 2004.
Smallwood, Stephanie. *Saltwater Slavery: A Middle Passage from Africa to American Diaspora*. Cambridge, MA: Harvard University Press, 2007.
Snyder, Terri L. "Suicide, Slavery, and Memory in North America." *Journal of American History* 97, no. 1 (2010): 39–62.
Soja, Edward. *Postmodern Geographies*. London: Verso, 1989.
Sorel, Georges. *Reflections on Violence*. Translated by Jeremy Jennings. Cambridge, UK: Cambridge University Press, 1999.
Spillers, Hortense. "Mama's Baby, Papa's Maybe: An American Grammar Book." In *Black, White, and in Color: Essays on American Literature and Culture*, 203–29. Chicago: University of Chicago Press., 2010.
Stein, Judith. *The World of Marcus Garvey: Race and Class in Modern Society*. Baton Rouge: Louisiana State University Press, 1986.
Steinberg, Philip E. "Free Sea." In *Spatiality, Sovereignty and Carl Schmitt: Geographies of the Nomos*, edited by Stephen Legg, 268–75. New York: Routledge, 2011.
Stephens, Michelle Ann. *Black Empire: The Masculine Global Imaginary of Caribbean Intellectuals in the United States, 1914–1962*. Durham, NC: Duke University Press, 2005.
Story, Brett. *Prison Land: Mapping Carceral Power across Neoliberal America*. Minneapolis: University of Minnesota Press, 2019.
Taylor, Eric Robert. *If We Must Die: Shipboard Insurrections in the Era of the Atlantic Slave Trade*. Baton Rouge: Louisiana State University Press, 2009.
Tenorio, Sam C. "White Carceral Geographies." *South Atlantic Quarterly* 121, no. 3 (July 2022): 515–39.
Thompson, E. P. "Time, Work-Discipline, and Industrial Capitalism." *Past & Present*, no. 38 (1967): 56–97.
Thrift, Nigel. *Nonrepresentational Theory: Space, Politics, Affect*. London: Routledge, 2007.
Tillery, Alvin B., Jr. *Between Homeland and Motherland: Africa, U.S. Foreign Policy, and Black Leadership in America*. Ithaca, NY: Cornell University Press, 2011.
Tiqqun. *Introduction to Civil War*. Los Angeles: Semiotext(e), 2010.
———. *This Is Not a Program*. Los Angeles: Semiotext(e), 2011.
Tocqueville, Alexis de. *Democracy in America*. Edited by J. P. Mayer. Translated by George Lawrence. New York: Harper Perennial Modern Classics, 2006. First published 1851 by Saunders and Otley (London).

Trouillot, Michel-Rolph. *Silencing the Past: Power and the Production of History.* Boston: Beacon Press, 1995.
Truong, Fabien. "Total Rioting: From Metaphysics to Politics." *Sociological Review* 65, no. 4 (2017): 563–77.
Ture, Kwame, and Charles V. Hamilton. *Black Power: The Politics of Liberation.* New York: Vintage,1992.
Turner, Jennifer, and Kimberley Peters. "Between Crime and Colony: Interrogating (Im)mobilities aboard the Convict Ship." *Social and Cultural Geography* 16, no. 7 (2015): 844–62.
———. "Rethinking Mobility in Criminology: Beyond Horizontal Mobilities of Prisoner Transportation." *Punishment & Society* 19, no. 1 (2017): 96–114.
Vargas, João H. Costa. *Never Meant to Survive: Genocide and Utopias in Black Diaspora Communities.* Lanham, MD: Rowman and Littlefield, 2010.
Wacquant, Loïc. "From Slavery to Mass Incarceration: Rethinking the Race Question in the US." *New Left Review*, 2002.
Walcott, Rinaldo. *On Property.* Windsor: Biblioasis, 2021.
Wallace, Erin. "Gordon Matta-Clark's *Anarchitecture*." In *Radical Gotham: Anarchism in New York City from Schwabb's Saloon to Occupy Wall Street*, edited by Tom Goyens, 180–200. Champaign: University of Illinois Press, 2017.
Walvin, James. *The Zong: A Massacre, the Law, and the End of Slavery.* New Haven, CT: Yale University Press, 2011.
Werlen, Benno. *Society, Action and Space: An Alternative Human Geography.* Translated by Gayla Walls. London: Routledge, 1998.
Wilderson, Frank B., III. "The Black Liberation Army and the Paradox of Political Engagement." In *Postcoloniality-Decoloniality-Black Critique: Joints and Fissures*, edited by Sabine Broek and Carsten Junker, 175–207. Frankfurt: Deutsche Nationalbibliotek, 2014.
———. "The Prison Slave as Hegemony's (Silent) Scandal." *Social Justice* 30, no. 2 (2003).
———. *Red, White & Black: Cinema and the Structure of U.S. Antagonisms.* Durham, NC: Duke University Press, 2010.
Williams, Kristian. *Our Enemies in Blue: Police and Power in America.* Chico, CA: AK Press, 2015.
Williams, Nick B. "The View From Watts Is Very Worth Taking." *Los Angeles Times*, October 10, 1965.
Wilson, Ivy. *Specters of Democracy: Blackness and the Aesthetics of Politics in the Antebellum.* Oxford: Oxford University Press, 2011.
Wilson, Mabel O. "The Multicultural City," In *Rethinking the American City: An International Dialogue*, edited by Miles Orvell, Klaus Benesch, and Holores Hayden, 49–69. Philadelphia: University of Pennsylvania Press, 2013.
Woolman, John. *A Journal of the Life, Gospel Labours and Christian Experiences, of that Faithful Minister of Jesus Christ, John Woolman.* Philadelphia: Friends Bookstore, 1883.

Yellin, Eric S. *Racism in the Nation's Service Government Workers and the Color Line in Woodrow Wilson's America*. Chapel Hill: University of North Carolina Press, 2013.

Young, Robert J. C. "Foucault on Race and Colonialism." *New Formations* 25 (1995): 57–65.

Zarmanian, Thalin. "Ordnung and Ortung/Order and Localisation." In *Spatiality, Sovereignty and Carl Schmitt: Geographies of the Nomos*, edited by Stephen Legg, 291–97. New York: Routledge, 2011.

INDEX

Page numbers *italics* indicate Figures

abjection, Black, 8, 12, 23–24, 61–63
abolitionism, 17, 45, 96, 149, 153; anticipatory, 23; prison, 133–34, 146–47, 172n74; of Shakur, 110; white, 20
accumulation, capitalist, 56, 106
Africa, 27–28, 53, 54, 59, 76–77
agency, 22, 45, 49, 153
agnosticism, 11, 21, 23, 42–44
Ahab (*Moby-Dick* character), 1–6
Alexander, Michelle, 17, 111, 146
alienation, 9, 82, 97–98, 101–2, 146
"alien," Black people as, 65–67
Alston, Ashanti, 44, 53, 104, 160n35
The American Commonwealth (Bryce), 65
Anarchism, 6, 75–77, 151, 154, 160n35; classical, 8–10, 23, 41, 69; white, 8, 10–12. *See also* Black anarchism
anarchitecture, 12–13
Anderson, Sean, 102–3, 147
Anderson, William C., 12, 103–4, 163n80
antagonism, 23, 99–100, 104, 151; racial, 3, 5–6, 9–10, 76, 107; structural, 5, 12, 14, 25, 34, 66, 87, 105, 111, 121, 133
antiblackness, 4, 6–10, 12–14, 16, 85–86, 104; Black mobility and, 150–51; carcerality and, 52, 119, 146–47; police violence and, 79–80, 83–85, 87–88, 100; vestibular subjection and, 110, 145; white dominion and, 93. *See also* carcerality
anticipation, 9–11, 18, 23, 108, 122, 135–37, 154
anti-citizens, 64, 67
anti-state, 15, 75, 130

architecture, 12–13; carceral, 117–19, 131–32; *defensible space* and, 16, 94–97, 99–101; of slave ships, 23, 25, 28–35, 42
archives of slavery, 22, 24, 48
arrests, 82, 111, 122–24
arson, 16, 80, 102
Assata (Shakur), 17, 109–10, 121–23, 127, 131, 136–38. *See also* autobiography
assimilation, 44, 91–94, 100, 102, 136, 167n20; Black diaspora and, 69–70; representation and, 137
asylum, political, 122, 139, 141
Atlantic Ocean, 17. *See also* Middle Passage
Australia, 66, 72, 118–19
authority, 6, 8, 23, 71, 78, 150; centralized, 11, 42; imperial, 15–16, 74; racial, 11, 15, 76, 104; state, 6, 69, 76, 102, 105, 128, 133, 135–36, 138; white, 7, 47, 57, 60, 84, 90, 120, 135
autobiography, 40; of Mulzac, 56; of Shakur, 17, 109–10, 121–23, 127, 131, 136–38
autonomy, Black, 52–53, 56, 58, 90, 106

Back-to-Africa movement, 4, 164n4
Bakunin, Mikhail, 103
Balagoon, Kawasi, 104, 160n35
banalization, 136
bankruptcy, 56
barricado (slave ship structure), 28–35
Bataille, Georges, 48
Belgium, 61
Bentham, Jeremy, 111, 114–15, 119
Best, Stephen, 138

189

Bey, Marquis, 12
Black anarchism, 9–10, 12, 14, 16, 41, 43–45, 150, 153; anticipation in, 154; Black diaspora and, 68, 73–78; Black liberation and, 21; carcerality and, 110; *cataclysmic critique* in, 80–81; collectivity and, 70, 73–78; destruction and, 103–4, 107; Garvey and, 53; paradox of, 151–52; refusal and, 8, 11, 15, 22; of Shakur, 145; socio-spatiality, 21–22, 78, 145
Black Angelenos, 79, 81–86, 93
Black Codes, 61–64, 121, 123–25, 128, 131, 165n34
Black criminality, 99, 121, 125–26, 142
Black dissent, 2, 4–5, 14, 44, 60, 62, 129–30, 142
Black Liberation Army, 104, 121–22, 129–30
Black Lives Matter, 145, 152
Black men, 52, 58, 84, 126; gendering of, 87–88
Black men (enslaved), 162n55; gendering of, 31–35; on slave ships, 19–20, 28
Black nationalism, 76–77
blackness, 41, 60, 67, 85, 94, 117, 120, 163n80; abjection of, 7, 28–30; criminalization of, 121, 123–27, 130, 140; gender and, 31–34; *Moby-Dick* and, 2–4; sexualization of, 33; structural antagonism of, 14; vagrancy and, 123; whiteness and, 98
Black Panther (film), 1–2
Black Panther Party, 104, 113, 129–30, 145
Black politics, 9–11, 17–18, 145, 150; criminalization of, 110; masculinity in, 60; racial boundaries and, 23; refusal in, 24
Black radical tradition, 10–11, 41, 46, 151–52
Black Reconstruction Collective, 102–3
Black Rose Anarchist Foundation, 8–9
Black social death, 13, 39, 109–10
Black Star Line (shipping line), 15–16, 51–52, 54, *55*, 56–60, 65, 68; Black diaspora and, 70–75, 77; Carnegie on, 164n6; Chief Sam's *Liberia* compared to, 164n4; hydrarchy and, 74; messianic framing of, 165n26. *See also specific ships*
Black women, 57, 59–60, 126–28, 144
Black women (enslaved), 171n54; gendering of, 31–35; jumping from slave ships, 19–20, 23–25, 41–42, 44
Bloch, Ernst, 134
bodies, Black, 44–45, 109; excess force used on, 83–84; gendering of, 19–20, 28–34, 126–27; police brutality enacted on, 83–84, 89–90; punishment of, 114–17; racialization of, 31–34; sexualization of, 126–27
Boston, Massachusetts, 56
boundaries, racial, 23, 67
bounties, 122, 142, *143*, 144
Brazil, 136
Britain, 61, 65–66, 72, 118–19
"broken windows" theory, 95
Brown, Pat, 86, 88
Browne, Simone, 13, 22, 115, 119–20
brutality, police, 83–85, 89–90
Bryce, James, 65–66
Bureau of Investigation, US, 61, 66–67, 70, 165n52. *See also* Federal Bureau of Investigation, US

California, 81–83, 86–90. *See also* Watts Rebellion of 1965
California Highway Patrol (CHP), 82–83
Camp, Stephanie, 28
Campt, Tina, 6
Canot, Theodore, 32
capitalism, 5, 56–59, 70, 106, 119
captivity, 2, 7–8, 13–14
carceral conditioning, 13–14, 110, 117, 122, 138–39
carcerality, 12–15, 22, 96, 109–21; antiblackness and, 119, 146–47; architec-

ture and, 117–19, 131–32; Black Star Line resisting, 68; following emancipation, 57; public housing and, 100–102. *See also* geography, carceral
carceral studies, 17, 110–12, 117–19
the Caribbean, 54, 59
Carnegie, Charles, 57–58, 60–61, 77, 164n6
caste system, racial, 111–12, 115–16
Castro, Fidel, 141
cataclysm, 23; the Watts rebellion and, 16, 102–8
centralized authority, 11, 42
Certeau, Michel de, 25–26
Cervenak, Sarah, 138
chaos, racial, 8, 18, 38
chattel slavery, 2–5, 9, 14, 33, 46, 60, 111, 119, 124; carceral studies on, 17; prisons in relation to, 133; spatiality of slave ships and, 22. *See also* enslaved people
Chesimard, JoAnne, *143*, 144. *See also* Shakur, Assata
Chicago, Illinois, 92
Childs, Dennis, 13, 22, 100, 119–20
CHP. *See* California Highway Patrol
Ciccariello-Maher, George, 75–77, 160n35
citizenship, 69–70, 73, 87, 102, 115, 151; white, 67, 85
civil rights, 11–12, 92, 94–95, 107, 145
civil society, 16, 67, 80, 85–86, 91, 102, 136
Civil War, US, 63–66, 165n34, 171n39
class (social), 9, 56, 64, 94, 120; middle, 97, 128, 141; surveillance and, 125–26; white master, 19–20, 30
Classical anarchism, 8–10, 23, 41, 69
Clotilda (slave ship), 13
coconuts, 56, 58, 74
COINTELPRO. *See* Counterintelligence Program, FBI
collectivity, 15–16, 18, 122; Black anarchist, 70, 73–78; of Black diaspora, 67, 70; Black mobility as, 150; Black Star Line, 58
Collingwood, Luke, 27
colonialism, 9, 18, 64–65, 67–68, 76–77, 118; in Brazil, 136; in the Caribbean, 59; ghettoization as, 97–98; modernity and, 72; settler, 53; "vestibular cultural formation" in, 15, 28
color line, 62, 65, 67
communism, 139–41
confinement, Black, 18, 146, 150
consent, 49
constructivism, 51–53
containment, 24, 28, 70, 125–26; after emancipation, 57; prisons as, 111, 120–21; sedentarizing practices of, 60–61, 101; slave ships and, 23, 30, 34–35, 120, 150; surveillance and, 13–14
convict ships, 118–19
Cooper, Cecilio, 86
Counterintelligence Program (COINTELPRO), FBI, 129, 145
COVID-19 pandemic, 152
crime, 94, 96, 98–100, 125, 144, 171n54; disorder and, 16, 95, 97
criminalization, 14, 17, 86–89 , 96, 98, 110–11, 150; of blackness, 121, 123–27, 130, 140; property and, 102, 105; of Shakur, 142, *143*, 144; vagrancy and, 121–30
criminal justice system, US, 111, 142
Cuba, 58; exile of Shakur to, 110, 122–23, 136–42, *143*, 144–47

Davis, Angela, 120, 128–30 172n61, 172n74
Davis, Mike, 101
death, 84, 101, 106, 111, 121–22, 150; Black, 14, 18, 63, 103–4; of enslaved people, 149, 160n54; on slave ships, 18, 23–24, 37–43, 46–49; by suicide, 20–22, 39–40; during the Watts Rebellion, 82–83. *See also* enslaved jumping ship

The Death and Life of Great American Cities (Jacobs), 95
decolonization, 172n61
defensible space, 16, 94–97, 99–101
dematerialization, 16, 44, 98
democracy, 66–67, 85, 139
Democracy in America (Tocqueville), 46
Department of Housing and Urban Development (HUD), US, 95–96
Department of Labor, US, 60
depoliticization, 13, 151, 164n4
deportation, 52, 56, 60, 66–67, 125–26
destruction, 12, 102, 106; Black anarchism and, 103–4, 107; as Black politics, 23; refusal and, 16; self, 22, 49; violence vs., 103–5; during Watts Rebellion, 80–82
diaspora, Black, 15–16, 67–73, 75, 77
Dillon, Stephen, 109
Discipline and Punish (Foucault), 111–15
discrimination, 62–63, 93, 111
dis-incarceration, 110, 130, 134–38, 146–47, 150; of Shakur, 17, 122, 144–45
disinvestment, 82, 85
disorder, 2, 6, 10, 12, 24, 94, 101–2, 128; crime and, 16, 95, 97
displacement, 4, 7–8, 18, 68, 88, 110, 140, 146
dispossession, 124, 146
disruptions, 6–7, 11–12, 15–16, 68, 74–75, 97, 102–4, 107, 129
double repression, 48
Douglass, Patrice D., 34, 85, 87, 122, 127, 144
Drogas Wave, 1
drowning, 3–5, 47
Du Bois, W. E. B., 51, 64
Dumaresq, Abraham, 19
Dutch West India Company, 160n54

Edwards, Brent Hayes, 71
electoral politics, 104, 107
emancipation, 57, 67, 121, 125–26
employment, 59, 64, 81; Black Star Line, 54, 55, 56

enslaved jumping ship, 1, 7–8, 14–15, 46–50, 55, 149–54, 162n64; Black women as, 19–20, 23–25, 41–42, 44; insurance litigation and, 36–37, 39–41, 45, 160n54; as refusal, 22–23, 40–43; suicide and, 20–22, 39–40, 43
enslaved people, 1, 2–3, 14, 19, 28, 62, 111; death of, 149, 160n54; dehumanization of, 23, 36; emancipation of, 57, 67, 121, 125; as human cargo, 27, 36–37; as property, 31, 34, 37–39, 79; slave ships taken over by, 7, 20, 35. *See also* abolitionism; transatlantic slave trade
epistemic violence, 9, 47
Equiano, Olaudah, 1, 14, 24
erasure, 59–60, 67–68, 75, 112, 136
Ervin, Lorenzo Kom'boa, 75–78, 152, 160n35
Eurocentrism, 76–77
Europe, 9, 67–68, 131, 166n65; imperialism, 119–20
exiles, 110, 123, 134, 139–42, *143*, 144–47
exploitation, 31–34, 59, 82

Falconbridge, Alexander, 24
Fanon, Frantz, 24, 76, 160n35
FBI. *See* Federal Bureau of Investigation, US
fear, 25, 49, 74, 87–88, 94, 98–100, 151
Federal Bureau of Investigation (FBI), US, 122, 129, 141–42, *143*, 144–45, 165n52
feminization, 19, 20, 34–35; of suicide, 40
Florida (slave ship), 24
Foster, Thomas, 33
Foucault, Michel, 17, 111–12, 119, 146
France, 61
Frank, Jason, 5
Fredensborg II (slave ship), 27
Frederick Douglass (Black Star Line ship), 54
free Black populations, 66, 123–24
freedom, Black, 7, 51, 75, 124, 134–35
Frye, Marquette, 82–83
Frye, Ronald, 82

fugitivity, Black, 135–36, 141
fungibility, 4, 46–47, 134

Garvey, Marcus, 15, 65, 164n6, 164n10; constructivism of, 51–53; deportation of, 52, 56, 60, 66–67; imperialism of, 16, 52–53, 59, 70, 78; mail fraud by, 56. *See also* Black Star Line (shipping line)
gender, 31–34, 60, 64; race and, 15, 23
gendering, 52, 151, 161n42; armed insurrections, 19–20, 35–37; of Black bodies, 19–20, 28–34, 126–27; of Black men, 65, 87–88; of enslaved people on slave ships, 19–20, 28–34; of suicide, 40
genocide, 62
geography, carceral, 15, 30, 110, 117–18, 124–25, 154; Black anarchism and, 145; vagrancy and, 142
Ghana, 78
ghettoization, 12, 16, 81–87, 92–93, 97–101; sedentarizing practices of, 104; Watts rebellion and, 106
Glissant, Edouard, 71, 74
global color line, 65, 67
globalization, 65
Goldman, Emma, 9
Gordon, Uri, 152
governance, race, 30–31, 42
government, US, 60–61, 66, 122, 128, 140, 144
Great Migration, US, 81
Great White Fleet, US Navy, 65

Hahn, Steven, 151
Haitian Revolution, 136
Hall, Stuart, 88
Hamilton, Charles, 98
Harris, Cheryl, 98
Hartman, Saidiya, 4, 12, 34, 45, 47, 127, 138, 161n42
heroism, 20, 35, 45
Hesse, Barnor, 84, 134–35, 166n65
heteropatriarchal violence, 33

heterosexuality, 60, 112
hierarchies, 62, 71, 74, 166n65; class, 9; gendered, 32–33, 60; segregation and, 67, 92; spatial, 97
Higgonet, Margaret, 43
Hinds, Lennox, 131
Hogg, James, 24–25
homeland, 69–70, 72–73
homelessness, 121
Hoover, J. Edgar, 61, 66–67, 129, 145
Horne, Gerald, 81–83
Houghteling, James L., 60
Housing Act (1949), US, 93–94
Howison, Jeffrey, 53
HUD. *See* Department of Housing and Urban Development, US
human cargo, 27, 36–37
Humus (Kanor), 1
Hurston, Zora Neale, 11
hydrarchy, 73–74
hypermasculinity, 35
hypersexuality, 126
hysteria, 47–48

Igbo, 153
immigration, 66
immorality, 81, 112, 126, 144
imperialism, 10, 44, 78, 138, 140–41; European, 119–20; of Garvey, 16, 52–53, 59, 70, 78
impoverishment, 81, 87–88, 100, 106
incarceration. *See* prisons
individualism, 42, 58–59, 96
individual rights, 96, 151
inequality, structural, 16, 97–98
infantilization, 88
insanity, 43, 150. *See also* madness
insurance litigation, slave ship, 36–37, 39–41, 45, 160n54
insurrections on slave ships, 7, 19–21, 28–29, 29, 32–33, 35–37, 45
integrationism, 91, 93, 138, 151

intercommunalism, African, 75–78
involuntary labor, 123–24
Ishmael (*Moby-Dick* character), 2–5, 7–8, 18, 149
Iton, Richard, 10–11, 44, 166n65

Jackson, George, 79, 106, 120, 128–30, 172n61
Jacobs, Jane, 95
Jagmohan, Desmond, 52–53
Jamaica, 52, 56, 88
James, C. L. R., 5–6
James, Joy, 129–30, 134
Jeffery, C. Ray, 95
Jim Crow laws, 61–64, 67, 87
Johnson, Lyndon B., 91–92, 95
Jones v. Schmoll (1785), 39
Jung, Moon-Kie, 7

Kanawha (Black Star Line ship), 54
Kanor, Fabienne, 1, 7–8
Kaspar, Johann, 107
Kelley, Robin D. G., 79–80
Kelling, George L., 95
knowledge production, 71, 136

labor, 43–44, 123–24, 165n34; of Black women, 60; James, C. L. R., on, 5–6; prison, 171n39; unproductive, 50
Laclau, Ernesto, 30
Lake, Marilyn, 64
landedness, 67–68, 153
LAPD. *See* Los Angeles Police Department
Latin America, 139
law-and-order society, 94–95, 99–102, 168n47
Lawrance (slave ship), 19, 24
Lee, John, 38
Lefebvre, Henri, 25
legitimacy, 12, 116, 130
Leusden (slave ship), 18, 160n54
liberalism, 4–6, 21, 23, 41, 44, 48, 98, 130, 146–47, 154

liberation, 7–8, 76; Black, 17, 20, 59, 68, 78, 92, 130, 140, 153
Liberia (ship), 164n4
linearity, 44
Linebaugh, Peter, 73–74
literacy tests, 66
locomotion, 58, 121, 139
Lombroso, Cesare, 126–27
looting, 80, 102
Los Angeles, California, 81–82, 86–87. *See also* Watts Rebellion of 1965
Los Angeles Police Department (LAPD), 82–85
Los Angeles Times, 79
Ludlow, Robert E., 83
Lupe Fiasco, 1
lynch mobs, 64, 142

madness, 3, 5, 150. *See also* insanity
mail fraud, 56
Marchart, Oliver, 30
marronage, 59–60, 139–40
Marxism, 5–6, 8–9
masculinity, 34–35, 57, 59–60; white, 65, 127–28
mass incarceration, 13, 109–12, 115–17, 132
Matta-Clark, Gordon, 13
McCone Commission, 83, 86, 88, 92–93, 106–7
McKittrick, Katherine, 26, 67
Melville, Herman, 1–8, 11, 17–18, 149
messianic framing of Black Star Line, 165n26
metamorphic capacity, 15, 28
middle-class, 97, 128, 141
Middle Passage, 19, 21, 27–28, 54
migration, Black, 81, 92
mobility, 57–58, 61–62, 150–51, 162n55; Black diaspora and, 67–75; carcerality and, 109–10; criminalization and, 121; in Cuba, 139; prisons and, 133; as refusal, 153
Moby-Dick (Melville), 1–8, 11, 17–18, 149
modernism, 59

Monroe Doctrine, US, 141
morality, 20, 106–7, 116, 126–28
moral panic, 86, 88–91, 170n1
Morgan, Jennifer L., 19–20, 42
Moses, Robert, 95
Mosnier, Louis, 1
Mulzac, Hugh, 56
murder, crime of, 33

National Association for the Advancement of Colored People (NAACP), 51
national borders, US, 72, 139–40, 145
national fable, US, 16, 98
nationalism, 57, 164n6; Black, 16, 52–53, 75–77, 160n35; white, 62, 66, 68, 73, 150
nationhood, 51–53
nation-state, 15–16, 54, 59, 68–71, 73–77, 150; Black, 52–53, 57; white, 57, 60–67, 72
Native Americans, 62, 98
Navy, US, 65
"negro problem," 65, 67
"Negro's cause," 91, 168n39
Negro World (publication), 58
neocolonialism, 75, 77
neoliberalism, 98, 105
New Jersey, 121–22, 145–46
The New Jim Crow (Alexander), 111, 115–17
Newman, Oscar, 16, 95–96, 98, 101–2
New York, New York, 51–52, 56, 58, 67, 93
Nickerson Gardens, 96–97, 99–100
Nixon, Richard, 168n47
nonbeing, Black, 3, 8, 14, 45–46, 98; slave ships and, 28
nonbelonging, 16, 64, 86, 106
nonrepresentation, 11, 18, 134–38
nonviolence, 92, 145
the North, US, 63–64

Occupy movement, 69
omissions, 48, 110, 128, 136–37, 145
ownership, property, 95, 98–99

Panama, 61, 66–67
panopticon, 111, 114–15, 118–19
Parenti, Christian, 140
Park, Robert E., 92
Parker, William, 84
Parsons, Lucy, 43–44, 48
paternalism, 57
patriarchy, 60, 132
Pease, Donald, 5
penal state, 96, 112, 117
performativity, 67, 107, 122
personhood, 46, 123
Peters, Kimberly, 118
Philadelphia, Pennsylvania, 56, 58, 61
Pip (*Moby-Dick* character), 1–8, 11, 17–18, 149
Pisacane, Carlo, 103
plantations, 19, 28, 34–35, 137–38, 162n55
police, 81, 95; antiblack violence by, 79–80, 83–85, 87–88, 100; brutality, 83–85, 89–90; state, 104, 144; surveillance, 85, 96, 99
policing, 14, 16, 82, 109, 140, 168n47; of Black diaspora, 72; punishment and, 61; racial, 85, 167n20 170n1; Reconstruction era, 64–65; on slave ships, 30; vagrancy and, 145–46
political: asylum, 122, 139, 141; participation, 8, 50, 68; prisoners, 75, 110, 113, 128–31, 172n61; subjectivity, 16, 52–53, 107
postrace, 100
Powell, Adam, 91–92, 100
power, 64–65, 76, 118–19; Black, 59, 70, 94–95; decentralization of, 78; racial, 12, 91, 93; spatiality and, 25, 42; white, 86–87
prefiguration, prefigurative politics and, 10–11, 44, 107–8, 152, 164n10
pregnancy, 24
Price, Rena, 82
prison industrial complex, 14, 111, 116

prisons, 14, 109–11; abolitionism, 133–34, 146–47, 172n74; architecture of, 117–19, 131–32; dis-incarceration of Shakur from, 17, 122; reforms, 130–34; slave ships as origins of, 22; temporality and, 120–21. *See also* carcerality
privatization, 16, 69, 96–97, 99–101, 105
Proctor, Brittnay, 12
property, 16, 93, 96, 98, 153; criminalization and, 102, 105; destruction, 81–82, 102–3, 106; enslaved people as, 31, 34, 37–39, 79; privatization and, 100; racialization and, 98; sentient, 34, 39, 49; "urban renewal" and, 92, 95, 100, 102, 105
Proudhon, Pierre-Joseph, 79
public housing, 16, 81, 94, 96, 100–102
public space, 97, 100
punishment, 46, 61, 88, 109, 130–31, 139; convict ships and, 118–19

race: engendering, 31–34, 161n42; relations, 91–94, 102
racial: antagonism, 3, 5–6, 9–10, 76, 107; authority, 11, 15, 76, 104; boundaries, 23, 67; capitalism, 119; caste system, 111–12, 115–16; chaos, 8, 18, 38; ideologies, 35, 62, 116; order, 1–2, 30, 43, 48; power, 12, 93
racialization, 60, 98, 111–12, 126–27, 141, 151; as a function of slave ships, 28–34; spatiality and, 26
racism, 62–63
Rai, Dhanwant K., 84
rape, 33, 87, 142
Reagan, Ronald, 95
recidivism, 121, 132
Reconstruction era, US, 1 25, 61–62, 64–65, 103
Rediker, Marcus, 73–74, 118–19
reformism, 102, 116, 130–34, 146
refusal, 2, 16, 74; Black anarchism and, 8, 11, 15, 22; Black liberation and, 68; in Black politics, 24; of carcerality, 52; enslaved people jumping ship as, 22–23, 40–43; by Pip, 6, 11, 18; reproduction and, 23, 44; ungovernability and, 151–53
reification, 14, 61–62
religion, 49
representation, 91–92 110; assimilation and, 137; refusal and, 23
repression, 48, 79, 111
reproduction, 17, 43–44, 151
revolt on slave ships, 19–21, 28–29, 29
Reynolds, Henry, 64
rights, 84, 131, 154; Black, 103; civil, 11–12, 92, 94–95, 107, 145; individual, 96, 151; property, 98
"riots," 79–80, 82, 86, 89–91, 103, 107
risk, insurance, 36–38
Roosevelt, Theodore, 65
Royal African Company of England, 36
ruination, 12, 16, 18, 81, 103–5
runaway slaves, 19

Sazmudi, Zoé, 163n80
securitization, 85, 95, 99, 101, 141–42, 145, 169n70
sedentarizing practices, 30, 60–61, 72, 74, 101, 104, 117–18
segregation, 121; ghettoization and, 62–67, 86, 101
self-destruction, 22, 49
self-determination, 51–53, 59, 78
self-empowerment, 16, 94, 96–97
self-sufficiency, 51
separatism, 51
settler colonialism, 53
sexualization, 33–35, 60, 87, 111, 126–27
sexual violence, 32–34, 87, 161n42
Shabazz, Rashad, 13
Shadyside, SS (Black Star Line ship), 54
Shakur, Assata, 131; autobiography of, 17, 109–10, 121–22, 121–23, 127, 131, 136–38;

in Black Liberation Army, 121–22, 129; dis-incarceration of, 134–38; exile of, 139–42, *143*, 144–47

Sharpe, Christina, 2, 33, 48, 67, 105, 154

ship takeovers, slave, 7, 20, 35

slave masters, white, 19–20, 30

slavery. *See* enslaved people

slave ships, 13, *27*, 60, 101, 110, 118, 119–20, 137–38; architecture of, 23, 25, 28–35, 42; barricados on, 28–35; captains on, 25, 27, 37; crews on, 25, 27–28, 47; deaths on, 18, 23–24, 37–43, 46–49; human cargo on, 27, 36–37; insurance litigation, 36–37, 39–41, 45, 160n54; insurrection on, 7, 19–21, 28–29, *29*, 32–33, 35–37, 45; Middle Passage journeys by, 19, 21, 27–28; as origin of prisons, 17; overpopulation of, *32*, *32*, 37; racial governance on, 30–31, 42; spatial technologies of, 15; temporalities, 120–21. *See also* enslaved jumping ship; *specific slave ships*

slave trade. *See* transatlantic slave trade

slave traders, white, 32, 45

social death, Black, 13, 39, 109–10

socio-spatial arrangements, 57, 81, 83; Black anarchism and, 21–22, 78, 145; of ghettoization, 101; of slave ships, 7, 23–24, 31–34; surveillance and, 101

La Soleil (slave ship), 7–8, 25

solitary confinement, 130–32

Sorel, Georges, 76

the South, US, 63–64, 66, 87

South Africa, 66

sovereignty, 42, 52, 69–70, 75–76, 153; white, 53–54, 62–63, 74, 85–86, 92, 106

spatiality, 12–14, 16, 23–24, 71, 86, 92–93, 98; Black diasporas and, 67–69; hierarchies, 97; post Civil War, 63–64; of prisons, 117–19, 131–32; public housing and, 100–102; of segregation, 63–64; of slave ships, 20, 22, 25, 27–29, 149–50; surveillance and, 125–26; technology and, 15, 28; violence and, 42–43, 62, 64; of Watts Rebellion, 80; of white dominion, 135. *See also* socio-spatial arrangements

Spillers, Hortense, 15, 28, 31

state: anti-state, 15, 75, 130; authority, 6, 69, 76, 102, 105, 128, 131, 133, 135–36, 138, 145; carceral, 22, 121–22; penal, 96, 112, 117; police, 104, 144. *See also* nation-state

stereotypes, 87–88

Story, Brett, 14

structural: antagonism, 5, 12, 14, 25, 34, 66, 87, 105, 111, 121, 133; inequality, 16, 98

Stubb (*Moby Dick* character), 3–8

suffering, Black, 4–5, 14, 102

suffrage, Black, 66

suicide, 20–22, 39–40, 43

surveillance, 13–14, 22, 119, 125–26, 140, 144; of Garvey, 61; ghettoization and, 97–98; police, 85, 96, 99; witnessing vs., 100–110

survival, 153; of enslaved people, 40, 49, 75; whiteness and, 65

Taylor, Eric Robert, 21, 35–36, 41, 45

technologies: carceral, 14; of death, 111; spatial, 15, 28

temporality, 18, 102, 120–21, 123

territoriality, white, 84–86, 84–88, 90, 94, 96

terrorism, 67, 89–90, 145; Shakur accused of, 122, 142, 144

theft, 16, 102; enslaved ship jumping as, 49–50

Thompson, Debra, 7

Tocqueville, Alexis de, 46–47

torture, 119

totalitarianism, 5, 172n61

transatlantic slave trade, 1, 24, 36, 118, 160n54; ships retrofitted for, 27–28; suicides in, 39. *See also* Middle Passage; slave ships
transience, 46, 87, 110, 121, 135, 139–40, 146
transnationalism, 52–53, 57–58, 73, 110
trauma, 48
Trouillot, Michel-Rolph, 134, 136
Trump, Donald, 122
Ture, Kwame, 98
Turner, Jennifer, 118

"unbuilding," 103
Underground Railroad, 137–38
ungovernability, 151–53
UNIA. *See* Universal Negro Improvement Association
United Kingdom, 61, 65–66, 72, 118–19, 131; moral panic in, 88–89
United Nations Commission on Human Rights, 131
United States (US), 16, 54, 56, 65, 73, 98, 106; government, 60–61, 122, 128, 140, 144; HUD, 95–96; mass incarceration in, 13, 109–12, 115–17, 132; national borders, 72, 139–40, 145. *See also* surveillance; *specific states, cities*
universalism, 9, 76
Universal Negro Improvement Association (UNIA), 15, 51–53, 61, 68, 75, 78. *See also* Black Star Line
unproductive labor, 50
urban malaise, 16, 97, 102
"urban renewal," 92, 95, 100, 102, 105
US Postal Service, 56, 61

vagrancy, 17, 110, 121–30, 128, 140, 142; policing and, 145–46
vandalism, 16, 102
Vargas, João H. Costa, 7
"vestibular cultural formation," 15, 28, 150

vestibular subjection, 15, 29–30, 48, 101, 120, 150–51; antiblackness materialized via, 110, 145; Reconstruction era, 64
violence, 2–3, 6–7, 10, 76, 120; antiblack, 79–80, 83–84, 89, 100; of assimilation, 44; of chattel slavery, 33; criminalization and, 111; destruction *vs*., 103–5; epistemic, 9, 47; ghettoized communities impacted by, 99–100; police, 79–80, 82–85, 87–88, 100; of the prison industrial complex, 14; of prisons, 111, 132; public housing and, 101; racial, 80, 104, 113; of sedentarizing techniques, 30; sexual, 32–34, 87, 161n42; on slave ships, 18, 28–30, 46–47, 49; in the South, 63; spatial, 26, 42–43, 62, 64; temporality and, 18; during Watts Rebellion, 82–83, 87, 90–91

Wagner, J. H., 60
Wallace, George, 168n47
"War on Crime," 95
"War on Poverty," 95
Washington, Booker T., 51
Watts Rebellion of 1965, 79–81, 80, 83, 84–85, 93–94, 168n39; cataclysmic vantage of, 16, 102–8; moral panic and, 89–90
welfare policy, 94
West Africa, 59
white: abolitionists, 20; Anarchism, 8, 10–12; authority, 7, 47, 57, 60, 84, 90, 120, 135; belonging, 16, 64; citizenship, 67; identity, 62, 85, 90; imperialism, 78; life, 9, 172n61; masculinity, 65, 127–28; nationalism, 62, 66, 68, 73, 150; panic, 86–91; sovereignty, 53–54, 62–63, 74, 85–86, 92, 106; territoriality, 84–88, 90, 94, 96; women, 87, 126–27
white dominion, 56, 62, 74–75, 86–90, 128, 144; Black death and, 46–47, 153;

Black diaspora and, 71–72; segregation and, 63–65; spatiality of, 135; surveillance and, 61; Watts Rebellion and, 90
white flight, 81
whiteness, 62, 64, 84–85, 87, 119; blackness and, 98; masculinity and, 60; property and, 98; survival and, 65
white supremacy, 21, 53, 67
Wilderson III, Frank B., 125
Williams, Kristian, 83
Wilson, James Q., 95
Wilson, Mabel O., 100, 102–3

witnesses, 4, 47–48; surveillance vs., 100–101
womanhood, 127
Woodruff, Barbara, 145
Woods, Clyde, 26
Woolman, John, 19
World War I, 54
World War II, 81

Yarmouth, SS (Black Star Line ship), 54, 56

Zong (slave ship), 18, 37–38, 160n54

ABOUT THE AUTHOR

SAM C. TENORIO is Assistant Professor of Women's, Gender, and Sexuality Studies and African American Studies at the Pennsylvania State University.

www.ingramcontent.com/pod-product-compliance
Lightning Source LLC
Chambersburg PA
CBHW020410080526
44584CB00014B/1260